HOW TO LIVE THE WONDERFUL CHRISTIAN LIFE

Compiled by: Henrietta Sutera

Copyright © 2009 by Henrietta Sutera

How To Live The Wonderful Christian Life
by Henrietta Sutera

Printed in the United States of America

ISBN 978-1-60647-739-7

All rights reserved solely by the author. Any part of this book may be reproduced in any form without the permission of the author. The views expressed in this book are not necessarily those of the publisher.

Unless otherwise indicated, Bible quotations are taken from The King James Version. Copyright © 1990 by Thomas Nelson Publishers.

Cover by: Patty Allen
Boiling Springs, SC

www.xulonpress.com

God bless you!
Henrietta Sutera
(Rom. 8:28-29)

TESTIMONIALS

This past Sunday school year, I attended the Foundations of Faith Class taught by Henrietta Sutera. This class provided me, and the other members, with a biblical foundation and practical application of biblical truths. The class looks, in detail, at both the joys and struggles of being a Christian, and provides guidance in everyday living that is backed up with scriptural reference. Henrietta's love for the Lord and her love for people are contagious, as the class grows in their relationship with God and their friendships with one another. Prayer time was very special, as it should be. Time and time again, we came together as a class to petition the Lord on behalf of a class member, family member, coworker, or friend. And, time and time again, we saw prayers answered. This class is truly the foundation that all Christians need, both new and seasoned alike. It has been a real blessing to me in my walk with the Lord.
Sandy Mankins
Foundations of Faith Sunday School Class 2007 - 2008

Boiling Springs First Baptist Church
Foundation of Faith Sunday School Class
The main goal for the Foundations of Faith class is to grow in your relationship with our Lord Jesus Christ through a scripture-based study of our Christian faith. This class is essential for new converts and a very useful class for "not so new" converts, such as me. In one year, I learned so much about what God reveals of himself and how he wants believers to live our daily lives for Him.

Weekly handouts, aided by "self-assessing" questionnaires were very beneficial to learning and growing.

Class members were very open and close as we shared prayer requests. It was often apparent when the Holy Spirit was guiding one other away from barriers or sins hindering our growth with God. No one worried about that; no judgment existed amongst us. Because of the spirit of God guiding the class, it made a member's age, race, marital status or any other earthly "status" irrelevant. The class is for anyone wanting to grow closer to God.
Rocky Mankins

Henrietta's demeanor and teaching style remain constant. She derives her material straight from the Bible and connects it with human nature. Her delivery is in such a way that she leads us to questions or it reminds us of past instances where we may have been perplexed. Then she gives us the answer - from the Bible.

It helps to have information that not only gives you lessons from the Bible, but also connects you so personally that you do feel more eager to learn more.

Henrietta is a wonderful instrument from God. I am sure I can say we all thank Him for bringing her to us.
Sandy Zimmerman

"She prays for me" "and I love her."
Bethanie Dalton

I joined the Foundation of Faith Sunday School Class in January of 2008. Henrietta and I had been a part of the Faith outreach program and she shared with me about her class. It took over a year for me to find myself in her class, but it was the most powerful thing I have ever done in my spiritual life.

The class is a Biblical blueprint of how and why we walk with the Lord. The lessons are dead on to meet the needs of us who struggle with our daily walk. Henrietta shows us where the Lord has made provision for our every need and thought. She shows us how clearly the Lord has defined the way we should live.

I have been in church my entire life. I have participated in Bible studies, including Experiencing God. However, I have never had anything strengthen my walk with the Lord as much as the lessons I've heard over the past months. Foundations of Faith should not be considered just a class for new believers, but a class for anyone who needs to be refreshed and strengthened in their walk with the Lord.

I know the Lord has a plan for me and He wanted me to be in this class at this time. I have needed the support and questions answered that this class has provided. It is a small intimate class and the prayer support is unbelievable. We have seen prayers answered and strength supplied through the prayers of our class. I feel selfish in saying that I have taken so much more from this class than I could ever give. I take away every Sunday a peace and a power that I know the week is not in my hands but His. I know that people are praying for me and my request and this give me the peace and the power to walk with God for that week. I come on Sunday knowing that I will be renewed and refreshed. When I have to miss a Sunday it hurts. I don't remember ever having these feeling about any other class that I have been part of. If you could find the combination of elements that makes this class what it is, you would be building Sunday School classrooms to the sky.

I will complete the first part of this class in the fall. I am deeply sorry that I won't share my Sundays this summer with this class. I am once again being selfish and Henrietta has told us the key is "death to self", but once you find a place like Foundations of Faith, you never want to leave.

Karen Mathis

Follow-Up
A Program for New Christians and Others Wanting to Know More About Victorious Living
(A Study Manual)
Compiled by: Henrietta Sutera

INDEX

Introduction xi

I. Have You Been Saved Or Deceived? 13
II. Repentance 19
III. Assurance 25
IV. What Happened When You Opened Your Heart To Jesus? 31
V. Open Confession Of Christ 35
VI. Christian Growth 37
    a. The Bible 39
    b. How To Have Devotions 49
    c. Prayer 53
    d. Scripture Memorization 103
    e. Witnessing 111
VII. Understanding The Spirit Filled Life 131
    a. The Two Kinds Of People 131
    b. The Two Natures 134
    c. Jesus As Lord 136
    d. Death To Self 143
    e. The Filling Of The Spirit 158

	f. Spiritual Gifts	182
VIII.	Overcoming Temptation	193
IX.	Putting On The Armor Of God	199
	a. Saying "No" To Addictions	221
	b. How To Say "No" To A Stubborn Habit	226
X.	Separation	233
XI.	Restitution and Reconciliation Guidelines	243
XII.	Causes and Cure For Fear And Anger	247
XIII.	Depression and Emotional Problems	265
XIV.	Sickness and Divine Healing	273
XV.	The Resurrection	289
XVI.	The Power Of The Resurrection	395
XVII.	Fellowship	303
	a. Sharing Burdens	303
	b. Church Membership	314
	c. The Lord's Supper	318
	d. Baptism	320
XVIII.	Tithing	325
XIX.	Knowing God's Will and Making Wise Decisions	335
XX.	How To Have Constant Victory In Christ	349
	(Praise and How To Handle Pressure Biblically)	
XXI.	The Second Coming Of Christ	359
XXII.	Recommended Books For Spiritual Growth	371
XXIII.	Recommended Books For Soul Winning	375
Bibliography		377

INTRODUCTION

Several years ago, in the church we attended, we were seeing people go to the altar, get saved and baptized, but before too long they were gone and you didn't see them anymore. At that time there was not a follow-up class for new believers. God seemed to lay this on my heart and for about two or three months, I felt compelled to do research and come up with a course that would help to ground these new believers in the things of God.

I read many books and they were all good, but I felt there were other areas that should be taught. I also felt that more time was needed to be with them, love them, and help them in times of need. And, they needed to see Christianity demonstrated.

In my study, I read that the Proverbs were not just Solomon's, but were a compilation of proverbs he had collected. That encouraged me because much of this course is a compilation of articles, etc., that I have collected and included in this study,

I have tried to give credit to everyone whose material I have used. If I have missed some, it hasn't been on purpose.

My desire is that this material can be used to make disciples in the true sense of the word, God grant that it will be so.

Follow-up, if done correctly, should lead one to understand that when we understand truth, we need to put it into action. We need to demonstrate it in our attitudes and actions. It is important that truth is taught in such a way that it becomes practical and functional. We need to teach in such a way that new Christians learn how to put truth they learn into action. It must be seen in those who are teaching. New babes need to observe that God's Spirit is living in and through a person who is knowledgeable about the Bible. As I teach, I want to encourage each student to realize their responsibility is to consistently apply the divine principles and truths they hear, and by God's enabling, to put them into practice.

As they meditate on the lesson each week, they need to ask themselves the following questions:

1. Do I need to change some of my beliefs, and does God want my actions to change?
2. What can I do to accomplish this change?
3. What is the first step I need to take to bring about this change?

As these questions are answered, change takes place and the new Christian is on the road to becoming a mature Christian.

CHAPTER I

HAVE YOU BEEN SAVED OR DECEIVED?

Many people believe they have been saved, but they have been deceived. Many believe that because they have been raised in a Christian home, because they have gone to church all their lives, have joined the church and been baptized, they automatically become Christians. Many do not realize they have not met God's conditions. Matthew 7:22-23 says, "Many will come saying 'Lord, have we not prophesied in thy name, and in thy name have cast out devils, and in thy name done many wonderful works?' But the Lord will say unto them, 'I never knew you, depart from me, ye that work iniquity.'" Even people who preach, teach Sunday School classes, and do other kinds of church work miss the mark. Many try to live a "good" life and hope their good deeds outweigh their bad ones. Some say, "I'm a pretty good person. Surely God won't condemn me to hell."

You might ask, how can this be so? I believe there are two reasons for this. Number one, people do not know their Bibles, and number two, Satan is a great deceiver. We need to understand what God says about every one of us. His word is very clear.

Romans 3:10 - As it is written, There is none righteous, no, not one.

Isaiah 64:6 - But we are all as an unclean thing, and all our righteousnesses are as filthy rags; and we all do fade as a leaf; and our iniquities, like the wind, have taken us away. (vs.7) - And there is none that calleth upon thy name, that stirreth up himself to take hold of thee: for thou hast hid thy face from us, and hast consumed us, because of our iniquities.

Psalms 14:1-3 - The fool hath said in his heart, There is no God. They are corrupt, they have done abominable works, there is none that doeth good. The Lord looked down from heaven upon the children of men, to see if there were any that did understand, and seek God. They are all gone aside, they are all together become filthy: there is none that doeth good, no, not one,

Titus 3:5 - Not by works of righteousness which we have done, but according to his mercy he saved us, by the washing of regeneration, and renewing of the Holy Ghost.

Romans 3:23 - For all have sinned and come short of the glory of God.

That is why it was necessary for Christ to go to the cross. If we could get to heaven by our good works or by "being good," then it was not necessary for Christ to die on the cross. Being good may make the world a better place to live in, but it doesn't get us to heaven. So, Satan deceives people into thinking they are pretty good and therefore will make it to heaven. We have no righteousness of our own that does us any good. **All** our righteousnesses are as dirty, filthy rags. But when we repent of who we are, then Jeremiah 33:16 tells us that the Lord becomes our righteousness. Daniel 9:7 says, "Oh Lord, righteousness belongeth unto thee..." In Galatians 2:21, Paul said, "I do not frustrate the grace of God: for if righteousness came by the law, then Christ is dead in vain."

I Timothy 1:15 - This is a faithful saying, and worthy of all acceptation, that Christ Jesus came into the world to save sinners; of whom I am chief.

Hebrews 7:25 - Wherefore he is able also to save them to the uttermost that come unto God by him, seeing he ever liveth to make intercession for them.

II Corinthians 5:17-18a - Therefore if any man be in Christ, he is a new creature: old things are passed away; behold, all things are become new. And all things are of God, who hath reconciled us to himself by Jesus Christ...

John 17:3 - And this is life eternal, that they might know thee the only true God, and Jesus Christ, whom thou hast sent.

Satan is the great deceiver. He deceives in many ways.

1. Satan deceives in conviction. How does he do that? He gets preachers to preach on "sins" instead of "sin." They preach about what you do, rather than what you are. Christ died for sinners. Some preachers preach about your sins of lying, stealing, drinking, cheating, cursing, adultery, divorce, etc. A person begins to feel terrible and condemned. This brings terrible regret. We feel embarrassed before God and even ourselves. This leads us to believe that this is true Biblical conviction. Holy Spirit conviction makes a man look, not so much upon his sins outwardly but upon himself inwardly. He sees himself as a sinner against God's will. This comes from preaching on what he has done. This brings to the sinner a feeling that he is **LOST**. Yes, we knew we had done wrong, but more than that, we knew we were hopelessly doomed because we were afflicted with the disease of sin, and that there is no remedy except Christ. This is Holy Spirit conviction. The conviction that the Holy Spirit gives is based on the truth of what we are, rather than on what we have done. What are we? We are sinners, and because of that we sin.

2. Satan deceives in repentance. Because of this terrible, morbid, undone feeling, a person is driven to do something about his sins. Now, what can you do about your sins? The only thing you can do is to be sorry for them. That is exactly what Satan wants. But being sorry is not repentance. Repentance is changing your attitude toward God, and agreeing that He is right in condemning you to hell because of what you are, not just what you have done. We are sinners by nature and by choice. Repentance is taking a sinner's place under the sentence of death, and submitting your case to the mercy of God. Being sorry for sin won't remove it. Only what Christ has done can do that. (Romans 6:23 - The wages of sin is death, but the gift of God is eternal life through Jesus Christ our Lord.) Satan would say, "Go on down to the altar. Cry and mourn and let God know how sorry you are and then you will feel better." Many times after this kind of experience, emotional relief comes. Emotional release can be mistaken for forgiveness. You hear people say, "Oh, I feel so much better."

3. Satan deceives in the experience of **salvation**. The sinner is led to believe that when "he feels better," he has been saved. The Holy Spirit, through the right kind of preaching, will direct the sinner not to try to do anything about his sins. He would tell the sinner to look to Christ who has already done all that can be done, or that is necessary, about his sins. He would tell the sinner to take his place before God as a sinner, submitting to God's judgment of him, and then look to Christ as the one who has satisfied the Father about his sin, and who, by His death, has redeemed him. Then, the sinner can say, "Because I have taken a sinner's place, and have looked to Christ to save me, on the authority of God's word I can declare I am saved. I know it is true because God says so, and I believe His Word."

Tract – By: B.H, Kazee
Have You Been Saved Or Deceived?

One can't be a Christian without becoming one. Being raised in "Christian America" doesn't make you a Christian. Many who say they are Christians in this "you-don't-suppose-I'm-a-heathen" sense, have never acknowledged their sinful estate and repented and received Christ as their Saviour. Some are even insulted if you ask them concerning their personal relationship with God.

To become a Christian in the Bible sense of the word demands **personal** faith in Jesus Christ as Saviour. Therefore, to become a Christian we must believe what is necessary to become one. "One becomes a Christian not by doing something for God but by believing that God has done something for him. The very heart of Christianity is the glorious good news that Christ died for our sins, and that salvation is a free gift which God grants on the simple condition of repenting of who we are and receiving Christ as one's personal Saviour.

"To commit the salvation of your soul to Jesus Christ involves, of course, a recognition of your need. In accepting Christ we, too, bowed before the verdict of God's word that we are sinners in need of salvation. We, too, renounced all our own efforts to please God as unavailing. We saw our character and our cherished 'good works' as falling miserably short of God's requirement. We faced the fact of the guilt of our sin and gladly believed that its dreaded penalty was borne for us by Christ in His death upon the cross.

"One who claims to be a Christian should also act like one. Christ-like character and conduct can be produced only by the indwelling presence of Christ controlling the believer's heart. The Christian should seek to walk even as He walked, by depending upon the transforming power of the living Christ."

Can You Be A Christian Without Becoming One?
By: Willard M. Aldrich

Don't even try to be a Christian without becoming one. It won't work. One cannot live the Christian life until they have received the gift of eternal life. Become one by meeting God's conditions and believing on the Lord Jesus Christ.

If a person has truly received Christ into his heart and life, **there must be a change in his life.** A true heart conversion produces a spiritual change in the life. Do you profess to being saved? Has there been any "about face" in your purpose and pattern of living? Jesus warned of the danger of profession without really being saved when He says in Matthew 7:21 "not everyone that saith unto me, Lord,

Lord, shall enter into the kingdom of heaven; but he that **doeth** the will of my Father which is in heaven."

Someone has said that there are three kinds of believers: true believers, unbelievers, and "make-believers." Which one are you? Have you been saved or deceived?

CHAPTER II

REPENTANCE

Many people believe that because they join a church and are baptized, or because they were raised in a Christian home, or Christian America, they are saved. That is far from the truth. For many there has been no true repentance and therefore no changed life. That is why the church is often weak and ineffective. That is probably why you hear people say there are too many hypocrites in the church,

A former pastor from our church in Ohio preached a sermon entitled, "The Lost Art of Repentance." He said there has never been a time in the history of man when repentance was needed more, and preached less. It is one of the most disliked, and consequently, most neglected subjects. Yet, if one is to find life and peace through the finished work of Calvary, there is no substitute for repentance.

Some seem to get the idea that if you just believe, you will be saved. They say they are saved, but go on living any way they choose. Christ said, "Except ye repent ye shall **all** likewise perish." (Luke 13:3)

What is true repentance then? Repentance doesn't mean merely shedding tears over our sin, but it lays strong hold upon the human will and brings the sinner into conformity with the will of God. "Repentance is changing your attitude toward God, and agreeing that He is right in condemning you to hell because of **what you are**, not just what you have done. Repentance is taking a sinner's place under the sentence of death, and submitting your case to the mercy of God. Being sorry for sin won't remove it. Only what Christ has done can do that."

The importance of repentance is seen in the fact that our precious Lord Jesus began His first sermon with an exhortation to repent. Matthew 4:17 says, "From that time Jesus began to preach, and to say, Repent, for the kingdom of heaven is at hand." Our Lord never once implied that salvation by grace could be obtained in any other way than by turning their back upon sin and the old life, and following Christ.

Let's look at some verses in the Bible to see what God has to say about repentance.

Luke 24:47 - "that repentance and remission of sin should be preached in His name among all nations, beginning at Jerusalem."

Acts 17:30 - "God commandeth all men everywhere to repent."

Luke 13:3 - "Except ye repent, ye shall all likewise perish."

Proverbs 28:13 - "He that covereth his sins shall not prosper: but whoso confesseth and forsaketh them shall have mercy."

Acts 3:19 - "Repent ye, and be converted that your sins may be blotted out."

Isaiah 55:7 - "Let the wicked forsake his way and the unrighteous man his thoughts; and let him return unto the Lord, and He will have mercy upon him, and to our God, for He will abundantly pardon."

"The need for repentance is emphasized 70 times in the New Testament. Repentance does not mean doing something to pay the penalty for having sinned. No man can pay the penalty for his sin and remain alive. Furthermore, Christ has already suffered for every man.

"Repentance means a complete change of mind toward God, toward sin, and toward others. The repentant sinner recognizes his disobedience to God's law, humbly confesses his sinfulness, and calls upon God for mercy. He turns his back on everything that displeases God. His attitude now is to please God in everything. The sinner is sorry for the wrongs he has done to others and endeavors to make restitution as far as possible. Restitution means correcting or undoing any wrong done to another person.

"Repentance always precedes faith. Faith without repentance is like telling a doctor that you believe he can cure you but that you intend to continue in the practice which produced the disease. The jailer at Philippi was struck with the fear of God and was then instructed to believe. However, to those who had no such conviction of their lostness, Jesus said, 'Repent ye, and believe the gospel.' (Mark 1:15)."

"The Highway & Hedge Evangel"
The Morning Glory

So why is repentance so important? Proverbs 14:12 says, "There is a way that seemeth right unto a man, but the end thereof are the ways of death." Also, "Strait is the gate, and narrow is the way which leadeth unto life, and few there be that find it," "Strive to enter in at the strait gate; for many, I say unto you, will seek to enter in and shall not be able. "(Matthew 7:14, Luke 13:24)

Repentance is necessary if sins are to be blotted out and we are to find favor with God. "When there is true repentance there is godly sorrow for sin, there is a determination to forsake it. It will lead to a complete change of conduct and to newness of life. II Corinthians 5:17 says, "If any man be in Christ he is a new creature. Old things are passed away, behold all things are become new." True repentance brings a sense of a Holy God who cannot look upon sin. A true child of God who has repented cannot enjoy sin, and continuously longs for deliverance. In desperation, Paul cried out, "O wretched man that I am! Who shall deliver me from the body of this death?" (Romans 7:24)

Unless there is repentance there is no changed life. If there is no changed life then there has been no new birth. Charles Spurgeon once said, "An unholy life is evidence of an unchanged heart. An unchanged heart is evidence of an unsaved soul." He stated that what value is there of grace that leaves us the same as before we received it. My belief must transform my behavior. It is not what I believe that saves me, but the one in whom I believe that saves. He must change my behavior."

True repentance will result in joy and peace in knowing our sins have been forgiven and that we have been made right with God.

Quote from Charles Spurgeon

"From the plain teachings of God's Word, there is no doubt that eternal souls pass from death unto life through a living faith in Jesus Christ. But ever and always this faith must be preceded by genuine repentance. Repentance ever precedes faith in New Testament doctrine, and there is no faith born into hearts apart from a repentance which is genuine in the sight of God who knows all hearts. Salvation comes to the sinning one when he, under the convicting power of the Holy Spirit, repents and forsakes sins. He then casts himself totally on Christ as his only hope. It is absolute committal, and such alone is true believing." (Mark 1:15, Luke 24:47, Luke 13:3, II Corinthians 7:10)

Superficial Believism
By: Rev. Paul Kenyon
Alliance Witness Magazine

Wherever Christ and the gospel has been preached, repentance and faith for the remission of sins has been preached, except by the modernists, who have, as they think, found a better way.

In our modern times many have been deceived into thinking that all one has to do is just "accept Christ," join the church and be baptized. There is no confessing and forsaking sin. When the heart and life remain unchanged, the canker of sin continues to operate and to lead to certain death.

Jesus said, "Ye must be born again." (John 3:7), at which time a new name is written down in the Book Of Life, and without which, joining every church under heaven will not accomplish anything. "For whosoever was not found written in the Book of Life, was cast into the lake of fire." (Revelation 20:12 and 15).

When one accepts Christ he also accepts His Word, and purposes to renounce sin and walk in His ways. If old things have not passed away, and all things become new, one has not truly accepted Christ in reality.

Another theory that has been around for some years now is the "Only Believe" theory. This is not possible until there has been true repentance and God's conditions have been met.

Have you repented? Is your name written in the Book Of Life?

Matthew 5:20 tells us that "our righteousness must exceed the righteousness of the scribes and Pharisees or we will in no case enter into the kingdom of heaven."

Romans 10:3-4 says, "For they being ignorant of God's righteousness and going about to establish their own righteousness, have not submitted themselves unto the righteousness of God. For Christ is the end of the law for righteousness to everyone that believeth." But, praise God, "Christ is made unto us righteousness,.." (I Corinthians 1:30)

II Corinthians 5:21 - "For he hath made him to be sin for us, who knew no sin, that we might be made the righteousness of God in Him."

Titus 3:5-7 - Not by works of righteousness which we have done, but according to his mercy he saved us, by the washing of regeneration, and renewing of the Holy Ghost; which he shed on us abundantly through Jesus Christ our Saviour. That being justified by his grace, we should be made heirs according to the hope of eternal life."

CHAPTER III

ASSURANCE

When I was a small child, I asked Jesus to come into my heart and to save me. I believe in my child-like way I repented and truly believed, but when I went forward to pray, no one came to pray with me or to council me. I wasn't talked to about it, or encouraged to write the date down or anything. I believe, as a result of that, and the devil trying to deceive me, there were times when I had real doubt about my salvation. I had doubt for a number of years. Finally, as a young teenager, I prayed one night and said to the Lord, "Lord I don't want to go to sleep tonight until I have a verse from the Bible giving me the assurance I need." In the wee hours of the morning, God led me to I John 5:11-15. It says, *"And this is the record that God hath given to us eternal life, and this life is in His Son. He that hath the Son hath life; and he that hath not the Son of God hath not life. These things have I written unto you that believe on the name of the Son of God: that ye may know that ye have eternal life, and that ye may believe on the name of the Son of God."*

From that day to this, I have not doubted my salvation.

We are all different, and God deals with us in different ways. If we fail to understand this, it can cause doubt and confusion. For instance, Paul and Timothy's conversions were very different. Paul's was probably very emotional and earth moving. Timothy's was probably very quiet. So, we can't just go on an emotional experience.

No matter what experience we may have, our faith must be placed in the person of God and in His holy, inspired Word, rather than in our feelings.

Many and probably most young Christians, at the beginning of their Christian life, make the mistake of relying too much on their feelings. One day they may feel close to God; the next day He may seem far away. They imagine their feelings accurately reflect their spiritual condition. This produces a frenzy of uncertainty. This is what I experienced. We must learn to mistrust our feelings. They change with the weather and vacillate with our health and circumstances. Our fluctuating feelings very often have nothing whatever to do with our spiritual progress.

[Bill Bright, **How To Be Sure You are a Christian**. Campus Crusade for Christ.]

There are a couple of other things we need to note at this point. Unless there is a genuine desire to obey and please the Lord Jesus, one has a right to question if he is truly a child of God. If willful sin is allowed to continue in our lives, we will begin to doubt our salvation and rightly so. In John 14:21, Jesus is saying that He will make Himself known to all who obey Him in such a way that they will experience the reality of His presence in their lives.

Bill Bright, in his writings, says there is a threefold confirmation. "The trustworthy Word, the confirming Holy Spirit, and a changed life." All three agreeing equal assurance.

So, repent and ask Jesus to be your Savior once, and then each day as an act of faith thank Him for doing what He said He would do. He promises never to leave us or forsake us. It is only then that we can experience His peace in our lives.

So how can we know we are truly saved?
1. We know by the Word of God. (I John 5:11-13; I John 2:3-5)
2. We know by the Witness Within. (Romans 8:16; I John 5:14; 5:10)
3. We know by the Works of our Lives. (Changed life)
    a. Obedience - (I John 2:3-4)
    b. Love for the brethren - (I John 3:11-12; 14)

    c. Love for God's Word - (Psalm 19:8-10)
    d. Desire to Worship God - (Psalm 122:1)
    e. Fruit of the Spirit - (Galatians 5:22)

Doubt brings torment. God does not want that for His children. He wants us to live in the reality of His presence, and to know that when we die we will go to Heaven to be with Him forever.

Lack of assurance is usually due to one or two things. It's either lack of information or misinformation concerning who God is, the true meaning of the crucifixion and the resurrection and what is involved in receiving Jesus Christ as one's Saviour.

Perhaps you have only recently become a Christian and you are still not sure that anything has really happened. You have no assurance of your salvation and have serious misgivings about where you will go when you die. Becoming a Christian involves repenting and receiving the Lord Jesus Christ, the gift of God's love and forgiveness - by faith. It results in a threefold commitment to a person, the person of the Lord Jesus Christ. It is a commitment to Him of one's **intellect, emotions** and **will**.

First of all, in order to become a Christian, or to be sure that you are a Christian, you must have a clear, intellectual understanding of what is involved. Christianity is not "a blind leap of faith." It is built upon historical fact, documented by centuries of scholarship and research. Many leading scholars have dedicated their lives to investigating the life, teachings, death, resurrection and influence of Jesus of Nazareth. As a result, we have more historical evidence proving His resurrection than we have of the fact that Napoleon was defeated at Waterloo. The intellectual commitment is a recognition of sin as personal guilt and defilement. (Romans 3:19-20; Psalm 51; Romans 1:32)

In order to become a Christian, then, you must honestly and squarely face the claims of Jesus Christ and believe **intellectually** that He is God, that He died for your sins and was buried, that He rose again, and that He wants to come into your life and be your Saviour and Lord. (Romans 10:8-10)

Second, being sure that you are a Christian involves the **emotions**. An emotion is a feeling or a reaction to a specific act, event or experience. Probably no one thing has caused more people to lack the assurance of a vital personal relationship with God through Jesus Christ than the wrong emphasis on emotions.

Man is an emotional creature by nature, and everything he does involves his emotions. Most young Christians, at the beginning of their Christian life, make a mistake of relying too much on their superficial feelings. One day they may feel close to God; the next day He may seem far away. They imagine their feelings accurately reflect their spiritual condition, and so they fall into a frenzy of uncertainty. Their Christian life becomes like a roller coaster ride. This is no good at all. Do learn to mistrust your feelings. They change with the weather and vacillate with our health. We are fickle creatures of whelm and mood, and our fluctuating feelings very often have nothing whatever to do with our spiritual progress. The emotional commitment should be heart sorrow for sin as committed against God. (II Corinthians 7, 9, 10)

Third is the **will**, God has made us in such a way that we can choose to commit our all to Him. That choice is the most important one we will ever make. It involves a renunciation of all sin.

"In ordinary life everything depends on the will, which is, as we all know, the governing power in a person's nature. By the will, I do not mean our wishes, feelings, or longings, but our choice, our deciding power, the king within us to which all the rest of our nature must yield obedience. I mean, in short, the person himself, the ego — that personality in the depths of the being which is felt to be the real self. A great deal of trouble arises from the fact that so few seem to understand this secret of the will.

HOW TO KNOW YOU ARE SAVED

1- You become interested in the Bible.

What God has to say in the Bible becomes increasingly important to you. You find yourself interested in his program and even detect the inclination within yourself to do things which you think will please Him. You may not always obey this inward tendency, but you will not question its presence. This new appetite for the Word (will) of God is a noticeable change that occurs when our lives become heaven bound. The words of the apostle John are stronger, but he is expressing the same truths. (I John 2:3-5)

When we note this change in our attitude toward God's will (Bible), we can be assured that the miracle has occurred.

2. You feel a Kinship with Other Christians.

When you become a Christian and are on God's side, so to speak, then His people become your people. You can't help feeling that they are one great family and unconsciously sense they somehow belong to you. This is not surprising when it is considered that you have the same life as they: the same destination (heaven): and have shared the same experience. This new attitude toward Christians and the feeling of oneness with them is another definite evidence of God's miracle in your heart. John puts it this way: *"We know that we have passed from death unto life because we love the brethren."* (I John 3:14)

This which you now feel toward them will grow and blossom into love and concern.

3. You Will have the Witness of God's Spirit Within Yourself.

This third evidence is just as definite as the others. It is the internal witness of the Holy Spirit that you belong to God. It takes the form of a conviction that arises within you. True, there is no way of proving or disproving the witness — it just is there. One may question it, dispute it, or even deny it, but he cannot change it. It is implanted the moment we are saved and remains steadfast through any attacks we suffer whether from within or without ourselves. Note how specifically John speaks of this witness. (I John 3:24; 5:10)

Find these three elements in your life and you will never be the same. It will be hard for you to turn your back upon the Lord and the Christian life once they are discovered in your own experience. One can never be the same after he has known the transforming miracle of receiving Christ. (I John 5:11, 12)

The common thought is that religion resides not in the will but in the emotions, and the emotions are looked on as the governing power in our nature. Consequently, all the attention of the soul is directed toward our feelings, and as these are satisfactory or otherwise, the soul rests or is troubled. The moment we discover that true religion resides in the will alone, we are raised above the domination of our feelings and realize that, so long as our will is steadfast toward God, the varying states of our emotions do not in the least affect the reality of the divine life in the soul. It is a great emancipation to make this discovery; and a little common sense applied to religion would soon, I think, reveal it to us all. (EDR, 68-69)

The will is the stronghold of our being. If God is to get complete possession of us, He must possess our will. When He says to us, "My son, give me your heart," it is equivalent to saying, "surrender your will to my control, that I may work in it to will and to do of my good pleasure." It is not the feelings of a man that God wants, but his will.

The "hidden man of the heart" (I Peter 3:4) is the Bible description of the will. Our feelings are not ourselves. What God desires is not fervent emotions but a pure intention of the will. The whole of his scrutiny falls on this "hidden man of the heart." Where He finds this honest devotion to himself, He disregards all the clamor of our feelings and is satisfied.

It is very possible to pour out our emotions on a matter without really giving our hearts at all. We sometimes see people who are very lavish with their feelings, but whose wills remain untouched. We call this sentimentality, and we mean that there is no reality in it. To get at reality, the heart, or in other words, the will, must be reached. What the will does is real, and nothing else is, (EDR, 72-73)

God Is Enough
By: Hanna W. Smith
Francis Asbury Press of
Zondervan Publishing House
Grand Rapids, MI 1986
Pg. 134-135

CHAPTER IV

WHAT HAPPENED WHEN YOU OPENED YOUR HEART TO JESUS?

HOW TO BEGIN YOUR CHRISTIAN LIFE

I. REALIZE WHAT HAS HAPPENED TO YOU.
A. You have been reborn. Titus 3:5
　　The rebirth has been defined as "the communication of life by the Spirit to a soul dead in trespasses and sin."
　　1. The realities of the new birth -
　　　　a. The new birth gives life to our spiritual capacity.
　　　　　　1. **Taste** - "O taste and see that the Lord is good!" (Psalm 34:8). We have now experienced the reality of God's love and goodness.
　　　　　　2. **Sight** - "having the eyes of your heart enlightened." (Ephesians 1:18)
　　　　　　3. **Touch** - "we have look upon and touched ... the word of' life "(I John 1:11)
　　　　b. The new birth gives us characteristics like our Father.
　　　　　　1. **Righteousness** - (John 17:25)
　　　　　　2. **Love** - (I John 4:7-8)
　　　　　　3. Holiness - (John 17-11)
How much do you look and act like the Father?

2. The results of the new birth -
   a. A new understanding of spiritual matters - (Colossians 1:9)
   b. A new life in Christ - (II Corinthians 5:17)
   c. A new purpose for living - (Ephesians 2:10)
   d. A release from the old way of life - (Ephesians 2:1-5)
   e. Peace with God - (Romans 5:1)

B. You have been forgiven - (Colossians 1:14)
   1. God has removed your transgressions - (Psalm 103:12)
   2. God made your sins as white as snow - (Isaiah 1:18)
   3. God placed your sins behind his back - (Isaiah 38:17)
   4. God remembers your sin no more - (Hebrews 8:12)

C. You have been justified - (Romans 5:9)
   Justification means that God accepts me "just-as-if-I'd" never sinned. It is a legal term showing you, the sinner, before God, the righteous Judge. Christ paid your penalty and you are pardoned, justified. You are pardoned because the demands of justice have been satisfied by Christ's death.
   1. You have been justified by faith - (Romans 5:1)
   2. You have been justified by God's free gift - (Romans 3:24)
   3. You have been justified through the death and resurrection of Jesus Christ - (Romans 5:9; 4:25)

D. You have been adopted into God's family - (Ephesians 1:3-6)
   1. God planned your adoption from the beginning - (I Peter 1:2)
   2. Christ died to make your redemption possible - (Galatians 4:4-7)
   3. You can now call God "Father" - (Romans 8:15) (I also like the next 2 verses 8:16-17)

E. You can now have the assurance of eternal life - (I John 5:11-13, Ephesians 1)
   1. You have the assurance of salvation - (John 6:47)

2. You have the assurance of victory over sin - (I John 5:5) – Romans 6:12 - Let not sin reign in your mortal bodies. God saves us from penalty of sin and from the power of sin and someday from the very presence of sin.
3. You have the assurance of answered prayer - (John 16:24)
4. You have the assurance of the Spirit that you are a child of God -(Romans 8:16)

CONCLUSION:

You are a babe in Christ. God loves you as a mother would love her newborn child - and more! Remember, he has plans for you! He dreams of your future just as other parents have dreams and plans for their children.

Let nothing hinder you from growing as a Christian. Be determined to be a child that will make your heavenly Father proud, and God will be with you each step of the way!

WHAT HAPPENED WHEN YOU OPENED YOUR HEART TO JESUS?

When you were born into God's family many wonderful things happened to you.
1. You were born into God's family.
2. God's Holy Spirit came into your life to dwell within your heart and soul.
3. Your sins were all forgiven.
4. A total new life began.
5. Fellowship with God was made possible.
6. You now have access to God's throne.

There are many more privileges that are yours now that you know Christ. I want to list for you a few of my favorites.

1. God will use everything in my life for good, conforming me into the image of Christ (Romans 8:28, 29) - (My life verses)
2. He will supply every need in my life (Philippians 4:19)

3. He already knows my needs before I ask Him (Matthew 6:32)
4. He will give me wisdom generously when I ask Him (James 1:5)
5. His peace is mine and He will superintend my thought life as I pray with thankfulness (Philippians 4:4-7)
6. He will always be with me (Matthew 28:20)

CHAPTER V

OPEN CONFESSION OF CHRIST

Once a person has repented and accepted Jesus Christ as his Lord and Saviour, the next step should be a public confession of that relationship. This is the first step in a newfound life in Christ. It is the first evidence of being born again.

Sharing what God did for you will help make it more real and exciting in your own life. How do we let others know what has taken place in our lives? Soldiers, pilots, firemen, and policemen all publicly identify themselves by their uniforms. A girl, when she marries, renounces her maiden name and receives a new name, the name of her husband. So when a person becomes a Christian there are steps that should be taken in our newfound faith. The first step should be a public confession. Rev. Billy Graham always had people go forward in his meetings to make a public confession of their faith.

Public confession seals the decision by bringing to a crisis a conscious committal of our lives to the Lord Jesus Christ. A new convert should witness his conversion by water baptism and aligning himself with a gospel and Bible preaching church. This is very important if one is to grow in their newfound life.

Christ knew how important an open confession was. In fact, He demanded it. He demands it for our own sake. This is the path of blessing. In Matthew 10:32-33, He said, "Whosoever therefore shall confess me before men, him will I confess also before my Father which is in heaven. But whosoever shall deny me before men, him will I also deny before my Father which is in heaven."

Some try to be secret disciples, but if one has truly been saved he cannot keep it to himself, nor should he want to. Matthew 12:34 says, "For out of the abundance of the heart the mouth speaketh." No one has ever succeeded in trying to be a secret disciple. If one is truly saved they can't keep it to themselves. The life of confession is the life of full salvation. It is the life of the only real salvation. When we confess Christ before men down here, He confesses us before the Father in heaven and the Father gives us the Holy Spirit as the seal of our salvation.

The apostle Paul believed very strongly in a public confession. He puts it first in the conditions of salvation. He says in Romans 10:9-10, "If thou shalt confess with thy mouth the Lord Jesus, and shalt believe in thine heart that God hath raised him from the dead, thou shalt be saved. For with the heart man believeth unto righteousness, and with the mouth confession is made unto salvation."

We need to confess Christ every chance we get, not just once. We need to make much of Christ, to lift Him up. He said, "If I be lifted up, I will draw all men unto me." (John 12:32) We need to let people know that we are on His side in our everyday living. Our lives should portray the fact that we glory in Christ as our Lord and King,

If we don't confess Christ frequently, we can so easily backslide. Christians get into new situations and relationships where people don't really know them, and know that they are Christians, and are sometimes tempted to hide the fact that they are Christians. They yield to the temptation and soon find themselves drifting. It will save one a lot of temptations and problems if you take a firm stand and let it be clearly known that you are a believer and you acknowledge Christ as Lord in all things.

CHAPTER VI

CHRISTIAN GROWTH

HOW TO LIVE A SUCCESSFUL CHRISTIAN LIFE

Once a person is a child of God, his growth largely depends on himself. It is impossible for you to become a successful and useful Christian unless you are willing to do the things that are absolutely essential to your spiritual growth. The Bible constantly gives injunctions designed to stir up God's people to develop themselves in the Lord. II Peter 3:18, *"But grow in grace, and in the knowledge of our Lord and Savior Jesus Christ."* (Read also I Corinthians 15:58; 16:13; Galatians 6:9; Hebrews 6:1). To this end, we believe the following suggestions will be found to be of vital importance.

CHRISTIAN GROWTH

The Christian has two natures: the old sinful nature he received at his first, or natural birth, and the new or Divine nature, which was communicated to him when he received Christ as Savior and Lord. There is a conflict going on because these two natures are diametrically opposed to each other. If the new nature is to have the ascendancy in the life of the Christian, it must be encouraged and strengthened by feeding on the Scriptures, communing with God by prayer, obeying God's will and separating oneself from all known sin. That is how we grow spiritually. The Bible is our spiritual food. If one stops eating they start dying. It's important what and how we eat. The Bible is the Word of God. "It reveals God, it uncovers sin, it proclaims the way of salvation, it presents a standard of life, it guides us with the truth of Hell and the hope of Heaven." (H. Lindsay, Jr.)

If we are going to be mature Christians, we must study the Word and learn to apply its principles to our lives. (**CONSERVE THE CONVERTS** - By: Charles Shaver)

God desires that His children should grow up to know Him more and more intimately. This can only be done as we are habitually in the Word. Most Christians today are ignorant of much of what the Bible teaches. New Christians need the milk of the Word. Other Christians need the meat, but we all need to feed upon the precious Word of God.

THREE ESSENTIALS FOR CHRISTIAN GROWTH

1. Proper **food** - (I Peter 2:1-2)
    a. Have a good reference Bible.
    b. Set apart an hour daily sacred to Bible Study.
    c. Study with a heart prepared for it. (Ezra 7:10)
    d. Ask the Author of the Book to guide you. (Psalm 119:18; John 16:13,14)
      e. Study for personal profit (I Peter 1:22, 23; Acts 20:32)
      f. Believe promises; heed warnings; obey directions
      g. Remember it is God's message to you

2. Proper **exercise.** (John 13:17)
      a. Confess Christ before men. (Matthew 10:32-38; Romans 10:9,10)
      b. Get into the visible church. (Acts 2:42-47; Hebrews 10:24, 25)
      c. Observe the Sacraments. (Acts 2:38-42; Luke 22:19)
      d. Pray daily in your family for God's Work. (Luke 11:9-13)
      e. Obey every Word of Christ (John 2:5; 14:23; 15:7)
      f. Use all your time and talents faithfully. (Ephesians 5:16)
      g. Give systematically as God has prospered you. (Proverbs 3:9-10)

3. Proper **associations**. (I Corinthians 15:33)
    a. Keep in the light. (I John 1:7; John 3:20, 21; I Thessalonians 5;5)
    b. Walk with the wise. (Proverbs 13:20)
    c. Stand aloof from worldly conformity. (Romans 12:2)
    d. Go only where the Spirit leads you. (Romans 8:9-14)

When Home Is Heaven
By: J. Wilbur Chapman
Fleming H. Revell Company

VI – A: THE BIBLE

BIBLE STUDY

In order to be able to really trust God and His Word, there are certain things one needs to know. One needs to be fully persuaded that **all** of the Bible is the inspired Word of God. One needs to be completely convinced that all the Bible is true or none of it is.

If someone said to you, "Prove to me that the Bible is the Word of God," what would you say? I want to give to you evidence that the Bible is the inspired word of God,

EVIDENCE OF INSPIRATION

Prophecy

First of all, think how amazed your unsaved friends will be when you show them from the Word a prophecy of the exact town in which a person would be born, written 700 years before his birth. Certainly no mere man could plan where he himself would be born, nor would it be possible for him to put the place down in writing centuries before and then have it come absolutely true. At Christmas time, people talk about Jesus being born in Bethlehem, so at least some will know where Jesus was born. Open your Bible to the book of Micah, the 5th chapter and the 2nd verse and show them in black and white the prophecy that was written so many hundreds of years before. They will have to admit that this could only be foretold as a miracle of God, who alone knows the future.

Scientific Accuracy

If your unsaved friends think the Bible is unscientific and out of date, ask them for an answer to this statement of scientific accuracy in Job 26:7: "He hangeth the earth upon nothing." The people of that day believed that the earth rested on elephants, which stood on the back of a turtle, which swam in a great sea. This was a so-called fact of science at the time and if the writer had been trying to impress those of his day with his knowledge of science, why did he not mention the turtle and elephants and the other ridiculous ideas which were accepted as true at that time? The God of all creation guided and protected every word put in Scripture so that no scientific inaccuracy would show up, even though the writers themselves were not, at the time they wrote, aware of the scientific facts which were not discovered until thousands of years later.

Testimony of Christ

Many of your friends who have never received Jesus Christ as Saviour will still admit as to His honesty, high moral character and purity of life. Put them on the spot as to whether or not they would believe the Bible to be the Word of God if Jesus did. Here are some ways in which we know Jesus accepted without question the entire Old Testament, for the Old Testament as it is in your Bible is exactly the same Bible Jesus used when He was on earth, and He commonly referred to the Old Testament as the Scriptures. In talking with two disciples in Luke 24:27, He put His complete endorsement on the Scriptures, "And beginning at Moses and all the prophets, he expounded unto them in all the Scriptures the things concerning himself." You can also show your friends that He referred to Noah's flood as an actual happening - Matthew 24:37-39; Jonah and the whale - Matthew 12:39-41; and the wisdom of King Solomon - Luke 11:31.

All these things Jesus believed to have happened just as recorded in the Old Testament. If he accepted them, who is any mere man to question them?

Circulation

The Bible has been the world's best seller year in and year out. I called Wycliff Bible Translators and asked them how many languages the Bible had been translated into. They told me that there are 6,912 languages in the world. The complete Bible has been translated into 2,529 of them. 2,377 do not have the whole Bible. Some don't need it. They can use another language or one similar to theirs.

Indestructibility

The Bible has been the most persecuted Book. Down through the centuries, men have burned it, cursed it, ridiculed it, and ignored it. These men have died but the Book lives on. Surely it is the "anvil that has broken a thousand hammers."

My husband and I were at a meeting one time when the wife of the president of OMS told this story.

During the second world war Russia confiscated all the Bibles they could find. They stored them in a warehouse. They were there for many years. After the war they finally decided they had to be moved somewhere else. Some college students were hired to move them. One of the college students hired was an atheist, and a young Communist. After he had worked for some time he sat down to take a short break. He picked up one of the Bibles and opened it up. To his utter amazement, he found that the very Bible he had in his hand had belonged to his own grandmother. Her name was in the Bible. As a result of that experience, he was converted. God uses even the wrath of man to praise Him. Of all the thousands of Bibles stored in that warehouse it certainly wasn't "by chance" that he picked up one that was his grandmother's.

God protects His Word.

Influence

The Bible has had a greater impact for good upon the history of nations than any book ever published. Every modern institution for the alleviation of human misery has had its origin in this Book. Throughout history, nations which have kept it an "open book" have experienced the greatest prosperity and success. "Them that honour me, I will honour"(I Samuel 2:30).

Power

The Bible does all that it claims to do. In Romans 1:16, we read, "it is the power of God unto salvation to every one that believeth." Here is your opportunity to bring your friend to Christ. Give him your testimony of how the gospel worked in your life and invite him to enjoy the same experience. Your friend may do this by personally receiving Christ, and he will discover that the gospel of Christ is the "power of God unto salvation," and that God keeps every promise in His Word.

WHY WE NEED THE BIBLE

Is it reasonable to believe that God would create a world of men and then stand off and not try to communicate with those whom He created (Ephesians 2:4-6)? Since He is a God of love, He desires fellowship with us (John 4:8). People will try to find Him in their own way and by their own efforts. If our planet be nothing but a speck in the heavens, how can man through his own efforts hope to discover the Creator and Ruler of it all? He cannot. Then too, though he is physically very small, God says that the soul of every man is of supreme value (Mark 8:36). Therefore, God must reveal Himself, which He has done in the Bible.

THE INSPIRATION OF THE BIBLE

By inspiration we mean that God so guided the men who wrote the book that every thought and word they expressed was exactly what God wanted man to know. Nothing was added. II Peter 1:21 says, "Holy men of God spake as they were moved by the Holy Ghost." All that was written was kept from error. In II Timothy 3:16 we read, "All scripture is given by inspiration of God." Literally, this means "all scripture is God-breathed." God breathed His own life into this Book. The Bible then is a living book because it is the Word of the Living God.

HOW THE BIBLE WAS PRESERVED

If His truth were passed on by tradition or word of mouth, it would most certainly have been changed or corrupted. Instead, we have an inspired Book that has been preserved in a marvelous way

(Matthew 5:18). Thousands of men over the years have made copies of the original manuscripts. They have taken minute pains to be accurate. Thousands of copies of the ancient manuscripts agree in content, although they were written at different times and places. By simply comparing these manuscripts, we can be certain that the copies which we now have are accurate.

If the Bible is not the Word of God, it is the greatest fraud ever perpetrated upon the human race. Some say it is merely a "good book" with some errors. What would be said of any book that claimed over 2,600 times to be "inspired" of God and was then shown to contain human error? Certainly you would not put your confidence in it. The Bible, however, makes this claim and stands ready at all times to back it up,

Moody Bible Institute
Correspondence School
Chicago 10, IL
By: S. Maxwell Coder
Youth Triumphant.

The Bible is without error on every subject it addresses. It couldn't be God's Word if there were errors in it. As a Christian, our greatest assurance is the knowledge that our faith is based on a trustworthy God who has given reliable evidence to all He wants us to know.

A BIBLE READING DISCIPLE

By: Michael Daves

The dynamic disciple must be a Bible reading disciple. The dynamic disciple does not read the Bible because it is colorful, or because it is interesting, or because it is exciting - although it is all these. He reads the Bible because it is God's Word to him. In its pages, he finds the history of God's association with man and concern for him. Here we read the strong words of Christ as He went about healing and preaching. Here we dedicate ourselves anew to Him as the Lord of Life.

But to read the Bible is not in itself enough. We must read the Bible intelligently. Thus, we should turn to some good commentary that will help us to interpret difficult passages and to relate them to the everyday experiences of life. So, too, we should read it with imagination, trying to recapture the Biblical scene as it actually appeared so many centuries ago. And, above all, we should take pains to read the Bible as a family, giving each member an opportunity to read from the Holy Writ and to share its meaning for him. So the Bible will become a lamp unto our feet and a light unto our path.

"The Bible does not reveal its secrets to the spasmodic reader." (Don McFarland)

HOW TO READ
DECISION - HELPS FOR NEW CHRISTIANS
By: Churches of Christ in U.S.A.

Do not make the mistake of reading too much at a time. Read SLOWLY! If you find yourself unable to understand it all, do not be unduly concerned; it will grow clearer with time.

Read along until you come to a portion that you do understand, then pause a moment and think about it. Take it as being spoken to yourself and determine if it has meaning and significance for your life. Some days you may read two or three chapters; other days only a single verse. The important thing is not so much to have read it, but to have appropriated its meaning for your life. Even as you read you will detect evidence of your new life, for you will understand things you never realized before and will find the spirit of God making things clear to you as you go along. The important thing is to persevere. Read a portion every day. It might be well to put your Bible by your bedside and it will be available for reading each night before going to sleep. If you run into problems, do not let them deter you. You can investigate them later with someone competent to help.

The Bible is "spiritual food" and absolutely essential to growth in the Christian life. Do not neglect it. We need to learn how to use the Word to solve our problems, to find guidance and encouragement, and to bring others to Jesus. One of the most important things we can do is to meditate on the WORD OF GOD each day and apply it to life.

You are a babe in Christ. God loves you as a mother would love her newborn child - and more! Remember, he has plans for you! He dreams of your future just as other parents have dreams and plans for their children.

Let nothing hinder you from growing as a Christian. Be determined to be a child that will make your heavenly Father proud, and God will be with you each step of the way!

In order to grow as a Christian, it is essential to be in the Word regularly. If your Bible study is regular and daily, it will become a habit in your life, a good habit. Find a place, if possible, free from distractions. That may not be easy depending on your circumstances. If you are a mother with young children, you may think it is impossible, but it isn't. God will make a way when we are determined. Remember, you want a relationship with God and you want to be able to talk to Him and He with you.

Don't read just for the sake of reading. To understand the spiritual teaching and lessons we need to learn, we need the Holy Spirit's leading. As you read the Bible, pray, asking God the Holy Spirit to make plain to you what He wants you to know. Read with an expectant heart and mind. God wants us to learn from His Word.

It's good to write down things the Lord teaches you. Writing helps to organize your thoughts, and to be specific about what God is saying. A daily quiet time is a very important part of your life. When I talk about living a happy Christian life, what do I mean? It means we are to live the life God has set out for us in the Bible. If we never read the Bible, we will never understand the plan God has for our lives. Someone once said, "If you only sample the Word of God occasionally, you will never acquire much of a taste for it." It is so important that we read it often. If we make a habit of taking our Bibles with us everywhere we go, we will find spare minutes throughout the day when we can read a few verses. That will help you to be more dependent on God and His Word. And it will help us to think more on the things of God.

The best way to start getting into God's Word is to just do it. The devil will try every way possible to keep you from doing that. Don't give into him. There is no other way if one wants to know God. God will bless the time you spend with Him and you will find yourself growing in your faith and your relationship with God.

PATTERN FOR BIBLE STUDY
(The Six Ps)

POINTS - What does this passage say?
PROBLEMS - What does it say that I don't understand?
PARALLELS - What similar thoughts are found elsewhere in the Bible?
PROMISES - What blessings may I claim?
PERILS - What warnings should I heed?
PRECEPTS - What commands should I obey?

Now What?
By: R.W. Harris

NOW THAT I'M A CHRISTIAN
(Moody Correspondence School)

BIBLE STUDY

1. **Survey Method** - Reading through the Bible, seeing it as a whole, and learning how the books relate one to another.
2. **Analytical Method** - Takes each separate book and breaks it down into its component parts. The survey method gives the overview, the analytical method, the details of the books of the Bible.
3. **Theological Method** - Trace through the Bible its major doctrines or teachings.
4. **Topical Method** - You explore a subject or theme such as "law" or "love, etc.
5. **Biographical Method** - Study of various characters. (Ex., Joseph and Caleb)
6. **Comparative Method** - Compare a passage with other scriptures which shed light upon it.

Bible study has rules. You need help of the Holy Spirit. One rule - who the speaker is in any given passage. Another who is spoken to.

The context is most important. No passage should be divorced from verses which surround it. Take into consideration the history and culture of Bible times. Buy a good concordance, dictionary, Bible handbook, a commentary, and a book on Bible doctrine.

STUDYING BY BOOKS

The study of individual books (also called "synthesis") is another good means of Bible study. Select a book of the Bible, preferably one of the shorter New Testament epistles to begin with. Master its contents by reading the entire book through several times. Read it each time at one sitting or even several times at a sitting. After the second reading, begin to look for the main teaching of that book. Then at the next reading begin to note how the theme is developed. In subsequent readings, make an outline of your own, keeping in mind the main theme.

STUDYING BIBLICAL CHARACTERS (Caleb)

The character method is also a helpful way of studying the Bible. A Bible dictionary (such as Unger's or Zondervan's) will give some assistance. Simply choose a Bible character and study exhaustively everything the Scriptures say about this person. Compile a list of facts about the person, such as:

1. His meeting with God (conversion or call).
2. His strong points (such as prayer, faith, preaching abilities, etc.).
3. His weak points (sins, failures).
4. His accomplishments and influence.
5. His name (note meaning and any changes).
6. Characteristics in his life you should imitate.
7. Characteristics in his life you should avoid.
8. What God said about him.

THE COMPARISON METHOD

The best commentary on the Bible is the Bible itself. By comparing one Scripture passage with another, difficult verses or passages will be seen in their true light and significance. When studying a difficult passage, try to find any other passage similar to it or at least dealing with the same subject, and let that help to explain the meaning. A concordance, a topical textbook, or a Bible dictionary will be helpful.

A LIFE THAT'S REAL
By: G. Christian Weiss

STUDYING BY CHAPTERS

Serious Bible study is essential to your spiritual development. (II Timothy 2:15; 3:16, 17). Bible study by chapters is one practical method. Select a book of the Bible and read it through, chapter by chapter, spending as much time as necessary to master the contents of each chapter. After reading, you should ask yourself these questions:

1. What is the main subject?
2. Who are the principal characters?
3. What truth is clearly taught or stressed?
4. What is the key verse?
5. Is anything taught concerning Christ?
6. What new truth (if any) have I discovered?
7. How does this chapter relate to my life?
8. What is God saying to me in this chapter?

It is also helpful to make a brief outline of the chapter. By going through book after book in this manner, you will greatly increase your knowledge and understanding of the Bible.

STUDYING BY TOPICS

The topical (or subject) method is both simple and valuable. You should have a good concordance (such as Cruden's, Young's or Strong's) or a topical textbook; however, the chain references, marginal references or subject index found in many Bibles will be of great assistance in this method of study.

Study all the Bible verses you can find on such subjects as the Holy Spirit, sin, grace, the blood of Christ, faith, the new birth, the resurrection, the love of God, Christian love, the coming of Christ, heaven, hell, angels and other important truths. With the aide you are using, see what the entire Bible says about each topic.

VI – B: HOW TO HAVE DEVOTIONS

HOW TO HAVE DEVOTIONS
By: Dr. Gedrick Sears

Devotions **MUST** become an intricate part of your life. Discipline yourself for it. Start every morning with the Lord. Make sure you will not be disturbed.

1. Start with a book and follow it through to the end.
2. Pray a prayer like this: "Father, feed me now."
3. Start to read - thinking about what you are reading.
4. Read until a verse says something to you, and STOP RIGHT THERE.
5. Re-read that verse a few times,
6. Think about what it is saying. Mull it over in your mind. (Memorize it, if possible.
7. Then pray it back to God, thanking Him for it. (Share it with someone if possible).
8. Then have your prayer time. (Include your wanting to love Jesus more and also that soul you should be concerned for). Finally give Him your body afresh for that day.

If you want more Spiritual food, keep reading until another verse is drawn to your attention and do as before. Doing this daily will strengthen you and help you to be a faithful follower of the Lord Jesus,

BIBLE READING (QUESTIONS TO ASK)
1. Is there a sin here I should avoid?
2. Is there something mentioned that I should accomplish in my life?
3. Is there a promise from God to me?

4. Is there a command I must obey?
5. Is there a blessing I can enjoy?
6. Is there a failure from which I can learn?
7. What thought in the passage made the greatest impression on me?

I have found that as I ask these questions I begin to understand what God's Word is saying to me.

Another very simple plan new Christians may want to use is the one we were taught in our High School BornAgainers Club. It's the ABC method.

A- Title
B- The Best verse that explains the title
C- Challenge.

Commando Course
By: High School Evangelism Fellowship, Inc.
NY, NY
1951

QUIET TIME SHEET

1. Consciously enter into God's presence. Ask Him to speak to you through His Word. Yield yourself to obey and respond to whatever He says.
2. Read Revelation 4 and 5 (you may want to read it aloud). As you read, try to visualize the scene that is being described.
3. Try to summarize this passage in one or two sentences.
4. What is the center of attention in heaven?
5. What does this passage reveal about God? (4:3-11)
6. What does this passage reveal about Jesus? (5:5-13)
7. List the different ways that the 24 elders, the four "beasts" (Literally, "living creatures"), and the angels worship God. (4:8-11; 5:8-13).
8. Join the angels and citizens of heaven in worshiping the One on the Throne and the Lamb. You may want to please Him by singing as well as with words. Suggestions: "Holy, Holy,

Holy" or "Crown Him With Many Crowns." These will assist you in your worship.
9. What should be the natural response of your life to the character of God as seen in this Throne-room scene?
10. Why were you created (4:11)? In what ways is your life bringing pleasure to God? In what ways is your life not bringing pleasure to God?
11. Take time to confess and repent of any sin God has revealed to you. Then commit every area of your life anew to Him as Lord.
12. Memorize one key verse from this passage that you would like to meditate on throughout the day.

Starting The Day With God

Our days so often go wrong because they do not START right. With the world, the flesh and the Devil all bidding for your time, you simply cannot afford the luxury of imagining that the day will go all right without guidance.

I would like to suggest some simple guidelines that have been a real blessing to many people across the land. You may want to adapt or change my suggestions somewhat and you are of course perfectly free to do so. Do not, however, change the BASICS. They are as follows:

1. Before I rise from my bed I begin my program. First of all, I simply give God thanks for the night's rest. Remember that many people do not even have a bed to lie down on. In Calcutta, India there are some two hundred thousand people who do not have a place they can call home. They live and die on the streets! You slept on a bed. Thank God.

2. The second thing I do is give the new day to the Lord. By an act of faith I just put the day into the hands of God in a very real and conscious way. The Bible says that my times are in the Lord's hand (Psalm 31:15). I want Him to have my entire day.

3. The next thing I do is pray the prayer found in Psalm 119:133: "Order my steps in Thy Word and let not any iniquity have dominion

over me." Proverbs 20:24 says that our goings are of the Lord. Jeremiah 10:23 declares that "I know that the way of man is not in himself; it is not in man that walketh to direct his steps." As I pray this prayer I do so in a very deliberate way and from the moment of prayer I BELIEVE that God will do what I have asked Him to do. While I know that I AM crucified with Jesus Christ (Galatians 2:20, 5:24) yet I know that the flesh is very strong at times and I do not take victory for granted. I pray that God will not allow any sin to be my master THAT DAY. When you ask a doctor how long you will be in the hospital, he will often say, "one day at a time." It would be good if every Christian could see that he must live his life in and for God just one day at a time. Micah 7:19 says that the Lord will subdue our iniquities. I am glad He does, for I cannot. There is a wonderful thought expressed in Isaiah 1:25: And I will turn my hand upon you and purely purge away your dross and take away all your sin." I want God to do this for me and He will as I ask and believe Him.

4. The last thing I do in this program is to ask God to fill me with the Holy Spirit. Remember that Dwight L. Moody, the great evangelist, used to say: "We are leaky vessels and we need to stay under the fountain all the time." I say, "amen" to that. When I ask the Lord to fill me with His Holy Spirit, I am of course relinquishing all rights to the control of my life for that day.

The simple program I have suggested will hardly take five minutes of your time. But if rightly done, it will bring blessing to you daily. This is not, of course, my entire devotional program, but simply a way to start the day with God.

A word of warning is perhaps necessary at this point. You may find your mind is wandering as you attempt to follow these steps. It is imperative that you be in real contact with the Lord BEFORE you begin. This may take a few minutes and mean a struggle, but it is absolutely necessary. As you continue in this plan, you will discover it becomes easier as time goes on to enter into the right spirit of faith as you begin.

May God bless you richly as you adventure in this area. I have found this system a great blessing and a real help and so have others. I pray you may also.

Bill McLeod
Canadian Revival Fellowship
Box 584, Regina, Saskatchewan
Canada S4P 3A3

VI—C: PRAYER

PRAYER

We come today to the subject of prayer. Is prayer a priority in your life? It should be because it is the only way we can have a personal relationship with. God. Hebrews 4:16 encourages us to "...draw near with confidence to the throne of grace, so that we may receive mercy and find grace in time of need." Probably, the greatest thing I can do for you is to teach you how to have an effective prayer life.

Prayer is how we invite God to use His power in our lives, to meet our needs, and to make us a blessing to others. It is during our prayer time that we grow the most in our relationship with the Lord. When our hearts are right with God, our fellowship with Him is sweet and precious. We look forward to our time alone with Him, and we miss it when we don't have it. When we are in love with someone, we look forward to our time alone with them. How much more should that be true with our Lord when He has done so much for us?

What a wonderful privilege we have of fellowshipping with the God of the universe, the King of all kings. He loves us more than anyone else loves us, and He wants a relationship with us. Just think of that!

Do we love Him in return and want to spend time with Him? How much do we love Him?

We were created to have fellowship with God and to enjoy Him forever. We will never be happy and content until that is a reality.

That is why prayer is so important. That is the only way it can be accomplished.

I am giving you prayer patterns and suggestions that cover every area of life. My desire is that you will take advantage of your privilege and use it for the glory of God,

* * * * *

What fresh air and breathing is to the physical body, prayer is to the spiritual body. There is nothing in all the world more wonderful than a human being communicating with the infinite and eternal God. We were made for this.

The greatest need in our lives, our homes, our churches and in our country today is **prayer**. We need to pray for ourselves and for each other. We have become a people characterized by indifference and a lack of involvement. As a result, even in our churches, people don't feel free to share their problems and burdens. We may even be guilty of making people feel that it's a sin to have a problem.

Some quotes:

"The greatest thing we can do for God or for man is to pray. We can accomplish far more by our prayers than by our work. We pray, God works."

"Prayer is also the hardest thing for us to do. I'm sure we all believe in prayer and we say we believe prayer changes things, but how many of us really pray?"

"The secret of all failure is our failure in secret prayer."

"Our spirituality, and our fruitfulness, are always in proportion to the reality of our prayers."

"No one can have very real and deep communion with God who does not know how to pray so as to get answers to prayer."

"Most Christians do not give God a chance to show His delight in granting His children's petitions; for their requests are so vague and indefinite."

"We all know how to pray, but perhaps many of us need to cry as the disciples of old, 'Lord, teach us to pray.'"

These are all quotes from the book, *The Kneeling Christian.* The author is unknown, but we can see that whoever it is knew something about prayer. (The Unknown Christian, *The Kneeling Christian.* Zondervan Publishing House, Grand Rapids, MI, 1971; pgs. 17, 12, 60, 44, 41, 17.)

Prayer is the means by which you talk to God and He talks to you. Its purpose is that you may have contact with God. This is why we were created.

We need to take time to put the Lord at the center of our attention. "First, do not try to pray like someone else. Just talk to God in a simple and natural way. Jesus taught that God is not to be thought of as someone far off, vague, stern, cold and unsympathetic. Rather, he told us to call God "Father," and when he used the term "Father," he meant just what he said. Just as you used to go to your earthly father when you were a child and needed something, or were hurt, or could not solve some problem in life, so you are to go to your heavenly Father.

"Just talk to Him. Tell Him in your own words whatever is in your heart, if you are all mixed-up, tell Him. If you have sinned, confess it. If you need help or guidance or strength ... just tell Him. More than you desire His help, He wants to help you. You are His child and He is more concerned about you than any earthly father ever could be. He is always ready to hear you, so do not hesitate or doubt. Just come to Him and have faith to know that, as surely as you pray -whether you are conscious of His presence or not - He is listening and guiding your life."

(National Council of the Churches of Christ in the U.S.A.. *Decision,* 475 Riverside Dr., NY 17, NY, p. 4-6.)

"God desires that His children should grow up to know Him better each day. After we have studied the Word of God, prayer follows naturally. Begin by speaking back to God on the same subject on which He has spoken to you. Don't change the conversation! If He has spoken to you of Himself and His glory, worship Him. If He has spoken to you of yourself and your sins, confess them. Thank Him for any blessings which may have been revealed in the passage, and pray that its lessons may be learned by yourself and your friends. When you have prayed over the Bible passage you have read, you will want to go on with other prayers. Commit to Him in the morning all the details of the day which lies before you, and in the evening run through the day again, confessing the sins you have committed, giving thanks for the blessings you have received and praying for people you have met."

(John R.W. Stott, *Being a Christian - Our Duty to God,* InterVarsity Fellowship Press, Downers Grove, IL, 1976; p. 20-23)

When You Pray

Let us come to the matter of prayer.

What Is Prayer?

It is the means by which you talk to God and He to you.

What Is The Purpose Of Prayer?

The purpose of prayer is that you may have contact with God. "I have discovered that prayer's real purpose is to put God at the center of our attention, and forget ourselves and the impression we are making on others." (***Prayer: Conversing with God,*** by: Rosalind Rinker)

PRAYER MOTIVATION

For believers characterized by love, confidence and obedience, it is only natural to ask their Heavenly Father for what they need (I John 3:22) - and be assured that He will grant their requests (John 16:23). Those who approach God with this supreme confidence will not want what is contrary to His will. They will not request anything that the Father would refuse.

There are occasions in which our prayers do not lead to the results for which we ask. How should we understand this?

When disappointed by the apparent lack of an answer to our prayers, we should ask certain basic questions. What did we request?

Did we ask according to God's Will (5:14)? Did we ask what pleases Him? Did we ask primarily for what we want or for what would glorify Him (John 14:13-15; 15:7, 16; 16:23-24)?

For God to do whatever we ask is a tremendous promise. Yet this can be easily misunderstood. It does not mean God is a genie who will cater to our every whim, whatever that might involve. God is unlikely to produce a divine painting job on my house. Nor is He likely to handle my workload through direct divine action when I feel lazy or tired.

The main purpose of the kind of prayer that is envisioned here is to ask God to work in and through us in the ways that will most effectively express and accomplish His will. As we discern how His will involves us, we may become increasingly specific in our request.

If this is really the motive behind our prayers, we should be content with whatever God does in response. God's will inevitably will bring honor and glory to Him. Any disappointment we feel in prayer should prompt us to ask whether our selfish desires are not too strong a factor in our motivations.

Our obedience and desire to please God is not entirely the basis for having our prayers answered.

Rather we may expect our prayers to be answered because we obediently pray for what coincides with God's will - in order to please Him.

Alliance Witness
Feb. 4 1981
By: Eldon Woodcock

ASK and ye shall...

Request	God's Answer

WHY BOTHER TO PRAY?

Have students share problems they have with prayer. Are these problems great enough so that they have ceased to pray regularly?

Discuss how they feel about public prayer. Are they embarrassed to pray publicly? Why? Discuss. Do they pray in private, but refrain from praying in a group? Discuss feelings of prayer habits.

What should we pray about? Can we be honest in our prayers? Can we complain to God if that's the way we feel? (Psalm 65:2; 66:18; Proverbs 15:8-9; 28:9; Matthew 5:44; 6:5-15; 21:22; 26:41; Romans 12:12; I Thessalonians 5:17; James 5:16).

Handbook for Spiritual Growth
By: Cliff Pederson

FAITH AND PRAYER

"What is the connection between faith and prayer? What that relationship is can be arrived at as we see what is the basis of faith. Romans 10:17 tells us, 'So then faith cometh by hearing, and hearing by the word of God.' Faith grows as our knowledge of the Word and obedience to it grows. We must get into the Word of God to find out what to pray for.

"Consider the difference between faith and feeling. This is a difference we must know. Faith is definitely a matter of the will based on the Word of God. When we go to the Word and find something that God says, we can rest on that because God has said it. What

God says settles it for us. We determine right then and there we will believe it. It makes no difference whether we feel like believing it or feel that it is true or not, our feelings do not change the fact of it. Feeling is a matter of emotion which is so closely allied at times to the self-life that it is not a safe guide. We must base our knowledge on the Word of God and set our will upon that.

"How can we come into this state of faith? The answer is, simply by searching the Scriptures and claiming the promises as we find them.

"Now what are we to believe with regard to our prayers? We are to believe that we will receive what we ask for. It will not be something equivalent to it, or something of comparable value, but the very thing we pray for. We have no right to believe something that the Word of God does not tell us we should believe. But when God clearly states the matter, that settles it.

"This means of course that our prayers will be based on the Word of God. Our wills will be subject to God. We will come into the presence of God by the blood of Jesus and in the authority of His name claim the promises. Appropriate the promises God makes. Faith not only claims, but faith actually takes the thing God has promised.

"We can exercise the authority we have in Jesus, bind the strong man, and set free the soul that Satan has bound. We can expect God to do something about it when we pray.

"God has told us to pray for the lost and holds us responsible to do so. Let us obediently fulfill this obligation so that we will be able truthfully to say as did Paul: *"I am pure from the blood of all men."* (Acts 20:26). "

Praying with Authority
By: Epp, Weiss, and Morrow
Chapter 8

I would like to give a summary of an article I read in the *Alliance Witness* a number of years ago, which has helped my prayer life. I hope it will help yours as well.

ASK QUESTIONS BEFORE YOU PRAY
By: Gordon Chilvers

Does your private prayer time have special meaning for you? Do you get answers to your prayers? Do you look for answers? These are serious questions because your attitude toward prayer reveals your attitude toward God.

Private prayer can degenerate into a religious exercise you engage in periodically because it seems the right thing to do. You scarcely are off your knees before your prayer has left your mind forever.

You can easily forget the majesty of God and speak to Him with less care than you speak to your friends.

No one hears you talking to God. Your concentration can lapse and you can spend minutes saying nothing.

If you were to hear your private prayers played back on a cassette recorder, would you be shocked?

Before you offer another petition, ask yourself these questions and see if your praying does not improve.

What Do I Want?

Do you keep to generalities or do you know precisely what you need from God? Are you as exact when you speak to God as when you talk to friends?

If your prayers are not specific, you cannot expect God to answer them specifically.

A blind man cried out to Jesus for mercy, in reply, Jesus asked him what he wanted from Him.

You may ask for God's blessing and fail to say in what way you need it. You may ask for victory over sin and not say which sin you want to overcome.

Jesus knew what the blind man needed and He was ready to give it to him, but He wanted him to make a precise request.

When the man prayed specifically, "Lord, that I might receive my sight" (Mark 10:51), he received his sight.

Definite petitions teach us to know our precise needs better. They help us discover what is our true need. They lead us to examine our desires to see if they are Scriptural.

Can God Grant My Petition?

You are loved by God, but so are millions of others. God will not grant your petition if doing so causes others to suffer.

Jack went to his pastor in great distress. "For six weeks I have been asking God to let me get the job of foreman at our plant. Instead, Carl got the job."

The pastor knew both men and their respective abilities. Carl's qualifications were clearly superior to Jack's.

He explained to Jack that his petition was wrong and that God could not answer it favorably because it violated at least one other person's deserved advancement.

James warns us: "Ye ask, and receive not, because ye ask amiss" (4:3). The selfishness that would be gained at another's expense is a hindrance to prayer.

Have I Done My Part?

Are you asking God to do something for you that you could do for yourself?

God is willing to do for us what we find impossible, but He expects us to use the abilities He has given us. He will never answer a prayer that would encourage us to be lazy.

When Jesus went to the tomb of Lazarus, He told the people to do two things while He did one. He asked them to roll away the stone from the tomb. They could do that; there was no reason for God to do it.

Then He used His miraculous powers to do the humanly impossible - raise the dead,

"Lazarus, come forth," Jesus cried (John 11:43, and the dead man emerged from the tomb, the grave clothes still binding him hand and foot.)

Jesus did not unwind the grave clothes or call on His Father to do so miraculously, He instructed the people to do that simple act.

The Lord will do for us what we cannot; but we must do what we can.

What is My Present Relationship With God?

A soured relationship can prevent God's answering your prayers.

"If I regard iniquity in my heart," the psalmist said, "the Lord will not hear me." (66:18). Sin moves us from God's wavelength. God is holy and sin is contrary to His nature, it is a bar to His hearing us.

Isaiah put it plainly: "Behold, the Lord's hand is not shortened that it cannot save; neither his ear heavy, that it cannot hear; but your iniquities have separated between you and your God, and your sins have hid his face from you, that he will not hear."

The word for "separate" is used of the curtain that divided the holy place from the most holy (Exodus 26:33). Behind the curtain was the Shekinah glory, the presence of God. In front of it were the priests.

Sin comes between God and His people's petitions as certainly as the curtain came between God's presence and the priests.

What is My Present Relationship With Other People?

If you have unnecessarily offended someone, you have put yourself out of touch with God.

Jesus spoke of the person who, while worshipping God, remembered he had offended a brother. He exhorted him to leave his worship and "first be reconciled to thy brother, and then come and offer thy gift." (Matthew 5:24).

God regards the removal of offenses between brethren so important that He requires even worship to be stopped so that a reconciliation can be made by confession and apology.

Equally, a man's wrong relationship with his wife can hinder God's hearing his prayer. (I Peter 3:7)

Have I Considered God's Interests?

If God responded precisely as you asked, would the answer be for His glory?

God answers prayer so that He can receive glory. Jesus explained, "Whatsoever ye shall ask in my name, that will I do that the Father may be glorified in the Son." (John 14:13)

God's glory is the supreme motive for all activity, whether divine or human. When Gideon was leading his nation against the Midianites, God reduced his army of 32,000 men to 300. Their weapons of pitchers, torches and trumpets were hopelessly inadequate for the job. The victory had to be from God.

When Paul became weakened through his "thorn in the flesh," it was obvious to all that his superb triumphs and achievements were brought about by God and not by his own ability. God received the credit.

Do I Expect An Answer?

Jesus insisted, "What things soever ye desire, when you pray, believe that ye receive them, and ye shall have them." (Mark 11:24)

So essential is faith when we pray that the writer of Hebrews emphasizes, "He that cometh to God must believe that he is, and that he is a rewarder of them that diligently seek him." (11:6)

Asking in faith is confessing that "with God all things are possible." (Matthew 19:26)

The nature of prayer makes faith an essential element in our praying. We cannot pray honestly for a specific blessing unless we believe God can grant it to us. Praying in faith is possible when we believe the whole world is in God's hands.

We have to be sure that God can intervene in any part of the world, in any circumstance, or we would have to limit our asking to what was within His sphere. We must be certain that God can touch the heart and move the will of any person, good or bad, or we cannot ask for what would depend on someone else.

Praying in faith demands our belief that God's power is adequate to bring about the desired results. Can we ask God to guide us to make the best decisions? We can.

Praying in faith is based on the conviction that God cares for us. Faith believes He loves us enough to use His power, wisdom and knowledge in our behalf.

Praying in faith is expecting God to answer our petition. We can count on the answer before we see the slightest movement toward it.

Alliance Witness
February 18, 1981

(Bill McCloud: Praying in unbelief is sin!)

Conclusion

Asking these questions and getting satisfactory answers to them will revitalize our praying. We will make the petitions God is so ready to grant, and our faith will be strengthened to expect evidence of His goodness in His answers to our petitions.

Our praying will become a rich experience that we joyfully anticipate as it enhances our fellowship with the Lord and with His people.

(Gordon Chilvers, *The Alliance Witness,* Prayer Motivation. Feb. 18, 1981.)

HINDRANCES TO PRAYER ITSELF

"Prayer," someone has said, "is a thing that most people talk about and very few people do."

There is a distinction to be maintained between hindrances to praying and hindrances to answered prayer. If the devil cannot stop us from praying, he will try to get us so tangled up and powerless that we receive no answers to our prayers.

One of those hindrances is our lack of awareness of the value of time. The Bible says, "Redeeming the time for the days are evil." We overlook this and give ourselves to things that are really not important and excuse our misuse of time by saying that prayer is not as important as other things. Since we have only a certain amount of time in which to get things done, we spend it doing what to us is more essential than praying. We do not realize how we can redeem the time through prayer.

Sometimes I think we do not pray because we are lazy. This is expressed forcibly in Proverbs 6:10: "Yet a little sleep, a little slumber, a little folding of the hands to sleep." We have to discipline ourselves before we do anything constructive, and extra discipline is needed with regard to prayer.

We want to be like everybody else. When we look around us and find, as we think, that other people do not pray, we will not pray either. We let the time slip by and do not do what we should.

Because we do not see the value of prayer, we do not pray. We live in a day and generation that wants to know what profit it gets out of doing anything. And so we say, "If I pray, what is it going to benefit me?"

The conclusion many reach is that there is little to gain through prayer. Some people have actually said to me, "Does anything really happen when you pray?" Most of them do not think so.

Prayer is a wonderful privilege. We would consider it a high honor to talk to the governor of our state, and even more so to talk to the President of the United States, or the king of some country. Such an event would be the subject of conversation with us for weeks and months. We would count it a high privilege to talk to any such leader face-to-face.

We count it a privilege to be able to speak to national leaders, but what a greater privilege it is to speak to God. He is our Creator. He put breath into our nostrils. He sent His son into the world to die for us. He is the God who loves us, calls us, cares for us, and has invited us to talk to Him. What a privilege, indeed! And let us not forget, He is the God to whom all must give an account.

Praying With Authority
Chapter 1
By: Epp, Weiss, and Morrow

HINDRANCES TO ANSWERED PRAYER

When we find our prayers are not being answered, we need to stop and consider the problem. God does answer prayer when His conditions are met; so if we are not receiving answers to prayer, then there is something in us that is causing the hindrance.

There are some specific things mentioned in the Scriptures that hinder the answer to prayer.

1. Unconfessed sin - Proverbs 28:13
2. Failure to Honor God - Malachi 1:6-10
3. Insincere Praying
4. Pride - Luke 18:13
5. Worldliness - I John 2:15-16

According to these verses, worldliness includes three things. There is first the lust of the flesh, which is self-dependence. Then there is selfishness seen in feeding ourselves on the wrong things, described as the lust of the eye. In the third place, there is the pride of life, which is self-will, or choosing the wrong things. So we depend on the wrong things, we desire the wrong things, and we choose the wrong things. This is worldliness. Worldliness is human activity with God left out.

6. Lack of concern for God's will - Luke 14:26; Hebrews 10:7; Romans 8:26-27; James 4:1-3
7. Failure to Sympathize - Job 16:4
8. An Unforgiving Spirit - Mark 11:25
9. Lack of Faith - Hebrews 11:6; Romans 14:23; James 1:5-8
10. Failure to Use Believer's Authority - Ephesians 6:11

We could sum up these matters in a positive way by saying that if we will walk humbly before God, fully accept His Word and let Him have complete control over our lives, we will pray as we ought, and we will receive the answers to prayer God intends us to enjoy.

Praying With Authority
Chapter 2 and 3
By: Epp, Weiss, and Morrow

HINDRANCES TO PRAYER

This is a summary of a message given by Dr. TV Thomas at the School of Revival and Prayer held in Regina, SK, July 18-20, 2007. From: Revival News, Regina, Saskatchewan, ISSN 1701-6673. Vol. XXVI No. 4, Fall 2007

The Scripture declares that there are times when God doesn't even hear our prayer. There are times when we go through what is sometimes called "The dark night of the soul." Psalm 66:18 teaches us that power in prayer is connected to purity in heart, John 15:7 reveals that daily confession of sin is necessary, the sins of omission and commission. This is why it is so important to pray "Lord, put the searchlight of your Holy Spirit on my heart." So that we may maintain a close and clean relationship with the Lord Jesus Christ.

There are at least 15 things that can hinder our prayers:

1. Rejecting the truth - Proverbs 28:9. The informed who choose unbelief and fail to walk or pray in faith.
2. Pride - James 4:6 and II Chronicles 7:14. The Lord opposes the proud. You and I cannot overcome Him so we must humble ourselves.
3. Hard-heartedness - Zechariah 7:12-13. When we harden our hearts the Lord gives us back what we have sown.
4. Lack of compassion - Proverbs 21:13. We cannot neglect justice and we must show compassion to others less fortunate than ourselves.
5. Unconfessed sin - Isaiah 59:2. This separates us from Him and hinders our prayers.
6. Wrong motives - James 4:3. Often our personal agenda is what we pray about. He is not our servant, rather we are His servants and we must keep our hearts and motives focused on His will.
7. Unbelief - Hebrews 11:6, Matthew 17:20-21, Matthew 21:22. Unbelief unchecked will produce uncertainty and distrust of God, the Church and cause us to become skeptics.
8. Not seriously asking - James 4:2. Thinking about it is not enough, we must ask, and ask in faith believing.
9. Broken relationships - I Peter 3:7. How often this hinders our prayers, personally, in marriages, homes, and in the Church.
10. Sinful lifestyle - Isaiah 59:2. If we refuse to give up our sin, the Lord cannot honour our prayers. Our life must be one of obedience and service to Him.
11. Vain repetition - Matthew 6:7. Many people pray the same things time after time, just going through the motions without

really opening their heart to God and or getting through to the heart of God.
12. Lack of forgiveness - Matthew 6:14-15. We need to cultivate a forgiving spirit. This is one of the greatest problems in churches today. With lack of forgiveness, how can God hear us and send revival?
13. Hypocrisy - Luke 18:9-14. The Pharisee felt he was so much better than the sinner, but the other man was justified, he prayed honestly with no reliance on self.
14. Double mindedness - James 1:5-8. Praying doubtfully is asking faithlessly. The Word says if we do this we should not expect an answer.
15. Idolatry - Ezekiel 14:3. We create our own idols, like prestige, power, leisure, wealth, work and family. We must remember God will not share His glory with another.

We must keep short accounts with God and ask the Holy Spirit to search our hearts and reveal issues. Then we can forsake them and repent of them. We must make every effort to live a Holy life.

PETITION

As we begin to grow in the Lord, we soon realize there is prayer and then there is prayer. There are three stages of prayer. Many never get beyond the first stage, which is petition. This is the first step of prayer in a person's experience. We have a need, we sense that need, and we come to God with that need.

The Bible word used to designate this stage of prayer is the word 'ask.' Ask of God, beg of God, beseech God.

This is prayer in its simplest form. Whatever you desire, ask of Him. Whatever you need, ask of Him. Whatever you lack, ask of Him, whether the need be spiritual, mental, physical, or material, whatever the need is, ask of Him. Jesus said, "Ask and it shall be given you," "Ask and ye shall receive ..."

Petition then is the first stage of prayer. But, we ought to get beyond the stage of personal petition. This form of prayer is mostly selfish and we need to go on to a deeper form of prayer. It doesn't have to be selfish if we are praying with the right motivation – that God's will *will* be done and that He will be glorified.

COMMUNION

Almost every person has some knowledge about prayer; and there are many people who would like to pray but who sense the fact that they have no access to God. To the true Christian, however, prayer in life's highest and holiest privilege and greatest delight.

Now we are concerned about the second and higher stage of prayer. There is a greater height of attainment in prayer than constant asking. True prayer goes further, deeper, higher and richer.

Of Jesus, Matthew said, "And He went a little farther ... and prayed." A more advanced and more glorious stage of prayer is communion. The Bible says a great deal about communion with God. Walking with God implies communion. It implies mutual conversation. In the book of John, Jesus said to his disciples, I don't call you servants, but friends: the friend relationship is one of communion and fellowship. Prayer on this level is communion with God. Communion and fellowship with God ought to be to the spiritual life what breathing is to the physical life. Prayer is an attitude and state of heart, involving one's very life and daily walk. A life of fellowship with God!

A Christian who has come to this stage in prayer, no matter what the experiences in life, no matter how he may be tossed about, automatically his soul within him turns to God. He has reached the second stage of prayer, that of Holy communion. This embraces a deep abiding, compassionate desire in the soul to walk with God.

This is the place where prayer becomes joyful, where prayer becomes sweet, where it becomes satisfying, where it is victorious.

Those who never get beyond stage one, the petition stage, seldom attain the joy and blessing and real satisfaction of the true prayer life and a real prayer ministry.

Have you really ever started a prayer life? How far have you gone? If you have begun, will you go a little farther, as Jesus did? Will you go a little farther seeking the face of your Heavenly Father? Will you go a little farther in submission to His will? Will you go a little farther in your walk with Him? A little farther in love, devotion, communion?

INTERCESSION

Now we come to a still higher plane and holier place in the experience of prayer. It is Intercession. Intercede means to go between. When as Christians we become intercessors, we are go-betweens, that is, people who stand in the gap between God and needy people,

It is when we reach this stage that we become truly Christ-like. Preeminently Christ, is our Mediator, our Advocate, our High Priest, our go-between. "He is able also to save them to the uttermost that come unto God by him, seeing he ever liveth to make intercession for them" (Hebrews 7:25). Jesus Christ is our Intercessor at the right hand of the throne of God and needy, sinful men.

This stage of intercession is the highest, holiest and healthiest form of prayer experience there is. First, because it pleases God the most. Jesus is an intercessor: the Holy Spirit, we are told, is an intercessor; and God has Himself commanded us to intercede for other men.

Intercession brings the greatest fruit of any kind of praying. Self is out of the way at this stage: others are in view instead.

But by intercession a Christian, even the most humble Christian, can touch the throne of God, and thus can touch the whole world. No great training or great talents are required for this. Even Satan trembles when he sees the weakest saint upon his knees praying. It has well been said that more has been wrought in the world by prayer than by any other means; more than any person, even the most brilliant historians, can ever know.

Intercession also brings the deepest personal reward and spiritual satisfaction to know that because we prayed, God worked. This is thrilling indeed. What joy or satisfaction could be greater than this? Intercessory prayer, while being the most costly, is certainly also the most rewarding.

This is the longest chapter in the book. That's because I feel it's the most important. If I can encourage you to get involved, and to enjoy your prayer life, then it will have been worthwhile. Prayer is hard work, but it's well worth the effort. So, start out with ten minutes or so, and as God burdens your heart, add more time.

Let me encourage you to make a prayer list. Write down the date next to each request as you see God answering that petition. That will encourage you to pray more.

Alliance Witness
By: Eldon Woodcock,
Prayer Motivation
Feb. 4, 1981

The principle of intercession is that Christians bear one another's burdens, and so fulfill the law of Christ (Galatians 6:2).

In the face of all adversity, sin, illnesses, satanic activity or whatever, God's Word to His people is to intercede (Isaiah 59:16). If we are not interceding, we will find ourselves criticizing, condemning, gossiping and growing bitter, resentful, spiteful and full of hate. This can only lead to trauma, tragedy and destruction.

To intercede in prayer and in the authority of Jesus is one of the greatest needs and obligations we have as Christians.

What Scripture Says

"Likewise the Spirit also helpeth our infirmities: for we know not what we should pray for as we ought: but the Spirit itself maketh intercession for us with groanings which cannot be uttered. And he that searcheth the hearts knoweth what is the mind of the Spirit because he maketh intercession for the saints according to the will of God ... Who is he that condemneth? It is Christ that died, yea rather, that is risen again, who is even at the right hand of God, who also maketh intercession for us." (Romans 8:26, 27, 34).

"I exhort therefore, that, first of all, supplications, prayers, intercessions, and giving of thanks, be made for all men." (I Timothy 32:1).

"Wherefore he [Christ] is able also to save them to the uttermost that come unto God by him, seeing he ever liveth to make intercession for them." (Hebrews 7:25).

"And he saw that there was no man, and wondered that there was no intercessor: therefore his arm brought salvation unto him; and his righteousness, it sustained him." (Isaiah 59:16)

"Is not this the fast that I have chosen? To loose the bands of wickedness, to undo the heavy burdens, and to let the oppressed go free, and that ye break every yoke? ... To deal thy bread to the hungry, and that thou bring the poor that are cast out to thy house? When thou seest the naked, that thou cover him; and that thou hide not thyself from thine own flesh?" (Isaiah 58:6-7)

How to Intercede:

The two aspects of intercession are: (1) To intercede with God; and (2) to stand against Satan, demons, sickness, ungodly circumstances, etc. in behalf of others. Ezekiel points out that an intercessor must be willing to feel and bear the burdens of those for whom intercession is made (Ezekiel 4:4).

These ten principles of intercession are tried and proven as being effective:

Some Principles for Effective Intercession
by Joy Dawson

1. Praise God for the privilege of engaging in the same wonderful ministry as the Lord Jesus. (Hebrews 7:25) Praise God for the privilege of cooperating with God in the affairs of men.
2. Make sure your heart is clean before God, by having given the Holy Spirit time to convict, should there be any unconfessed sin. (Psalm 66:18; Psalm 139:23-24) Check carefully in relation to resentment to anyone. (Matthew 6:12; Mark 11:25) Job had to forgive his friends for their wrong judging

of him, before he could pray effectively for them. (Job 42:10)
3. Acknowledge you can't really pray without the direction and energy of the Holy Spirit. (Romans 8:26). Ask God to utterly control you by His Spirit, receive by faith what He does, and thank Him. (Ephesians 5:18; Hebrews 11:6)
4. Die to your own imaginations, desires, and burdens for what you feel you should pray (Proverbs 3:5, 6; 28:26; Isaiah 55:8)
5. Deal aggressively with the enemy. Come against him in the all-powerful name of the Lord Jesus Christ and with the "Sword of the Spirit" - the Word of God. (James 4:7)
6. Praise God now in faith for the remarkable prayer meeting you're going to have. He's a remarkable God and will do something consistent with His character.
7. Wait before God in silent expectancy, listening for His direction. (Psalm 62:5; Micah 7:7; Psalm 81:11-13)
8. In obedience and faith, utter what God brings to your mind, believing. (John 10:27) Keep asking God for direction in relation to whom or what you are praying, expecting Him to give it to you. He will (Psalm 32:8). Make sure you don't move on to the next subject until you've given God time to discharge all He wants to say to you regarding this particular burden; especially when praying in a group. Be encouraged from the lives of Moses, Daniel, Paul, and Anna, that God gives revelation to those who make intercession a way of life.
9. If possible, have your Bible with you should God want to give you direction or confirmation from it. (Psalm 119:105)
10. When God ceases to bring things to your mind to pray for, finish by praising and thanking Him for what He has done, reminding yourself of Romans 11:36.

A WARNING: God knows the weakness of the human heart towards pride, and if we speak of what God has revealed and done in intercession, it may lead to committing this sin. God shares His secrets with those who are able to keep them. There may come a time when He definitely prompts us to share, but unless this happens, we should remain silent. (Luke 9:36; 2:19)

As You Pray

Ask God to reveal those needs for which intercession should be made. Thank and praise Him for calling intercessors and equipping them with gifts for lifting burdens and delivering the saints and the needy.

References/Homework

Study the Scripture references above.

List those you know who need your intercession. In each case, record the date you begin to intercede as well as the date God begins to answer. As you see God answer, you will build your faith and that of others.

Keep a log (diary) of Scripture, circumstances, words of knowledge, wisdom or prophecy, impressions and thoughts that come to you.

PRAYER

Introduction

"Prayer is talking with Jesus." - answer given by Westminster student in Sunday School.

"Prayer is an offering up of our desires to God for all things lawful and needful, with humble confidence that we shall obtain them through the mediation of our Lord and Savior Jesus Christ."

"Prayer is worship addressed to the Father, in the name of Christ, and the power of the Holy Spirit." (Dr. H.W. Frost)

"Prayer is the soul of man talking to God."

"Prayer should consist of at least four parts - ACTS - remember the word ACTS.

Adoration - praise and worship of the soul to God. (Psalm 95:6)

Confession - repentance from every know sin. (Psalm 32:5)

Thanksgiving - be thankful for anything, everything. (Philippians 4:6)

Supplication - intercession, requests, petitions and desires. (I Timothy 3:1)

Our prayers should be directed to God the Father (Acts 12:5); In the name of Jesus Christ (John 14:13); Through the power of the Holy Spirit. (Ephesians 6:18).

I. Where to Pray.
   1. Everywhere. (I Timothy 2:8)
   2. In the Closet. (Matthew 6:8)
   3. In the Temple (Church) (Luke 18:10)

Private prayer will be made in the secret place.
Family prayer will be made with a small group.
Public prayer will be made before the congregation.

II. When to Pray.
   1. Always. (Luke 18:1; I Thessalonians 5:17)
   2. In the Morning. (Luke 18:1; I Thessalonians 5:17)
   3. At noon and in the evening. (Psalm 55:17)
   4. Daily. (Psalm 86:3)
   5. Day and night (Psalm 88:1)

Daniel prayed three times a day. (Daniel 6:10)

III. Subjects for Prayer.
   1. (Matthew 6:9-13) The Lord's Prayer - the second coming of Christ, the will of the Lord, daily bread, forgiveness, guidance, victory over temptation and sin.
   2. (James 5:13-16) Pray for the sick.
   3. (I Timothy 2:1-4) Pray for all men, for kings, for all in authority, for our own personal lives, and for the salvation of sinners.
   4. (Isaiah 38:1-5) Pray for a longer life.
   5. (Daniel 6:18-23) Pray for personal safety and the safety of others.
   6. (I Kings 3:5-9) Pray for wisdom and understanding.

      7. (Matthew 6:25-34) Pray for clothing, shelter and food.
      8. (Romans 1:10) Pray for a prosperous journey.
      9. (Colossians 1:28) Pray for every Christian to be made perfect in Christ Jesus.
     10. (Matthew 5:38-48) Pray for them that despitefully use you and persecute you, pray for your enemies.
     11. (I Timothy 5:17) Pray for those over you in the church.

IV. How to Pray.
      1. (Romans 8:26-27) We should be guided by the Holy Spirit in our praying.
      2. (Hebrews 11:6) We must pray with faith in the existence of God.
      3. (Hebrews 11:6) We must believe that God rewards faithful intercession.
      4. (Luke 18:1-8; 11:1-13) There must be persistence in prayer.
      5. (II Chronicles 7:14) We must pray with humility.
      6. (II Chronicles 7:14) We must be prepared to repent of our sins.

V. Conditions of Prayer.
      1. (Romans 8:27; Matthew 26:39) We must pray in the will of God.
      2. (Mark 11:25) We must forgive others before God will hear and answer our prayers.
      3. (Mark 11:24) We must pray in faith believing.
      4. (I John 3:22) We must keep His commandments.
      5. (John 15:7) We must abide in Christ
      6. (Jude 20) We must pray in the Holy Ghost.
      7. (John 16:24) We must pray in Jesus' name.

VI. Hindrances to Prayer.
      1. (James 1:6-7) Unbelief.
      2. (Mark 11:25) An unforgiving spirit
      3. (Psalm 66:18) Iniquity.
      4. (James 4:3) Ask amiss (asking with wrong motives or out of the will of God).

VII. Some Prayer Promises.
(Mark 11:24; John 15:7; I John 5:14-15; Ephesians 3:12, 20; Philippians 4:19; Matthew 7:7-8; Luke 11:9-13; Hebrews 4:16).

Conclusion

What answer does God give to prayer? God gives one of three answers: 1) Yes; 2) No; 3) Wait.

(Isaiah 65:24) "And it shall come to pass, that before they call, I will answer; and while they are yet speaking, I will hear."

(II Corinthians 12:7-10) Paul prayed for healing and God said, "No." We must wait for God's will and God's time.

The one prayer of a sinner that God promises to hear. (Luke 18:13; II Peter 3:9).

We will never learn to pray by reading books on the subject. We must pray. Be sure to thank Him constantly for answered prayer.

Does God Answer Prayer?

"Have you ever doubted that God would answer your prayer? Perhaps you have prayed for the salvation of a friend, and he still does not know Christ. Perhaps you have prayed that you would be the star of the basketball team, and you are still not the star. Is God not hearing your prayers, or is there some reason why you have not received an answer? If you have a prayer that has not been answered, try to decide the reason as several people speak on the topic of prayer."

TOPIC A: Who can pray? Can just anyone expect an answer to prayer?
1. Those who know Christ as Savior. (I John 14:6)
2. Those who come in faith. (Hebrews 11:6)
3. Those who do not live in sin. (Psalm 66:18)

Give an illustration of how God answered prayer in your life.

TOPIC B: How should I pray? Is there a right and a wrong way to pray? As you speak, explain each Scripture, pointing out the right and wrong ways to pray.

1. Pray in the Holy Spirit (Jude 20)
2. Pray without ceasing. (Romans 1:9)
3. Pray with others. (Matthew 18:19)
4. Pray about everything. (Philippians 4:6)
5. Pray in faith. (Matthew 21:22; Mark 11:22-24)
6. Pray boldly. (Hebrews 4:16)

Give an illustration of how God answered prayer in your life.

TOPIC C: For what should I pray? Can I pray for just anything? Give an illustration for each point.
1. Pray for leaders. (I Timothy 2:1-2)
2. Pray for Christian workers. (Matthew 9:38)
3. Pray for strength to overcome temptation. (Mark 14:38)
4. Pray about all things. (Matthew 21:22)
5. Pray for great things. (Jeremiah 33:3)
6. Pray unselfishly. (James 4:3)

Give an illustration of how God answered prayer in your life.

Faith, mighty faith the promise sees
And Looks to God alone;
Laughs at impossibilities,
And cries, It shall be done!
C. Wesley

A-C-T-S PRAYER PATTERN

"If my people, who are called by My name, will humble themselves and pray and seek My face and turn from their wicked ways, then will I hear from heaven and will forgive their sin and will heal their land." II Chronicles 7:14

A
ADORATION – "I praise You, Heavenly Father, that You are ..."
Omnipotent, Omniscient, Omnipresent, Unchanging, Transcendent, Sovereign, Eternal, Holy, Righteous, Just, Loving,

Merciful, Patient, Trustworthy, Gracious, Forgiving, Wise, Truthful, Faithful, Wrathful, Creator.

C

CONFESSION – "Moved by Your holiness and forgiveness, I confess my ..."

Failure to pray, Disobedience, Willfulness, Lack of love, Unbelief, Ignoring the Bible, Jealousy, Complacency, Pride, Lack of discipline, Materialism, Anger, Fear, Bitterness, Dishonesty, Unforgiveness, Gossip, Critical spirit, Immoral thoughts, Immoral behavior, Not standing for You.

T

THANKSGIVING – "For these things, and in everything, I thank You ..."

Jesus Christ, Holy Spirit, Salvation, The Bible, Truth, Moral absolutes, Answered prayers, Family and friends, Church, Guidance, Provision, Protection, Opportunity to serve, Freedom to worship, My country, State/Province, The Constitution, Founding fathers, Elections, Faithful Christians, Trials and discipline.

S

SUPPLICATION – "According to Your will, I pray for these concerns ..."

President / Prime Minister, Congress / Parliament, Supreme Court, Governor / Premier, Legislators, Local officials, Business community, Church leaders, Family leaders, Others' needs, Personal needs, Spreading the Gospel, Conviction of sin, Revival and renewal, Earnest prayer, Obedient hearts, Unbelievers, Pastors, Empowering the Church, Church unity in truth, Wisdom, Turning to the Bible, Abortion, Drug and alcohol abuse, Divorce, Sexual immorality, Child abuse, False religions, Anti-Semitism, Government corruption, Economic sins, Crime, AIDS, other diseases.

Author Unknown

PRAYER OUTLINE
Hour of Prayer

1) **GREET THE LORD** - Address Him as though you can actually see Him on the throne and you are walking into His presence. Stand before Him with your spiritual eyes and then Spiritually fall at His feet.
   a) Acknowledge who He is. (Read Matthew 6:9)
   b) Mention the name of Jesus. (Read John 5:19 & John 14:14)
   c) Acknowledge that He is in control. (John 5:30)
   d) Submit to His Word and will. (Read John 4:24 & 25)

2) **REPENTANCE** - Tell Him you realize that His kingdom is at hand and that you realize that He is in control of everything. Say it in your own words. (Read Matthew 4:17). Go to Him with a clean and pure heart, free of any sin or guilt.
   a) Confess your sins, shortcomings or faults. (Read I John 1:9)
   b) Tell Him he is more important than your needs or requests. (Read Matthew 6:33).

3) **HEAVEN AND EARTH** - Acknowledge that the way He does things in heaven is the right way and that's the way you want things to be done here on Earth.
   a) Tell Him that is your desire to see things accomplished here on Earth the same as it is done in Heaven. (Read Matthew 6:10)
   b) Mention that God governs justly and ask Him to do so according to the needs that you are about to express.

4) **GOD IS THE SUPPLIER** - (Read James 1:17) If we expect good things to happen, those things have to come from God.
   a) Mention your specific requests. (Read Matthew 6:11)
   b) Acknowledge that He is the supplier of everything we need from our basics to our desires.

5) **PRAY FOR OTHERS** - Be specific. Mention those that you pray for and tell God something about them.

1) Pray for your Church. Mention the name of the Church specifically.
2) Pray for your Pastor. Speak his or her name.
3) Pray for members of your congregation,
4) Pray for another Church that you know of.
5) Pray for another Pastor that you know.
6) Pray for unsaved loved ones by name.
7) Pray for the lost of the world.
8) Pray for our nation. Mention specific people or areas that concern you.
9) Pray for your neighbors.
10) Pray for those who have hurt you.
11) Pray for your enemies.
12) Pray for your own specific needs.
13) Pray for someone in the hospital or that you know is sick.
14) Pray for a child that you know.
15) Pray for those in authority.
16) Pray for our missionaries and other Christian workers
17) Pray for those being persecuted.

READ PSALM 56 (All 13 verses) - Then pray over the Word. Lay your hands on the scriptures and ask God to be Glorified.

6) **FORGIVENESS** - Forgive others who have hurt you. Ask God for the strength to do so. Ask God to forgive you for anything that you might have done to hurt someone else, even if you didn't mean to do so.
   a) Mention those who have hurt you by name. Forgive them and ask God to forgive them. (Read Mark 11:25 & 26)
   b) Ask for forgiveness for those you have wronged intentionally or unintentionally. (Read Matthew 25:35-46)
7) **TEMPTATION** - Pray for understanding concerning temptation. (Read James 1:13). Understand that temptation in and of itself is not of the Lord.
   a) Put on the full armor of God so that you can withstand the attacks of the devil. (Read Ephesians 6:13-18)

b) Pray that temptation would be removed from you. (Read Luke 11:4)
c) Pray for wisdom to recognize the difference between temptation and limitation. Pray for strength to reject temptation and accept your limitations. (Read I Kings 3:9-12)
d) In the name of Jesus, reject Satan and all he would try to throw in your path or upon you. Take authority over the devil and lean on Jesus for strength. (Read James 4:7)

8) **THANKSGIVING** - Thank God for having heard you. Thank Him for listening to you and for responding. (Read John 11:40 & 41)
   a) Thank Him for answering prayer even if you can't understand the answer. (Read Daniel 3:17 & 18)
   b) Thank Him for answered prayer. (Read Mark 11:24)
   c) Tell Him that you realize that all final authority rests with Him. (Read Matthew 6:13)

READ PSALM 23 (all 6 verses) - Then pray over the Word. Lay your hands on the scriptures and ask God to be Glorified.

9) **AMEN** - Close your prayer with reverence.
   a) Mention who God is:
      1) Jehovah - Jireh - "GOD IS MY PROVISION"
      2) Jehovah - Nissi - "GOD IS MY BANNER"
      3) Jehovah - Rohi - "GOD IS MY SHEPHERD"
      4) Jehovah - Rophe - "GOD IS MY HEALER"
      5) Jehovah - Shalom - "GOD IS PEACE"
      6) Jehovah - M'Kaddesh - "GOD SANCTIFIES"
      7) Jehovah - Tsidkenu ~ "GOD IS OUR RIGHTEOUSNESS"
   b) So be it. Let it be so. Believe that it is done. (Read Romans 11:36)

PRAYING FOR OTHERS

1. This is a guide for whom we should pray.
    A. Ephesians 6:18- Fellow Christians
    B. Colossians 4:3-4 - Christian Workers
    C. I Timothy 2:1-2 - Those in authority
    D. I Timothy 2:3-4 - Non-Christians
    E. James 5:14-15-The sick
    F. James 5:16 - Those who confide in us or ask for prayer.
    G. James 5:19-20 - Sinning Christians

2. For what should we ask? (Jesus' prayer for His disciples)
    A. He asked that His followers be kept as those who are not of this world. (John 17:15-16)
    B. He asked that His followers would be sanctified, or set apart, to do God's will. (17:17-19).
    C. He asked that His followers would be one in love (17:20-23).

Paul's prayers for the Ephesians.
  1. Ephesians 1:15-23
     A. He asked that they would know God. (Ephesians 1:17)
     B. He asked that they would know God's calling. (1:18)
     C. He asked that they would know God's riches. (1:18)
     D. He asked that they would know God's power and authority. (1:19-23)
  2. Ephesians 3:14-19
     A. He asked that the Ephesians would be strengthened through the Holy Spirit's power. (Ephesians 3:16).
     B. He asked that spiritual strength would make it possible for Christ to dwell in their hearts (3:17)
     C. He asked that they would be able to grasp the greatness of Christ's love (3:18-19) D. He asked that they would be filled with the fullness of God. (3:19)

It's important that our prayers for others be accompanied by actions of love. These actions spring up out of the great concern we have for people. This is the same concern that motivates us to pray for them.

Praying for others, which is sometimes called intercession, is a lot more than just a nice thing to do for people. Praying is a responsibility God Himself has given us. Are we living up to that responsibility?

HOW TO PRAY FOR THOSE WHO MINISTER

Ministers are basically "elders" as shepherds of God's flock and need to be ministered to and built up as part of the "Body." The Early Church existed to build up the body of Christ as God built the assemblies. In what ways can we pray for any who handles the Word of God and ministers to the congregation?

1. To become a man of **PRAYER.**
2. To be sensitive to what the Holy Spirit is saying in his **PREACHING**. Being sensitive to the Holy Spirit is not always easy.
3. To be available and sensitive to "hurting" **PEOPLE**. Pray that he will not only be available for people to "make an appointment" to see him, but he will be sensitive to initiate contacts where needs exist.
4. To be flexible for God to deal with the "rough spots" and mold his **PERSONALITY.**
5. To be open to God's direct will as a **PERSON** – his future, how long to stay in the church; decisions, etc. This is not always easy.
6. To be constantly making spiritual **PROGRESS** "growing in grace" and not merely in knowledge.
7. To be honest enough to share personal needs as **PETITIONS**, such as priority problems, personal problems, pride potential, practical life-style problems, etc.

31 DAYS OF PRAYING FOR YOUR PASTOR

(c) 2005 Life Action Ministries(tm)
Life Action Revival Ministries
P.O. Box 31
Buchanan, MI 49107
1-800-321-1538
www.lifeaction.org

Brothers, pray for us.
1 Thessalonians 5:25 ESV

There is no greater gift you can give your pastor and the spiritual leaders of your church than to pray for them.

Pastors cannot win the battle alone; they need committed intercessors to lift them up in fervent, specific prayer. Imagine how the power of God might be released in our churches if we were to pray faithfully for our pastors.

Pastors are human – they face the same challenges that their people do, with some additional ones! They grow tired in ministry, are tempted to sin, and may find it difficult to balance their many roles and responsibilities. They need the encouragement and support of those they lead.

Prayer for your pastor is crucial to the spiritual health of your pastor, his family, and your church. God will reward your efforts to cover him in prayer.

If you want to encourage your spiritual leaders (and their wives!) let them know you are praying for them. Ask them periodically for any specific prayer requests and assure them you will pray accordingly. Use the following prayer guide with accompanying Scriptures, to suggest practical ways to pray for those who provide spiritual leadership for the flock.

"Let the thought sink deep into the heart of every church, that their minister will be such a minister as their prayers make him ... How perilous is the condition of that minister ... whose heart is not encouraged, whose hands are not strengthened, and who is not upheld by the prayers of his people! ...

"It is at a fearful expense that ministers are ever allowed to enter the pulpit without being preceded, accompanied, and followed by the earnest prayers of the churches. It is no marvel that the pulpit is so powerless, and ministers so often disheartened when there are so few to hold up their hands ... When the churches cease to pray for ministers, ministers will no longer be a blessing to the churches." Gardiner Spring (1785-1873)

Day 1
Pray that your pastor will love God with all his heart, soul, mind, and strength. Pray that God's Spirit will work in his heart in power and that he will value and follow biblical priorities. (Deuteronomy 6:5; Matthew 6:33)

Day 2
Pray that your pastor will cultivate strong character and uncompromising integrity. Pray that his testimony will be genuine, and that he will never do anything that he would need to hide from others. (I Timothy 1:5, 3:7; Ephesians 6:10-12)

Day 3
Pray for his personal walk with God - that his soul and spirit will be nourished and strengthened in his quiet time with God, beyond his sermon preparation. Pray that he will spend more time in the Word of God rather than reading Christian books and articles. (Mark 1:35; II Timothy 2:15-16)

Day 4
Pray that your pastor will counsel and teach with discernment through the wise use of Scripture and faith in God's power to work. Pray that he will be protected from the effects of sinful or negative attitudes that he encounters as he counsels. (Malachi 2:7; James 1:5-6; John 17:15)

Day 5
Ask God to protect your pastor's marriage and keep it strong as a model of Christ's relationship with the Church. Pray that your pastor will tenderly cherish and lead his wife, and that she will respect and encourage her husband, submitting to his leadership. (Ephesians 5:23-33) (If your pastor is not married, pray for his relationships with loved ones and those who are close to him.)

Day 6
Pray that God will protect your pastor's wife from bitterness when her husband is criticized. Pray that her prayer and devotional life will be consistent, and that she will guard her mind and heart. (Hebrews 12:15; Proverbs 4:23)

Day 7
Pray for your pastor's children, and especially that the pressures of the ministry will not discourage or embitter them. Pray that your pastor will provide godly leadership in the home, not based on fear of what others will think, but according to Scriptural truth. (Ephesians 6:4; Colossians 3:20-21) (If your pastor does not have children, pray that God will give him many "spiritual children" as he shares the Gospel.)

Day 8
Ask God to protect your pastor from the evil plots of Satan. Pray that he will not be corrupted as he rubs shoulders with the world in the course of ministry. (John 17:15; Isaiah 54:17; II Corinthians 2:11; I Peter 3:12; Psalm 9:9-10, 91:9-11)

Day 9
Pray that God will build a hedge of protection around your pastor's marriage, and that he and his wife will be aware of the potential for any improper relationships. Pray that their family time will be protected. (Ezekiel 22:30a; II Corinthians 10:4-5; Matthew 19:6)

Day 10
Pray that your pastor will use discernment in the use of e-mails, the Internet, and the media. Ask God to guard his heart concerning the use of free time. Pray that he will be morally pure and that he will wear the armor of God so that he will not fall into sexual temptation. (Romans 13:14; I Peter 1:16; Ephesians 6:10-18; II Corinthians 10:4)

Day 11
Pray that God will bring godly friends and encouragers to your pastor and his family to strengthen them for the ministry and provide meaningful fellowship and times of rest (Philippians 2:19-25)

Day 12
Pray that your pastor will be humble and authentic in his faith, not given to pride or hypocrisy. Pray that he will have pure motives and give God glory for every gain and victory. (Micah 6:8; Galatians 6:14; John 7:17-18; I Corinthians 10:13)

Day 13
Pray that your pastor will make wise lifestyle choices in order to protect his health, especially in the areas of exercising, eating moderately, and getting sufficient rest. Pray for times of relaxation and renewal to balance the stress of ministry. (Romans 12:1-2; I Corinthians 9:27, 10:13, 6:19-20; James 3:1-2)

Day 14
Pray that your pastor will focus on the Word of God and walk in the fear of the Lord - rather than fear of man - as he prepares his messages. Pray that he will seek to please God rather than men, and pursue holiness rather than the praise of men. (Acts 6:4; Proverbs 19:23; II Timothy 2:15; Hebrews 11:6; II Timothy 4:1-2)

Day 15
Praise God for your pastor's leadership and pray that he will make godly decisions. Pray that he will lead with a shepherd's heart, and that he will always speak the truth in love. (I Kings 3:9; I Peter 5:2; Romans 12:6-8; Jeremiah 3:15)

Day 16
Pray that your pastor will be courageous in proclaiming Christ from the pulpit and confident in his use of the Word of God. Ask God to help him preach with insight, transparency and humility. (Colossians 1:28, 4:3a; Ephesians 6:19)

Day 17
Pray that your pastor will be a "Great Commission man" - committed to personal evangelism and the equipping of the saints to seek the lost. Pray that he will have a heart to develop a thriving missions program in the church. (Romans 10:15; Matthew 28:19-20; Luke 19:10)

Day 18
Pray that your pastor will be a man of prayer and worship, and that he will lead by example - teaching the congregation how to

walk in a close relationship with the Father. (I Thessalonians 5:17; Acts 1:14a; Matthew 4:10; Mark 1:35; Luke 22:46)

Day 19

Pray that your pastor will use wise time management and that he will seek God's perspective for his schedule, guarding his time against unnecessary interruptions. (Ephesians 5:15-16; Colossians 4:5; Psalm 90:12; John 9:4)

Day 20

Pray for a fresh, divine anointing on your pastor's ministry. Pray that God's working will be powerfully evident both in his personal life and in the spiritual life of the congregation. (I Corinthians 9:27; II Timothy 1:7; Romans 15:18-19a)

Day 21

Pray that your pastor will not give in to discouragement but will deal with inevitable criticism and conflict by committing himself into the hands of God, who judges righteously. (I Peter 2:23)

Day 22

Pray that your pastor will practice servant leadership, edifying the congregation with wisdom and serving with God's "agape" love. (Galatians 5:13b; Ephesians 6:7; Luke 10:43b-45, 9:23-24; John 13:5-9: Philippians. 2:3-4)

Day 23

Pray for spiritual unity in the church staff and among the spiritual leadership of the church (elders, deacons, etc.). Pray that the enemy will not be allowed to create divisions, strife, or misunderstanding among the church leaders. (Romans 14:19; I Corinthians 12:25)

Day 24

Pray that God will give your pastor a clear, biblical vision of what your church can and should be for His glory, and that he will communicate that vision clearly and confidently to the church. (Proverbs 29:18; John 15:16, 17:17; II Timothy 3:5; Malachi 3:11)

Day 25

Pray that your pastor will seek God for personal revival, and revival in your church and community. (II Chronicles 7:14; Psalm 69:32)

Day 26

Pray that your pastor will think biblically with the mind of Christ. (I Corinthians 2:16; Colossians 2:6-8; Ephesians 4:17)

Day 27
Pray that your pastor will earnestly seek God's will and be committed to instant and complete obedience - ready for God to work powerfully in and through his ministry. (II Corinthians 10:3-5; Luke 9:23-24)

Day 28
Pray that your pastor will strive for personal excellence and will believe God for all He wants to do in the congregation. (II Peter 1:3; Colossians 3:23-24)

Day 29
Pray that your pastor will be a man of faith and have a passionate love for God, not giving in to worries, fears, or an uptight and anxious spirit. (1 John 4:1 8; Proverbs 3:5-6)

Day 30
Ask God to provide for the financial needs of your pastor and his family. Pray that he will be a wise steward of both personal finances and church funds. (Philippians. 4:19; Hebrews 13:5; I Timothy 6:11; Psalm 37:25)

Day 31
Ask God to heal any hurts that your pastor has suffered in the ministry. Pray that he will serve the Lord with gladness and encourage the congregation to worship God with a joyful, surrendered spirit, (Isaiah 61:3)

PRAYING SCRIPTURALLY FOR NON-CHRISTIANS

Note: Personalize your prayer by putting the person's name in each blank as you pray.

1. That God will draw _____ to Himself. (John 6:44)
2. That _____ would sense the void in his (her) life and seek to know God. (Acts 17:24-27)
3. That _____ may believe the Scriptures. (I Thessalonians 2:13; Romans 10:17; II Timothy 3; 15)
4. That Satan is bound from blinding _____ from the truth. (Matthew 13:19; II Corinthians 4:3-4)
5. That the Holy Spirit works in _____. (John 16:8-13)

6. That God will send His messenger to lead _____ _____to Christ.
   (Matthew 9:37-38; Romans 10:13-18)
7. That _____ may believe in Christ the Messiah as Savior. (John 1:12; 5;24)
8. That _____ will repent of his (her) sin. (Acts 3:19; 17:30-31)
9. That _____ will confess Jesus as Lord. (Romans 10:9-10
10. That _____ will yield all to follow Christ (II Corinthians 5:15; Philippians 3:7-8)
11. That _____ will take root spiritually and grow in Christ. (Colossians 2:6-7; II Peter 3:17-18)

HOW TO PRAY FOR YOUR MISSIONARIES

"And this is the confidence that we have in Him, if we ask anything, according to His will, that He heareth us, and if we know that He hears us, whatsoever we ask, we know that we have the petition that we desire of him." (I John 5:14,15).

Very little is accomplished in this life unless we have an organized plan and consistently work at that plan. The same is true when it comes to praying for your missionaries. Very little will be accomplished if it is hit and miss. Set aside a very specific time to pray.

The missionaries have many needs, but they can only be met through the consistent, effectual prayer of those warriors holding the ropes at home. Your missionaries will be grateful if you will be faithful in your prayer life on their behalf. "The effectual fervent prayer, of a righteous man availeth much" (James 5:16). All of us have been guilty of praying, "Lord, bless all of the missionaries around the world." In I Samuel 1:11, Hannah asked for a male child. In II Kings 3:9, Solomon asked for wisdom. God honored these very specific requests. We encourage you to call your missionaries by name when you pray, but we also encourage you to pray for them in specific areas. You might pray for one of these areas each day of the week.

1) Pray for their health. On many mission fields there are inadequate medical facilities, poor sanitation, contaminated water and limited diets. All of these factors can lead to disease that has long been controlled in this country but is still prevalent in much of the world. Human life is very cheap in many countries.

2) Pray for safety. Government problems abound around the world. Many lawless bands are well armed today and terrorizing the population in many countries. All foreigners are probably targets. Missionaries by nature of their work lead very visible lives. They are out among the people and are predictably in the same location often. Travel safety should be a prayer priority, both for the missionary in the U.S. on deputation and furlough and especially while on the field where driving conditions often defy description. It is impossible to calculate how many cumulative miles our missionaries will spend traveling by car and plane each year; only the grace of God and the faithful prayers of His people have given us a remarkable safety record. Pray that this will continue to be true.

3) Pray for finances. Adequate monthly support is essential but so are church buildings, homes and vehicles. Worldwide inflation and the fall of the American dollar on the world money market have made finances an even more pressing problem than in the past. The exorbitant cost of education for missionary children on the field forces many more children to be schooled at home, thus tying up the mother and giving the children limited social contact.

4) Pray for missionary children. Education of the missionary child is the number one problem on the mission field today. Pray for the many problems associated with adjustment on the field and then another adjustment on returning to the states. Most missionary children move an incredible number of times before they enter college. Deputation and furlough are hard on the children. Either they have no father at home for prolonged periods of time or they travel together as a family unit with no natural home stability. Imagine what your children might say if they were in church services almost every night of the week.

5) Pray that the missionary will use his time wisely. Often it takes so long to accomplish the most minor errand. The rest of the world does not move at the same pace we do. Everything takes longer, from shopping to preparing meals. Government red tape abounds, seemingly just to take up their time. The Devil would like to keep them so busy on day-to-day matters that there is no time left for the essentials of prayer and Bible study.

6) Pray for their cultural adjustment and language aptitude. Pray that God will give them an unusual ability to learn the language, especially the wives. If they are home schooling their own children, they have little time for language study. No one can adjust to a new culture, much less minister to the people, without language. Pray for their cultural adjustment. There will be strange plumbing, food, smells, shopping methods and often inadequate water and electricity. Pray that they will have comfortable housing. Their home is their refuge from everything around them that is strange. Home is where you shut the door at night and can just be yourself in a strange world.

7) Pray for the missionaries' spiritual life, emotional well-being and the power of God on their ministry. It is easy to neglect their own spiritual life when they must think always of feeding others.

HOW TO PRAY FOR YOUR CHILDREN AND GRANDCHILDREN

PRAY...
1. That they will be saved early in life. (Psalm 63:1; II Timothy 3:15)
2. That they will develop a hatred for sin. (Psalm 97:10)
3. That they will be caught when guilty. (Psalm 119:71)
4. That they will be protected from evil in each area of their lives: spiritual, mental, social, and physical. (John 17:15)
5. That they will have a responsible attitude in all interpersonal relationships. (Daniel 6:3)
6. That they will respect the authorities in their lives. (Romans 13:1)
7. That they will desire right friends and be protected from wrong friends. (Proverbs 1:10-11)

8. That they will be kept from the wrong mate and will be saved for the right mate. (II Corinthians 6:14-17)
9. That both they and those they will marry will be kept pure until marriage. (II Corinthians 6:18-20)
10. That they will actively resist Satan in all circumstances. (James 4:7)
11. That they will be single-hearted - willing to be sold out to Jesus Christ. (Romans 12:1-2)
12. That they will be hedged in so they cannot find their way to wrong people or wrong places - and that wrong people will not find them. (Job 1:10)

Let us as parents take heed and beware of a carnal complacency that subtly desensitizes us to the needs of our children. Passivity never won a child's heart for Christ. It is urgent to cultivate closeness with our children. Some practical suggestions would include:

Travail: In Isaiah 66:8, the Scripture says that "as soon as Zion travailed, she brought forth her children." If we intend to see God's power revealed in the lives of our children, we must part company with casual prayer. Mere words and "vain repetitions" in prayer never conquered unbelief in the life of a child. Effectual, fervent prayer still avails much.

Transparency: Our children learn more of grace when they see the grace of God revealed in our own struggles. Confessing of faults before them will do far more to amplify grace in the eyes of children than just merely talking about it.

During a meeting in Oklahoma City a few years ago, a son had been praying with his father at the conclusion of the service. When the pastor asked for testimonies, the son responded by sharing that his father had asked him to forgive him for the first time in twenty-three years. The joy on the young man's countenance was indescribable, as he had been liberated by his father's transparency and humility.

Training: The training in Proverbs 22:6 suggests instructing by exercise, drill, to make obedient to orders, to put or point in an exact direction. It entails instruction, discipline and example. John Flavel warned, "If you neglect to instruct your children in the way of holiness, will the Devil neglect to instruct them in the way of wickedness? No; If you will not teach them to pray, he will teach them to curse, swear and lie; if the ground is not cultivated weeds will grow."

Tradition: Deuteronomy 6 addresses the importance of establishing a tradition of teaching our children the words and ways of God. Nothing produces security in our relationship with them and affirms the reality of truth in their lives more than when we diligently teach them Biblical principles.

ACTION STEP ONE
Pray with a Pencil

The teacher starts a lecture, but the students are staring into space. Finally, one raises a hand and asks, "Is this gonna be on the exam?" Well, yes, of course. Only then do the students get out their pencils and start taking notes.

We write down the things we need to remember, whether notes in a classroom or phone numbers on the refrigerator door or deductions for the IRS. If it's important, we write it down.

So, why not have a pencil handy when you pray?

Prayer is dialogue. It's not like we're ordering items in some divine deli - "I'll take one pound of healing and half a pound of traveling mercies." Yes, the Lord does want to hear our requests, but often he's giving us orders - marching orders, if you will. He instructs us in the way we should go.

So it's important to listen as we pray. But it's also important to remember what he tells us. Maybe we ought to write it down. Many people have learned to record their prayer requests so they can check back later to see how God has worked. That's great! But we should also be jotting down what God is telling us about how to live, how to get closer to him, what he wants us to do, who he wants us to reach out to with the light of Christ.

What to Do

Set aside a time each day to talk with God - and grab a pencil and a journal as you do. Start with the "Show Me Prayer" (at the end of this section), pausing after each request to listen for what God might say. There's also an opportunity to add whatever specific question or need comes to mind.

As the day or week unfolds, write down whatever the Lord shows you. Set aside a page for recording what you "see" or "hear" at the end of each week in this journal.

Prayer is a personal matter, so you can "pray with a pencil" in different ways. Here are a few additional suggestions you might try:

Prayer Model A: Get the Lead Out. Before you begin your day in prayer, take out a pencil or pen and a blank sheet of paper. Jot down the overriding concerns you have for the day. Begin your prayer time making reference to those issues right from the start. As you talk to the Lord about your preoccupying thoughts, write whatever ideas come to you. It could be a verse from Scripture, a plan of action, or something to think about later. Be especially mindful of what the Lord seems to be saying about your concern. Write down some aspect of his character that will clarify your ability to trust him in this area.

Prayer Model B: Use Sparking Questions. Ask yourself a few questions to spark your conversations with God. Ask questions about the past that God might use to show you his plans for the future. For instance, "What were the five times in your life you've felt closest to God?" As you write your answers, you may receive some guidance about how to draw close to God again.

Prayer Model C: Keep a People File. As we pray, God often brings certain people to our mind. Jot down the names of those you think about as you talk with God. Pray for their needs, and see if you ought to reach out to them in some way.

Prayer Model D: Journal Your Prayers. Write down what you're saying to God - not only your requests, but also your thanks and praise. You might think of it as writing a letter to God.

Choose any prayer model you like, or create your own, but be sure to use the "Show Me Prayer" to connect with the great Teacher - and take notes as you listen.

The Show Me Prayer
Lord, please show me the way today.
Show me some aspect of your greatness I tend to overlook.
Show me what makes you smile and what makes you sad.
Show me people I can touch with your love.
Show me who I need to forgive and from whom I should seek forgiveness.
Right now I especially need you to show me _____
Thank you for showing yourself by sending your Son, Jesus.
AMEN

YOU MAY HAVE ANYTHING

Some of God's promises are absolutely breathtaking. They almost seem to be too good to be true. They suggest that there is nothing He will not do for those who love Him.

If you want to feel like a millionaire, open your Bible and read Psalm 84:11: *"No good thing will he withhold from them that walk uprightly."*

The same pledge is given in Psalm 34:10: *"They that seek the Lord shall not want any good thing."*

And look at this in Psalm 37:4: *"Delight thyself also in the Lord; and he shall give thee the desires of thine heart."*

Now turn to the book of Deuteronomy and read what God was prepared to do for Israel in the days of Moses: *"If thou shalt harken diligently unto the voice of the Lord thy God, to observe and to do all his commandments ... all these blessings shall come on thee and overtake thee ... Blessed shalt thou be in the city, and blessed shalt thou be in the field ... Blessed shall be thy basket and thy store. Blessed shalt thou be when thou comest in, and blessed shalt thou be when thou goest out."* (Chapter 28:1-6) *"The Lord shall open unto thee his good treasure."* (verse 12)

It was as though God said to them, "I will give you all these blessings, and if there is anything else you need, it is yours for the asking. Just come and take it. My treasury is open to you."

That these amazing promises were not intended only for His people in ancient times is made abundantly clear in the Scriptures.

Again and again the glorious truth is repeated that God wants to be equally generous to everybody in every age. *"Whatsoever ye shall ask in my name,"* said Jesus, *"that will I do, that the Father may be glorified in the Son."* (John 14:13)

Notice the word *whatsoever*. It recalls the wonderful whosoever of John 3:16. It is equally limitless. It suggests infinite wealth and an infinite willingness to share it with others.

To make sure that no one would mistake His intention or underestimate the extent of His promise, Jesus added: *"If ye shall ask anything in my name, I will do it."* A little later He repeated the assurance in these words: *"If ye abide in me, and my words abide in you, ye shall ask what ye will, and it shall be done unto you."* (John 15:7)

Here are some of the most remarkable promises of help and blessing ever made. Read them again in the Revised Standard Version.

"Whatever you ask in my name, I will do it."
"If you ask anything in my name, I will do it."
"Ask whatever you will, and it shall be done for you."

If words mean anything, then God has made provision for every holy wish of ours to be granted. If our lives are wretched, impoverished, and spiritually emaciated, the fault must be ours, not His. He has planned greatly for us. He stands ready to be very gracious to us and fill our lives with blessings. If we "have not" it is because we "ask not," See James 4:2.

One reason why Jesus came to this earth and died on Calvary's cross was to make rich those who accept and love Him. *"You know the grace of our Lord Jesus Christ,"* wrote the apostle Paul, *"that though he was rich, yet for your sake he became poor, so that by his poverty you might become rich."* (II Corinthians 8:9 RSV).

Not rich necessarily in material things, for these count but little in the sight of God, but rich in the things of the Spirit, which, after all, alone have lasting value. Through Him we can become rich in wisdom, in knowledge, in faith, in mercy, in love. *"Has not God chosen those who are poor in the world to be rich in faith and heirs of the kingdom which he has promised to those who love him?"* (James 2:5)

> *"If any of you lacks wisdom,"* wrote James, *"let him ask God who gives to all men generously and without reproaching, and it will be given him."* (James 1:5).

This emphasizes again God's attitude to all our needs and requests. He is generous. Very generous. And His generosity is measurable only by His love, which is infinite.

With this thought in mind, the apostle Paul asked, *"He that spared not his own Son, but delivered him up for us all, how shall he not with him also freely give us all things?"* (Romans 8:32).

It seemed only reasonable to him that if God loved us enough to give His Son to die for us, He would never withhold anything else that might contribute to our present and eternal happiness.

His reasoning was right, of course; and it helps us to appreciate more fully the infinite weight of eternal truth behind Christ's promise: *"If you ask anything in my name, I will do it."*

Of course, the word "anything" does not mean anything bad, or anything harmful to us or to others. But it does imply anything that will be good for us, anything that is in harmony with the will of God, anything that will advance His cause and His kingdom.

And because He says "anything," we should not hesitate to bring large requests to Him. By so doing we shall honor Him, for it will demonstrate that we believe He is able to grant them.

Judging by some people's prayers, one would think they believe that God is only concerned with the smaller interests of life. They seem afraid to mention the great burdens they are carrying, or the real desires of their hearts. But God wants us to bring all such larger matters to Him. It is His joy to do great things for His children, for *"he is able to do exceeding abundantly above all that we ask or think."* (Ephesians 3:20).

Notice that Jesus did not say, *"If you shall ask any little thing in My name, I will do it,"* but *"If you ask any thing."* And that surely takes in the great things, the seemingly impossible things, and the things that seem far beyond our reach.

"Call unto me," the Lord said to the prophet Jeremiah, *"and I will answer thee, and shew thee great and mighty things, which thou knowest not."* (Jeremiah 33:3).

That is what He wants us all to do - to call upon Him in faith, expecting mighty results from our prayers.

Many people have accepted this invitation, and, as a result, have seen God work for them in marvelous ways.

Your Bible tells the story of the prophet Elijah, who asked that fire be sent from heaven - not for his glory, but for God's.

"Lord God of Abraham, Isaac, and of Israel," he prayed, *"let it be known this day that thou art God in Israel, and that I am thy servant, and that I have done all these things at thy word."* (I Kings 18:36).

It was a very short and simple prayer, but it revealed the complete consecration of the prophet, and his single-minded desire to bring honor to God's holy name. As a result, there and then, *"the fire of the Lord fell."*

This is the kind of prayer God answers. As John says, *"If we ask anything according to his will he hears us."* (I John 5:14 RSV)

King Hezekiah prayed a similar prayer when he received a letter from the king of Assyria demanding the immediate surrender of Jerusalem. He took the letter *"and went up unto the house of the Lord, and spread it before the Lord. And Hezekiah prayed unto the Lord, saying, O Lord of hosts, God of Israel, that dwellest between the cherubims, thou art the God, even thou alone, of all the kingdoms of the earth. Incline thine ear, O Lord, and hear; open thine eyes, O Lord, and see; and hear all the words of Sennacherib, which hath sent to reproach the living God ... Now therefore, O Lord our God, save us from his hand, that all the kingdoms of the earth may know that thou art the Lord, even thou only."* (Isaiah 37:14-20).

As a result of this prayer, which was also for the glory of God, the Assyrian army was mysteriously destroyed and Sennacherib returned to Ninevah without so much as shooting an arrow at Jerusalem.

Examples of great results from earnest prayers uttered by faith-filled men and women are not confined to Bible characters.

Everybody has heard of George Muller and his world-famous orphanage at Bristol, England. When he began his work for orphans in 1836, he resolved to depend solely upon God for help. From then to the end of 1959, his institution received in free-will gifts more than three million pounds sterling - about $9,000,000 - solely in answer to prayer and without anyone's being asked for a donation. Think of praying for $9,000,000! But God sent it and more than 17,000 orphans have been blessed thereby.

Muller's faith became almost proverbial, and inspired countless others to put their trust in God. All his needs, great and small, he spread out before the Lord, with absolute assurance that they would be supplied.

On one occasion when he was crossing the Atlantic, his ship ran into a fog. Approaching the captain, he said, "I have come to tell you that I must be in Quebec on Saturday afternoon."

"Impossible," said the captain.

"Very well," replied Muller, "if your ship cannot take me, God will find some other means. I have never broken an engagement in fifty-seven years."

"I would willingly help you if I could," said the captain, "but there's nothing anyone can do."

"Let us go to the chartroom and. pray," said Muller.

"Do you know how dense the fog is?" asked the captain.

"No," was Muller's answer. "My eye is not on the density of the fog but on the living God, who controls every circumstance of my life."

Together they went to the chartroom and Muller prayed: "O Lord, if it is consistent with Thy will, please remove the fog in five minutes. You know the engagement You made for me in Quebec on Saturday. I believe it is Your will."

When he had finished, the captain was about to pray, but Muller touched him on the shoulder and told him not to do so. "First," he said, "you do not believe He will; and second, I believe He has, so there is no need for you to pray about it."

The captain looked amazed and Muller continued: "Captain, I have known my Lord, for fifty-seven years, and there has never been a single day that I have failed to gain an audience with Him. Get up and open the door. You will find the fog gone. "

The captain opened the door. The fog had disappeared!

Many similar stories have come out of the trials and anguish of our fighting forces. Chaplain W.H. Bergherm tells of meeting a devout admiral who once sent up twenty-five planes on a reconnaissance flight and lost sight of them in impenetrable midst. Anxiously he waited for their return, but they couldn't find the carrier. Knowing their gas was running low, he began to lose hope of saving the gallant young pilots. Then he thought of God. Going to his cabin he prayed for a break in the fog. Returning to the deck he saw that a streak of blue sky had appeared. Through this the planes came hurtling down one after another, till all were safely aboard. Then, just as suddenly and mysteriously, the sky closed in again.

In his book, **We Thought We Heard the Angels Sing,** Lt. James C. Whittaker tells of the days he spent on a rubber raft after his plane had crashed in the ocean. Hungry, thirsty, and blistered with the heat, he and his companions turned to God for help.

On the thirteenth day of their terrible experience, hope revived as a rain squall blotted out the scorching sun and moved toward them. Then, when the cloud was less than a quarter of a mile away, the wind blew it in another direction! The disappointment was crushing. "But somehow," says Lieutenant Whittaker, "my faith did not die. For the first time I found myself leading the rest in prayer. Like many of the others, I didn't know how to address God properly. I talked to Him, therefore, as I would have to a parent or a friend.

"'God,' I prayed, 'You know what that water means to us. The wind has blown it away. It is in Your power, God, to send back that rain. It's nothing to You, but it means life to us.'"

Nothing happened, but he continued to pray. In agony of soul he cried out: "'God, the wind is Yours. You own it. Order it to blow back the rain to us who will die without it.'"

They waited, watching and hoping. Then the miracle happened. Says Lieutenant Whittaker:

"There are some things that can't be explained by natural law. The wind did not change, but the receding curtain of rain stopped where it was. Then, ever so slowly, it started back toward us - against the wind!

"Maybe a meteorologist can explain that to your satisfaction. One tried it with me; something about crosscurrents buffeting the squall back. I tell you that there was no buffeting. It moved back with majestic deliberation. It was as if a great and omnipotent hand was guiding it to us across the water."

They caught a great store of rainwater, washed the salt from their poor, blistered bodies, and gathered courage for the rest of their ordeal. They knew then that God would not desert them.

Some years ago, a woman told me this personal experience: Her father, a farmer in Canada, and a faithful servant of God, had fallen upon hard times. It was winter, and there was food enough for but one last meal for the family of five. In desperation, he called them all to prayer, not seeing any escape from starvation. After praying, he sent one of the boys through the snow to the post office, several miles away. The lad brought back a letter, and in it was a draft for one hundred dollars - money the father had lent to a man thirteen years before!

Would you like to see God work for you? You may. He loves you very dearly. He wants to help you. He wants to do great things for you. Just give Him a chance. Tell Him your needs, your hopes, your dreams. Ask for specific blessings and watch them come to pass.

"Call," He says, "and I will answer."

"If you ask anything in my name, I will do it."

I don't know where I got this article, but I chose to use it to encourage and challenge people to believe God for great and mighty things.

VI-D: SCRIPTURE MEMORIZATION

One of the greatest things we can do for ourselves is to memorize Scripture. When our children were small, one of the things we did was to work with them on memorizing verses. I was told as a young person that sin would keep me from the Word or the Word would keep me from sin. So I believed the more verses we learned the better. It would give the Holy Spirit something to work on in times of need. There are other good reasons we need to learn Scripture.

"Memorizing the Scripture has great value - in this way we can best retain and make use of them. The Word committed to memory will restrain us from sinning. A memorized verse will flash into the mind at the moment of temptation and prevent us from sinning.

"Verses and passages of the Scriptures committed to memory also equip one to be a witness and a soul winner. God always honors and uses His Word. When human persuasion and reasoning fail, statements from the Word will convince, convict and convert people. Therefore we should quote it.

"Various methods and aids for Scripture memorization have been developed. A simple suggestion is to memorize each day a verse selected from your regular Bible reading - the verse that means the most to you. Underline it in your Bible or Testament, and review it at various times during the day. Keep reviewing verses previously learned, for constant repetition is the secret of memorization. If one verse a day seems too much for you, start with one verse a week."

A Life That's Real
By: G. C. Weiss

VARIOUS PLANS FOR MEMORIZING
Keep in Memory
By: N. A Woychuk

There are several ways in which Bible memorizing may be followed:

1. One plan that some people follow is that of memorizing certain verses in connection with the daily Bible reading and quiet time. The most significant verses are checked or underlined and an effort is made to memorize them. This seems to work for some people very nicely. However, for the most part, although it seems good in theory, it fails in actual practice. I recall a statement from a friend in Kansas a few years ago: "I tried to memorize verses as a part of my devotions each day, but I felt lost in the project. I realized that I needed some specific guidelines." (Kathleen Regehr).

2. Memorizing a certain chapter or an entire book in the Bible is often undertaken. I tried it a number of times, but seldom got very far with it. This has some real advantages. There is generally a sequence of thought, and there is no question but that following

such a plan, you will understand the verses in that chapter or book better as you memorize all the verses in their context. This significant factor must not be overlooked. A few people succeed in memorizing all the Psalms, some absorb other long books or even the entire New Testament, and they do so with great profit. Thomas Cranmer, the first Protestant Archbishop of Canterbury, memorized the whole of the New Testament on his journey to Rome. Frances Ridley Havergal, one of the outstanding hymn writers of England who lived only 42 years (1836-1879), committed to memory all of the New Testament, the entire Book of Psalms, and the Book of Isaiah while she was still a teenager. Later, she added all the Minor Prophets. She had in memory a total of 12,935 Bible verses.

Although this plan has some distinct advantages, it has to be organized and implemented with systematic effort. John Ruskin tells about the outstanding chapters of the Bible which his mother selected for him to memorize. Among them was Psalm 119, which is the longest chapter in the Bible. Not only did she insist upon daily pursuit of it, but it had to be done word-perfect and recited with expression so as to indicate that he really understood what he had memorized. He said that as a boy he just knew that he would always dislike the Bible and that the one chapter that he would most assuredly detest would be Psalm 119. On the contrary, he attributed his greatest achievements in life to the reverence of the Scriptures that his mother had instilled in him as a boy: "All that I have taught of art," he said, "everything that I have written, every greatness that has been in any thought of mine, whatever I have done in my life, has simply been due to the fact that when I was a child, my mother daily read with me a part of the Bible, and daily made me learn a part of it by heart."

Elsewhere he stated that although he loved the entire Bible, yet the one Scripture which was like a river of delight to him was Psalm 119. To quote him exactly: "It is strange that of all the pieces of the Bible which my mother taught me, that which cost me the most to learn, and which was to my child's mind most repulsive - the 119th Psalm - has now become of all the most precious to me in its overflowing and glorious passion of love for the law of God."

3. Typing or printing the desired Bible verses on small cards has been used by many quite successfully in memorizing the Word. The Scripture text generally printed on one side and the reference on the other. Many individuals have developed such for themselves, but it has been best perfected and used by the Navigators and by the Young Life Campaign, who have arranged the verses under topical headings and assembled them in packs for handy use. This plan has certain merits and many, particularly adults, have been blessed in following such a system.

4. Another plan is that of memorizing key verses in the books of the Bible and in many of the outstanding chapters. This also facilitates learning the contents of the Bible inasmuch as the key verses often shed light on the entire chapter or book.

MEMORY VERSE STUDY

REMEMBER:
1. Think through the verse.
2. Apply the verse personally.
3. Say the verse out loud.
4. Repeat the reference before and after each verse.
5. Check yourself for word perfection.
6. Use the verse in your daily meditation and witness.
7. Review your verses each day: the real secret of memorization.
8. Learn at least two new verses each week.

Be accountable to someone in learning your verses, until it becomes a habit for you. It is so easy to let this slip, and we become the losers. Don't miss out on the exciting times you will have as you experience the Holy Spirit using these verses in your life to minister to you and to others.

This is just another way we grow!

THE KEY TO MEMORIZATION

When you think of actually memorizing, you may ask yourself, "How can I memorize verses when I have such a terrible memory?"

Psychologist Tim LaHaye explains that our apprehension about memorization is not so much from a mental block as it is with an ambition block: "If I were to ask you for your address or phone number, you would have no trouble recalling it. Anyone who can do that can memorize Bible verses. Very honestly, memorization involves hard work but it pays greater dividends to your spiritual life than any other known method of Bible Study."

All of us can memorize Scripture. Some may memorize faster than others, but we are all capable of memorization.

The key motivation for memorizing Scripture is realizing how important it really is. I hope it won't take a squadron of torpedo bombers to awaken you to this. Perhaps just understanding what the Bible says about memorizing will be sufficient!

Why Memorize?

Psalm 1 describes the person who memorizes God's Word and then thinks about it often (meditates upon it):

Oh, the joys of those who do not follow evil men's advice, who do not hang around with sinners, scoffing at the things of God: But they delight in doing everything God wants them to, and day and night are always meditating on his laws and thinking about ways to follow him more closely. (Psalm 1:1,2).

When you care enough about knowing God's Word to memorize it, it becomes a part of your thoughts. You find yourself suddenly remembering it throughout the day. If you awaken at night full of anger or fear, you can choose to mentally review verses in God's Word that deal with those emotions.

The psalmist explains the result in a person's life because of such meditation: "They are like trees along a river bank bearing luscious fruit each season without fail. Their leaves shall never wither, and all they do shall prosper" (Psalm 1:3). Those who meditate upon God's Word keep going when the going gets tough. They don't wilt under pressure. They are consistent.

Jesus exemplified that consistency in His life. We can't claim to live exactly as the sinless, incarnate God did, but we can value what He valued. Pick up any of the Gospels and begin reading about Jesus. He is often quoting Scripture - from memory! Nearly 10 percent of the words of Jesus in the Gospels are quotations from the Old Testament. By having Scripture memorized, Jesus could use the right Scripture for the need of the moment, like a craftsman who instinctively reaches for the right tool. The same can occur in your life.

Romans 12:2 says, "Do not conform any longer to the pattern of this world, but be transformed by the renewing of your mind. Then you will be able to test and approve what God's will is - his good, pleasing and perfect will" (NIV). Memorizing Scripture and then consciously thinking about it gives you a grid with which to evaluate all the messages you receive from advertising, friends at work, your family...everything you are exposed to. Instead of remaining conformed to the world, you are transformed as God's Word renews your mind.

HOW TO MEMORIZE

Let's get started. Look at your watch and note the time. What follows will require some effort, but you will be surprised by how little time it actually takes to memorize a verse or two letter perfect. (Even those who have memorized thousands of verses began by memorizing one verse at a time.) Let's try Philippians 4:6,7:

Do not be anxious about anything, but in everything, by prayer and petition, with thanksgiving, present your requests to God. And the peace of God, which transcends all understanding, will guard your hearts and your minds in Christ Jesus (NIV).

Memorization begins first with **familiarization.** Read the verses aloud several times. This involves your mind in three ways: seeing, speaking and hearing. Next, copy the verses down on a 3x5 card or a large self-stick type note. By writing the verses on a note card you will have a handy reminder to place on the refrigerator or the bathroom mirror.

Carefully compare your own copy with the version in this book. You may be surprised to find that you omitted or added a word in copying the verses!

AMPLIFICATION

Amplification involves gaining the fullest meaning from the text. This involves looking up definitions to words that aren't totally clear, as well as reading the verses in their context to determine meaning. You may have been hindered in memorizing Philippians 4:6, 7 because you didn't entirely understand what the verses were saying. In particular, the meaning of several of the words may be unclear. What does it mean to **petition** God? And what does **transcend** mean?

Webster's Dictionary reveals that petition is an earnest request, with a second meaning of a formal request made to a superior. Transcend means "to rise above or go beyond the limits of."

Philippians 4:6, 7 is saying that if you present your request to God, who is your superior, He gives you His peace. It becomes God's job to worry about your problem! That does not free you from personal responsibility, but it does free you from personal anxiety. You still have to work through the problem, but the worry is given to God.

PERSONALIZATION

Personalization applies the verse to your own situation. Consider how Philippians 4:6,7 applies to you:

"I will not be anxious about anything, but in everything by prayer and petition with thanksgiving, I will present my requests to God. And I know that the peace of God, which transcends all understanding, will guard my heart and my mind in Christ Jesus."

Writing and thinking about how this verse applies to you allows God's Word to change patterns in your life. When you become fearful or sense a lot of stress, tell God your problems. These needs are presented with thanksgiving and the confidence that God's peace will guard your thinking.

To make it even more personal, you might write out, "What situations cause me to be anxious?" and then list specific situations or areas that make you stressful. Include the things that make you lie awake at night or wake you early in the morning with a tight knot in your stomach. Decide to pray over these things, recalling that prayer is not limited to "spiritual" areas, but includes talking to God about the money you need to get the car fixed or your kid's problems at school.

REVIEW

It will not help much to memorize these verses today, only to forget them tomorrow. The key to effective memorization is review. Putting your memory verses on 3x5 cards allows you to place them in a file box for review. Here is one method of review that many have found helpful:

Review once a day for seven days;
once a week for seven weeks;
once a month for seven months.

I hope you will set aside time today to begin memorizing and meditating on Scripture. The first week will be the hardest, but also the most important. You'll begin to learn firsthand the value of this practice.

Francis Cosgrove Jr., like Roy Robertson, has memorized Scripture extensively. He gives this encouragement:

"Why do I memorize Scripture? Because I have convictions about it. I know God wants me to know His Word, and He wants me to share it with others, so I discipline myself to add more verses to my biblical vocabulary. I keep adding verses, but I remember that there was a day when I had only one verse memorized."

Of course, Scripture memory alone won't guarantee a healthy, growing spiritual life, but it does provide a powerful resource when you're tempted. Yet, even with this tool, you still need to live a life of total dependence on God. And, as we will see in the next chapter, you really can't live the Christian life - even with memorized verses - in isolation.

VI-E: WITNESSING

Are you growing? For spiritual growth, a Christian not only needs good food, the word of God, and good, fresh air, which is prayer, but he needs exercise. This comes in working for Christ. The main work of a Christian is to witness and win others to the Lord. "The fruit of the righteous is a tree of life and he that winneth souls is wise" (Proverbs 1:30). Christian maturity leads a person to be able to stand alone and to reproduce. Every living organism has a God-given ability to reproduce itself. It is the same with the Christian. We are guilty of spiritual manslaughter when we let souls go out into eternity unprepared without a warning or a wooing word. (Ezekiel 3:18, 33:8) Witnessing is natural (John 4:28-29), scriptural (Mark 16:15), helpful (John 4:39) and necessary. We need to remember that the task before us is never greater than the power behind us. (Matthew 28:18-19)

The most important thing we can do is to witness for the Lord by holy living. All the talking in the world will be of no avail if the life is not consistent. "What you do speaks louder than what you say."

"I'd rather see a sermon, than hear one any day;
I'd rather one would walk with me than merely tell the way.
The eye's a better pupil, and more willing than the ear;
Fine counsel is confusing, but example's always clear.
The best of all the preachers are the men that live their creeds;
For to see good put in action is what everybody needs.

I soon can learn to do it if you'll let me see it done;
I can watch your hands in action, but your tongue too fast may run.
The lectures you deliver may be very wise and true,
But I'd rather get my lesson by observing what you do.
But there's no misunderstanding how you act, and how you live."

By: Edgar Guest

If one is truly born again, they are sincerely concerned that others become saved too. This is what God expects of His children and God has given us the wonderful privilege of spreading the Gospel of Christ. Because of that privilege, we should give ourselves over immediately to the interesting and absorbing task of fitting ourselves to be a good witness for the Lord.

You might ask, "How can I do that?" There are many plans or outlines one can use to help you. We should choose one and study it. We should memorize the Scripture verses that go along with the outline. I am going to give several plans that have been used and which you might find helpful. Remember, the more you witness, the easier it becomes, and "practice makes perfect."

There are only five ways that I know for anyone to witness:

1. By what he is most of all.
2. By what he does.
3. By what he says.
4. By what he gives.
5. By what he prays.

I was taught that "If you are not a missionary, you are a mission field." In other words, if you are not witnessing to someone, someone should be witnessing to you.

So every Christian can be a witness. You need not be someone special. It doesn't take any unusual gifts or miraculous powers to be a witness for Christ.

I would remind you that the lost souls with whom you work or those that live next door to you, or even those who may go to church with you, are as lost as those in dark Africa or anywhere in the world. God loves them as much as He loves you or anyone. Jesus died for them too. They are under bondage to sin and the devil and are headed for the same hell as any lost soul in the world.

The majority of Christians never win a soul to Christ. In fact, they never even try. Worse, yet, many never let their neighbors, friends and fellow employees know that they are Christians. Matthew 5:16 tells us to "Let your light so shine before men that they may see your good works and glorify your Father which is in heaven."

A poll taken several years ago resulted in the following startling facts: "Only 28% of Christians are witnessing with any degree of regularity to their friends. A mere 8% are responsible for 70% of the professed conversions." From: *Christian Life Magazine*. This reveals that Christians have put their lights under bushels. But Jesus tells us to put them on candlesticks so that it gives light to others. (Matthew 5:14-15)

The unsaved want to know whether Christianity really works in our lives, our homes, at the shops, with our neighbors, in our daily living. A true Christian doesn't become one, but is one by the way he lives and what he truly is. Are we living the claims of Christianity? Are we enjoying its fruits, and giving our lives to spreading its message? That is the real test of Christianity.

"God has made a tremendous investment in you. He expects a return. You were chosen 'that you might go and bring forth fruit, and that your fruit should remain' (John 15:16). He not only saved you from sin; He saved you for His work. He has a job for you. You were created in Christ Jesus unto good works.

"Your good deeds, of course, are not the basis of your salvation. You are saved only by the grace of God through faith. But having been redeemed, you start working for God. Now others, seeing your good works, give glory to your Father in Heaven. God gets the credit for it, but someday you will get a reward for it.

"God is counting on you. You are His instrument in ministering to the needs of the world. Look around for these opportunities for service. Surely there is something that you can do. He will give you the strength to do His work, if you will only trust Him, and let Him lead you on.

"Above all, God wants you to represent Him before those who do not know His grace. This was the supreme mission of His Own Son when He came to earth, 'not to be ministered unto, but to minister, and to give His life a ransom for many' (Mark 10:45). Now in the power of His Spirit He sends you out to be His witness 'unto all men of what thou hast seen and heard' (Acts 22:15).

"The love of Christ constrains you to this task. It is your reason for living. You are born to reproduce. What a thrill! You are a co-laborer with Christ in telling the good news of salvation to the ends of the earth and unto the end of time."

Established By The Word Of God
By: Robert E. Coleman

Since 95% of Christians have never won a soul to Christ, they are missing out on the greatest thrill in the world.

A plan that I have enjoyed using is **The Romans Map To Heaven.**

Who is Good?

Romans 3:10 - As it is written. There is none righteous, no, not one,

Who has sinned?

Romans 3:23 - For all have sinned, and come short of the glory of God,

Where Sin comes from

Romans 5:12 - Wherefore, as by one man sin entered into the world, and death by sin, and so death passed upon all men, for that all have sinned.

God's Price On Sin

Romans 6:23 - For the wages of sin is death, but the gift of God is eternal life through Jesus Christ our Lord,

Our Way Out

Romans 5:8 - But God commended his love toward us, in that, while we were yet sinners, Christ died for us.

Romans 10:9-11 - That if thou shalt confess with thy mouth the Lord Jesus, and shalt believe in thine heart that God hath raised him from the dead, thou shalt be saved. For with the heart man believeth unto righteousness; and with the mouth confession is made unto salvation. For the scriptures saith, Whosoever believeth on him shall not be ashamed.

Romans 10:13 - For whosoever shall call upon the name of the Lord shall be saved.

Pray to receive Christ now and you will begin the great adventure of life that God has for you.

"Lord Jesus, I need you, I have sinned against you. Forgive me of my sins. I receive You now as my Saviour and Lord, Make me the kind of person You want me to be. Thank You for giving me the gift of eternal life. Amen,"

Take God at his word and claim his promise for your salvation.

AN EFFECTIVE PERSONAL WITNESS

QUALIFYING

I. Cultivate essential personality traits.
   1. Develop Spiritual mindedness.
   2. Practice patience.
   3. Use tact.
   4. Be courageous.
   5. Employ persistence.
   6. Guard confidences.

II. Make personal preparation.
   1. Present a pleasing appearance.
   2. Have normal health.
   3. Display a pleasant personality.
   4. Develop enthusiasm.

III. Make Spiritual preparation.
   1. Pray before going.
   2. Exercise faith; go expecting them to be saved.
   3. Go in the strength of the Lord. (Joshua 1:9)

IV. The witness must realize what it means to be lost.
   1. The lost person is guilty of sin. (Romans 3:23)

2. The lost person is dead in sin. (Ephesians 2:1, Ezekiel 18:4, Romans 6:23)
3. The lost person is condemned before God. (John 3:18, John 8:44)
4. The lost person is without God or hope. (Ephesians 2:12)
5. The lost person is facing eternal hell. (II Thessalonians 1:7-9)

V. The witness must know the plan of Salvation.
 1. All are lost. (Romans 3:23, Isaiah 53:6)
 2. All lost persons are condemned. (John 3:18, Ephesians 2:12)
 3. All lost persons are bound for eternal death. (Romans 6:23, Acts 4:12)
 4. All lost persons may be saved by faith in Christ. (Ephesians 2:8-9, Acts 3:19, John 3:16, Acts 16:31, John 1:12)
 5. All saved persons should confess Christ. (Romans 10:9-10, Matthew 10:32-33)
 6. Consecration.
 7. Keep an active prayer list.
 8. A compassionate heart.

HOW TO WITNESS EFFECTIVELY

Often the first reaction a person has when he receives Christ into his heart is a desire to tell someone else. When Andrew met Christ, he immediately told his brother Simon Peter (John 1:40-41), When the Samaritan woman realized she had met Christ, she ran to town to tell others (John 4:28-30). According to the Bible, the urge to witness is natural. But as a new convert you may be fearful of witnessing to others. In this lesson you will learn how to witness effectively.

1. We Must Know Why To Witness
 A. The Commission of Christ.
 "You are witnesses of these things" - Luke 24:28

The first reason for witnessing is that Christ has commanded it. He promised in Matthew 28:19-20 that he will be with you as you witness. Jesus announced to the disciples in Luke 24:47-48 that they were witnesses of his miracles and teachings to the whole world. This command of Christ should be the only reason the Christian needs to witness to the lost around him.

B. The conscience of a Christian.
"If I say to the wicked, O wicked man, you shall surely die, and you do not speak to warn the wicked to turn from his way, that wicked man shall die in his iniquity, but his blood I will require at your hand" - Ezekiel 33:8

God warns us that as Christians we are responsible to warn the sinner of his sinful ways. Because we know what sinners ought to do, our conscience commands that we witness and try to lead them to Christ.

C. The consequences of sin.
"For the wages of sin is death, but the free gift of God is eternal life in Christ Jesus our Lord" - Romans 6:23

The Bible says we earn and deserve from a life of sin eternal death - separation from God forever. Realizing spiritual death comes to those who die without Christ is another motivation to be witnesses as Christ wants us to be.

D. The coming of Jesus Christ.
"Watch therefore, for you do not know on what day your Lord is coming" Matthew 24:42.

"Therefore you also must be ready; for the Son of Man is coming at an hour you do not expect" - Matthew 24:44.

"For you yourselves know well that the day of the Lord will come like a thief in the night" - I Thessalonians 5:2.

And what will take place when Christ returns?
"For we all shall appear before the judgment seat of Christ, so that each one may receive good or evil, according to what he has done in the body" - II Corinthians 5:10.

These verses and many others warn us Christ's second coming could be at any moment. We ought to be ready. Because Jesus could come any time, we should be sharing with others the Gospel, so they will be prepared to meet Christ when he appears.

E. The changes in one's life.
"For I am not ashamed of the Gospel: It is the power of God for salvation to everyone who has faith, to the Jew first and also to the Greek" - Romans 1:16.

"Therefore, if any one is in Christ, he is a new creation; the old has passed away, behold, the new has come" - II Corinthians 5:17.

Since the Gospel has power to change lives, we ought to share it with those in need. If a doctor finds a healing medicine, duty demands he share it with those who are suffering. Knowing the changes Christ can bring to those in sin around us, duty demands that we witness.

F. The cost of a soul.
"For what is a man profited, if he shall gain the whole world, and lose his own soul? or what shall a man give in exchange for his soul?" - Matthew 16:26 (KJV).

This verse shows us the value of a soul, worth more than the whole world. Thereby if a man dies without Christ, it is the greatest loss he can experience. For that reason we should witness.

G. The certainty of death.
"And just as it is appointed for men to die once, and after that comes judgment" - Hebrews 9:27.

"But God said to him, 'Fool! This night your soul is required of you; and the things you have prepared, whose will they be?'" - Luke 12:20.

Although we do not know when we will die, if Jesus tarries, we will all die. And after death, we will all be judged. Thus, all men need to hear and respond to the Gospel. And the only way men will hear the Gospel is for Christians to be witnesses.

H. The cheers in heaven.
"Just so, I tell you, there is joy before the angels of God over one sinner who repents" - Luke 15:10.

What causes heaven to rejoice? It is not your good life, how much you give, how much you have learned from God's Word, or how long you pray, though God is interested in each of these. The only thing that makes heaven rejoice is when men and women repent of their sins and begin to live for God.

II. We Must Know To Whom To Witness.
Now that you have accepted Christ, God expects you to witness to those around you. Who are those to whom you should witness?

A. Your friends.
"Go home to your friends, and tell them how much the Lord has done for you, and how he has had mercy on you" - Mark 5:19.

B. Your family.
"He first found his brother Simon and said to him, "We have found the Messiah" (which means Christ). He brought him to Jesus..." John 1:41-42.

C. Your neighbors.
"Come, see a man who told me all that I ever did. Can this be the Christ?" — John 4:29. The Samaritan woman left the well and water pot when she met Christ and immediately began to tell the people of the city, her neighbors, about Christ. As a result, John records that:

"Many Samaritans from that city believed in him because of the woman's testimony,,." - John 4:39

D. Everyone.
"Go therefore and make disciples of all nations..." - Matthew 28:19

"Repentance and forgiveness of sins should be preached in his name to all nations..." - Luke 24:47.

"You shall be my witnesses in Jerusalem and in all Judea and Samaria and to the end of the earth" - Acts 1:8.

III. You Must Know How To Witness

A. Some practical helps for witnessing
1. Witness by a good life.
2. Realize you will learn to witness as you continue to witness.

3. Begin like the demoniac of Mark 5 - go home to your friends and tell them what great things God has done for you.
4. Pray for opportunities to witness.
5. Be alert to opportunities to witness.
6. Relax - as you persuade men to receive Christ (II Corinthians 5:11) the Holy Spirit is also convincing men of their need (John 16:8).
7. Be sensitive to the Holy Spirit's leading - Acts 8:26-40.
8. Learn a definite plan of salvation.

You may want to learn how to effectively use such a tool as the "Salvation by Appointment" flip-chart or the shorter "Four Spiritual Laws."

B. A definite plan of salvation.
 1. Three opening questions:
    a) All have sinned - Romans 3:23
    b) The sinner's responsibility -
       (1) Repent - Acts 17:30
       (2) Believe - John 3:36
       (3) Confess - I John 1:9
       (4) Receive - John 1:12
    c) Follow-up the new believer by having him read II Corinthians 5:17 and having prayer with him. Encourage him in the Christian life.

95% of all Christians have never led a soul to Christ.

I. SALVATION IS A PERSON
 A. The ONE TRUTH that must fill the heart and mind of the soul-winner is that Jesus Christ is NOT A DOCTRINE. The Lord is a living person whom the grave could not hold and at this very moment, is alive and waiting to meet men in a personal encounter.

II. SOUL WINNING IS INTRODUCING
   A. The soul-winner is the introducer of Jesus Christ.
   B. The Holy Spirit makes Christ real.

III. THE NATURE OF MAN
   A. He is intellectual – he has a mind and is a thinking creature.
   B. He is emotional – he has feelings that move him and prompt his actions.
   C. He is volitional – he is capable of making decisions.

   It is not enough to know about the Lord, one must know about men too!

IV. YOU NEED A PLAN
   A. Approach
   1. "Are you interested in spiritual things/"
   2. "Have you ever thought of becoming a Christian?"
   3. "What if someone were to ask, 'What is a Christian?' What would you say?"

   B. Four verses that may be used as a plan
   1. Romans 3:23. "For all have sinned, and come short of the glory of God."
   2. Romans 6:23. "For the wages of sin is death; but the gift of God is eternal life through Jesus Christ our Lord."
   3. John 1:12. "But as many as received him, to them gave he power to become the sons of God, even to them that believe on his name."
   4. Revelation 3:20. "Behold, I stand at the door, and knock; if any man hear my voice, and open the door, I will come in to him, and will sup with him, and he with me."

V. HINTS THAT HELP THE SOUL-WINNER
   A. Get the prospect alone.
   B. Stay on target.
   C. Do not defend the Bible.
   D. Learn to distinguish between resistance and resentment.

E. Do not teach a Bible lesson in the middle of an introduction.

Do we understand about Hell? It is torment, it is agony, it is burning, it is eternal separation from God and anything that is good and decent, and it is never-ending.

There is a powerful verse found in Ezekiel 33:8 that should motivate us to be witnesses. It says, "If I say to the wicked, O wicked man, you shall surely die, and you do not speak to warn the wicked to turn from his way, that wicked man shall die in his iniquity, but his blood I will require at your hand."

The Bible gives evidence that the desire to witness is natural. It is often the first reaction a person has when he receives Christ. A couple of examples are the Samaritan woman (John 4:28-30), and Andrew (John 1:40-41).

As a new convert, you may be afraid of witnessing to others. To help alleviate the fear, one needs a plan to go by. There are many plans available. Here are a few.

1. The Four Spiritual Laws - Tract
2. The Evangelism Explosion Program
3. The Roman Road to Life – (Romans 3:10; 3:23; 5:12; 6:23; 5:8; 10:9-13)
4. Soul Winner's Guide – Five Steps to Salvation
    a. Acknowledge – Psalm 51:3; Romans 3:23
    b. Confess – Proverbs 28:13; I John 1:9
    c. Repent – Mark 1:15; Luke 18:13
    d. Forsake – Isaiah 55:7; John 8:11
    e. Believe – John 3:16; Acts 16:29-34
5. Four verses that may be used as a plan – Romans 3:23; Romans 6:23; John 1:12; Revelation 3:20
6. Outline of Plan of Salvation
    Intro. The need – John 3:3
    1. Our condition – Sinners – Romans 3:23, Revelation 20:14-15
    2. God's Provision – The Gospel – I Corinthians 15:3-4
    3. Commitment – Romans 10:13

(Suggested Prayer: "Almighty God, believing I am a lost sinner for whom Christ died, was buried and rose again, I now repent of my sin and receive Him into my heart and will trust Him forever as my Lord and Saviour, in Jesus' name, Amen.")
    4. Assurance – The know-so salvation – I John 5:13.

Outlines Presenting Plan of Salvation

A.   The A-B-C Plan:
    I. Salvation Needed
        A. All have sinned (Romans 3:23)
        B. Sin brings death (Romans 6:23)
    II. Salvation has been Provided
        A. Sin may be cleansed (I John 1:7-9, Isaiah 1:18)
        B. Whosoever will may be saved (John 3:16, Romans 10:13)
        C. Salvation is a free gift of grace through faith (Ephesians2:8-9)
    III. Salvation can be Accepted
        A. Through repentance and faith (Acts 20:21)
        B. Repent or perish (Luke 13:3,5)
        C. Believe or be condemned (John 3:36)

Explanation:
1. This outline is just a suggestion. Make one that you feel is adequate explaining the plan of salvation.
2. Allow the letters N, P, A represent the words "Needed, Provided, Accepted" respectively.
3. Write the first Scripture reference in your outline somewhere in the front of your Bible in the following way. According to the outline above the first reference is Romans 3:23. Write: "N – Romans 3:23. The "N" signifies to you that Romans 3:23 is to be used to show the individual his need of salvation.
4. Turn to Romans 3:23 and explain the verse thoroughly. Directly above this reference right at the top of your Bible page, write the next reference in the same way. The proper letter in front of the reference will remind you about the

thought you are to present in that reference. Do this through your entire outline and you will be clearly presenting the plan of salvation without even having any verses memorized. Can it be made easier?

B. The Four "R's" of Salvation: (Good for use even without a Bible)
  1. Realize what sin has done - separation man from God (Isaiah 59:1-2)
  2. Recognize what God has done - sent His Son to Calvary to unite man with God (John 3:16, Romans 5:8, II Corinthians 5:21)
  3. Repent of your sin - the sin of rejecting Christ. All other sin is the result of rejecting Christ. (Luke 13:3,5, Acts 17:30-31)
  4. Receive Christ as your personal Saviour (John 1:12)

Assurance of Salvation

A. Emotional feeling is the wrong foundation. Never discredit feeling in the salvation experience to anyone, but make sure that a person's assurance is not depending on his feelings. Our feelings are changeable.

B. Only foundation is God's Holy Word, the Bible... God's Word is unchanging, unfailing, and unending.

C. Lack of assurance is actually not believing the Bible. It is calling God a liar! (Psalm 138:2, Matthew 24:35, Romans 3:4)

D. Point people to the Word of God.
  1. Forgiveness of sin (I John 1:9)
  2. Salvation (Romans 10:13)
  3. Assurance (John 5:24) (An explanation of this verse is wonderful to show what Jesus says we have received. Notice the present tense used and the absence of mention of personal feelings.)

E. Assignment for young Christians to help bring assurance of Salvation - Read I John and underline every use of all the forms of the word "know."

F. Word of the poet:
    Three men were walking on a wall, Feeling, Faith and Fact;
    When Feeling got an awful fall and Faith was taken back,
    So close was Faith to Feeling, He stumbled and fell too;
    But Fact remained and pulled Faith back, and Faith brought Feeling too.

These are all good plans, but many times one doesn't know how to get started. We need an approach. A good question can often get the conversation started. Here a few examples:
1. Are you interested in spiritual things?
2. Have you ever thought of becoming a Christian?
3. What if someone were to ask, 'What is a Christian?' What would you say?
4. If you died today, would you have the assurance of going to Heaven?
5. Would you like to know how you can have that assurance?
6. If I can show you in the Bible how you can know you are going to Heaven, will you be willing to do what God's Word says?
7. Have you ever had a personal experience with Jesus Christ?
8. Has anyone ever taken the Bible and shown you what you must do in order to be saved?

If you are just starting to witness, it may be encouraging to know that the more you witness, the easier it becomes. We learn by doing.

"Jesus wants to use you in winning others to Himself. Start telling your family and friends today about the new peace you have in Christ. Pray about bringing others to Jesus. Ask the Holy Spirit to give you the power to speak the right words at the right time. He will guide you to people hungry for the gospel.

"Every time you have the opportunity to speak for Christ, do it. Faithfulness in witnessing strengthens your faith and gives great joy. As you read your Bible, mark the verses that will help you explain the plan of salvation to others. Get a supply of gospel tracts and be prepared to use them as tools in expressing your faith." (Keith M.

Bailey, *Learning to Live*, Christian Pub. Inc., Harrisburg, PA, pg 45-46.)

HOW TO PRESENT THE GOSPEL
By: Larry Moyer

Opening Question - Has anybody ever taken a Bible and shown you how you can know that you're going to heaven? May I?

Transition Point - The Bible contains both bad news and Good News. The bad news is something about yourself. The Good News is something about God. Let's discuss the bad news first.

I. Bad News.
   A. You are a sinner.
      1. The verse - Romans 3:23 says, "For all have sinned, and come short of the glory of God."
      2. The illustration - When the Bible says you and I have sinned, it means we lie, we lust, we hate, we murder, and we steal. The word "sin" in the Bible actually means "to miss the mark." In other words, God is perfect and we aren't. Let me explain! Suppose you and I were to each pick up one rock. Then I say to you, "I want you to throw that rock and hit the North Pole." Well, you might get it farther than me or I might get it farther than you, but neither of us would make it. Both of us would come short. When the Bible says, "All of us have sinned, and come short of the glory of God," it means God has set a standard He expects every one of us to meet. That standard is God Himself. He expects us to be as holy as He is holy, as perfect as He is perfect. But it doesn't matter how religiously we live, how good we are, how hard we work; we cannot meet that standard. All of us have sinned and come short of the glory of God.

   B. The penalty for sin is death.
      1. The verse - Romans 6:23 says, "For the wages of sin is death..."

2. The illustration - Suppose you were to work for me one day and I were to pay you fifty dollars. Fifty dollars would be your wages. It represents what you have earned. The Bible is saying that because you and I have sinned, we have earned death. We are going to die and be eternally separated from God.

Transition Point - Since there was no way you could come to God, **the Bible says God decided to come to you.**

II. Good News.
   A. Christ died for you.
      1. The verse - Romans 5:8 says, "But God commendeth his love toward us that, while we were yet sinners, Christ died for us."
      2. The illustration - Let's say you were in the hospital dying of cancer. I could come to you and say, "I want to do something for you. We'll take the cancer cells from your body and put them into my body and I'll die in your place." What would happen to me? (pause) Right! I would die. What would happen to you? (pause) Right! You would live. Why? (pause) Yes! Because I took the thing that was causing your death, placed it upon myself and I died as your substitute. The Bible is saying that Christ came into the world and He took the sin and the guilt that was causing your death. He placed it upon Himself and He actually died in your place. He was your substitute! The third day, He arose, as proof that sin, death, and the devil had been conquered,
   B. You can be saved through faith.
      1. The verse - Ephesians 2:8, 9 say, "For by grace are ye saved through faith; and that not of yourselves, it is the gift of God, not of works, lest any man should boast."
      2. The illustration - Now you may be wondering, "What is faith?" The word "faith" means "to trust." For example, you were not here when that chair was made and you didn't examine how it was built before you sat down. You are simply trusting the chair to hold you. Putting your faith in Christ means trusting Him to save you - not trusting your church membership, your good life, or your baptism to get you to heaven, but trusting

Christ and Him alone. Your trust has to be in the One Who died for you and arose again. It is then God gives you heaven as a free gift.

III. Conclusion.
    A. Question - "Is there anything that is keeping you from right now trusting Christ as your Savior?"

Note: If the person seems hesitant, take a 3X5 card and number from one to five on the left hand side. Ask the individual to list three to five things that he feels is keeping him from trusting Christ right now. Then answer each objection. For example, if he writes, "I don't know what my wife will say," you might say to him, "I can understand that, but let me ask you something. Do you love her? (pause) Then, obviously if you knew you were going to heaven, you'd want her to know she was going to heaven, too. But just as you can't come back from some place you've never been, you can't share somebody you don't know. So what you ought to do is trust Christ and then tell her about Him."

CHAPTER VII

UNDERSTANDING THE SPIRIT FILLED LIFE

VII-A: THE TWO DIVISIONS OF MANKIND

I find from my study of the Bible that man is divided into two groups. These divisions are based entirely upon the spiritual condition of man's heart. He is either saved or lost, God's child or a child of the devil, on his way to heaven or hell, one who has had one birth or two. It's just that plain.

Paul tells us there is the natural man and the spiritual man. The natural man is the person who has been born only once! He is alive physically, but spiritually he is dead. He is motivated mainly by his physical desires. He is unbelieving, and unsaved. Paul describes his characteristics in Galatians 5:19-21. *"Now the works of the flesh are manifest, which are these: adultery, fornication, uncleanness, lasciviousness, idolatry, witchcraft, hatred, variance, emulations, wrath, strife, seditions, heresies, envyings, murders, drunkenness, revellings, and such like: of the which I tell you before, as I have also told you in time past, that they which do such things shall not inherit the kingdom of God."*

Jesus defined the natural man, saying: "That which is born of the flesh is flesh." (John 3:5) Jesus Christ is not in the life. Self is supreme. The natural man is ego-centered. He basically functions and seeks his fulfillment in the five human senses. His spirit has never been touched by the Holy Spirit, and he is separated from God. To him, the things of God are foreign and he cannot understand them. I Corinthians 2:14 says, *"The natural man does not understand the things of God because they are foolishness unto him, neither can he know them because they are spiritually discerned."*

Paul speaks of the second division of mankind in I Corinthians 2:15-16, *"He that is spiritual judgeth all things, yet he himself is judged of no man."*

The Bible divides all of mankind into two groups. God's divisions of mankind are based entirely upon the spiritual condition of the human heart: In the New Testament book of I Corinthians 2:13-3:4, Paul writes about the great divisions of mankind.

I. The NATURAL MAN
   A. Who is the natural man? (I Corinthians 2:14)

   B. What are his characteristics?

II. The SPIRITUAL MAN
   A. Who is the spiritual man? (I Corinthians 2:15-16)

   B. What are his characteristics?

Carnal: Romans 7:14, Romans 8:7, I Corinthians 3:1, II Corinthians 10:4, I Corinthians 9:11, Colossians 2:18, Hebrews 7:16, Hebrews 9:10

THE CARNAL MAN

The second major division of mankind is that of the carnal man. The natural man is one totally alienated from God, whereas the carnal man is a Christian under fleshly control. He has experienced God's salvation but he is not experiencing God's sovereignty. He has been born physically and spiritually. Christ is in the life, but self is still supreme! Ego still sits in the driver's seat.

In I Corinthians 3:1, Paul tells the believers at Corinth that he was forced to speak to them as "carnal, even as unto babes in Christ."

Now, of course, there is nothing wrong with being a spiritual baby. That's where we all begin. Peter, speaking to new Christians, writes, "As newborn babes, desire the sincere milk of the word, that ye may grow thereby" (I Peter 2:2). We all must start our Christian experience as infants - as new babes.

But the tragedy occurs when a person remains an infantile Christian. A mother is understandably alarmed if her baby fails to develop normally. A farmer is financially ruined if his crops do not grow and bring forth fruit. The first law of life is expansion. Without growth there can be no life!

Why is it important that we grow as Christians? Because it is God's plan for us. In Romans 8:29 we read that "whom he did foreknow, he also did predestinate to be conformed to the image of his Son." God desires that we be made like unto Jesus Christ. Wretched and miserable is the Christian who resists God's plan for development.

Let's look for a moment at the characteristics of the carnal man. Like an infant, he is easily offended and hurt. The small baby will cry at the slightest provocation. Any unusual activity is likely to disturb him. The carnal Christian is shortsighted. As with the young child, he lacks judgment and is immature. As these characteristics are normal for the child, they are also normal for the young Christian. It is only as the Christian fails to grow that carnality expresses itself. Unfortunately, many Christians remain spiritual infants throughout their lives. Their growth has been arrested and stunted.

Envy, strife, and divisions are characteristics of the carnal man. In I Corinthians 3:3, Paul says, "For whereas there is among you envying and strife, and divisions, are ye not carnal, and walk as men?" Children often quarrel and fight. They are impatient and lack self-control. Many times they are unable to get along with one another.

It was carnal Christians who caused many of the problems in the New Testament Church.

Much of Paul's time and many of his letters were devoted to clearing the confusion and strife created by carnal believers. Why? They were more concerned with the physical than they were with the spiritual issues of life. They did not know the centrality and sufficiency of Jesus Christ.

My friend, where do you stand today? Are you growing? Is your spiritual life fruitful or unfruitful? Are you a carnal Christian - saved yet so as by fire? The carnal man is the second division of mankind - converted but ruled by self.

By: Bill Bright

VII-B: THE TWO NATURES

Each born again person possesses two natures. The first, called "the flesh" is that sinful nature he received at his first, or natural birth. This nature he received at his first, or natural birth. This nature is unchanging in its enmity to God, is incurably depraved and totally incapable of pleasing God. (Romans 8:7-8)

It is the origin of his evil desires, and responds to every temptation if allowed to do so. (James 1:13-15)

This nature is never eradicated, but remains in the believer during his whole lifetime on earth.

The second nature, called "the Divine nature," was communicated to him upon his acceptance of Christ as Savior and Lord. (II Peter 1:3, Romans 8:9)

This nature is incapable of sin and leads the believer to think, say and do those things that are pleasing to God. (Galatians 5:16-26)

Through the indwelling of the Spirit, the Christian has thus been made a partaker "of the Divine nature." (II Peter 1:4)

Joy And Peace In Believing
By: Good News Publishers

DELIVERANCE FROM THE POWER OF SIN

After conversion, the young believer is usually filled with peace and joy for a time, until he discovers that his sinful nature is still in him. Then follows a struggle with indwelling sin, with many and bitter failures. Finally, if the soul is earnest, he finds God's remedy to be Christ Himself, operating in the life by the Holy Spirit.

God does not improve the old nature, the flesh. He condemns it. (Romans 8:7)

This explains my failures to change or improve the flesh. It simply cannot be done. God Himself does not attempt it.

What then is the way out?

Simply to let the Spirit of God have His way, counting the old man, the flesh, to have died with Christ. Here is the victory: "The Spirit of life in Christ Jesus has set me free from the law of sin and death." (Romans 8:2)

THE NEW POWER AND ITS RESULTS

"The experience of deliverance from the power of sin has been so startling in some believers, that it is like a second conversion, and some have called it the "second blessing." God intends that His children should have this deliverance from the day they believe, but in many cases there is a hard struggle and an interval of time before the soul gives up its efforts to improve the flesh, and accepts God's sentence of death on the "old man" and all his works."

The New You
By: Harold Myra

"Thus, in each child of God, dwells these two natures, diametrically opposed to each other. The result is a conflict. (Galatians 5:17)

Which of these natures is to have the ascendance in the life of the Christian? It all depends on the believer himself. In the measure in which he grasps the fact that:
1. His old nature has been crucified with Christ. Romans 6:6
2. Reckons himself to be dead unto sin. Romans 6:11
3. Refuses its claim to recognition. Romans 8:12
4. Makes no provision to fulfill its lusts. Romans 13:14
5. Keeps it in the place of death. Colossians 3:5
6. Yields himself unto God. Romans 6:13

In that measure he will be delivered from its dominion in his life.

The new nature, needless to say, must be encouraged and strengthened by feeding on the Scriptures, communing with God by prayer, obeying God's will and separating oneself from all know sin. This is what is termed "walking in the Spirit," and only by this means can the Christian avoid fulfilling the lust of the flesh." (Galatians 5:16)

VII-C: LORDSHIP

I believe that the "three divisions of mankind theory" came about as a result of not teaching that becoming a Christian means making Christ Lord of our lives. Who wouldn't want a fire escape from hell and yet be able to continue in their old sinful way of living.

The main thrust of Romans 6-8 is that in Christ there is no condemnation to those who walk not after the flesh but after the Spirit. We are free from the law of sin and now have power to live above the deeds of the flesh.

The issue that has to be dealt with in making Christ Lord of our life, is our will. In the natural, none of us wants to let someone else tell us what to do. We like to make our own decisions. Our will is our decision-making faculty. It is often caught between our thoughts and our desires. Our will tells what we want.

Before we can bring our will into harmony with God's purposes, we need adequate goals for our lives. When our goal is to live for the Lord and to honor and please Him, and when we surrender our will to God, we finally discover the resources to do what God requires. As we give ourselves to Him, we receive His power. The power of the Word of God is unleashed when we bring ourselves under its authority.

(A tract has been printed entitled *Can Christ Be Savior Yet Not Lord?* I feel it is so important that I want to give you the whole thing.)

CAN CHRIST BE SAVIOR YET NOT LORD?

"It is very significant that two of the titles given to Jesus Christ, Lord and Savior, are inseparably linked together."

The Greek word *soter*, always translated "Savior," occurs twenty-four times in the New Testament. In two of these instances Christ is called "the Savior of the world" (John 4:42 and I John 4:14). There are also eight miscellaneous references, such as when Paul told those gathered at the synagogue in Antioch of Bisidia that "God according to promise brought unto Israel a Savior, Jesus" (Acts 13:23 ASV) or when Peter spoke before the high priest, "Him (Whom Ye Slew) hath God exalted with his right hand to be a Prince and a Savior" (Acts 5:31).

At all other times it is "Lord and Savior" or "God and (my) Savior." You will notice also that the title "Lord" always precedes the title "Savior." It is never "our Savior and Lord." In other words, Christ is always Lord and God before He is Savior.

Again, notice that Christ is never addressed as "Savior," He is always addressed as "Lord" or "Master." The common title "Lord" (kurios) occurs 745 times in the New Testament; 719 times the word is translated "Lord," fourteen times "master," thirteen times "sir," and once "Owner." "Lord" is the title which is used most often in addressing Christ.

Then there is a stronger Greek word, *despotes*, from which we get our word despot. This word occurs only ten times in the New Testament, e.g., when Paul speaks of "a vessel unto honor, sanctified, and meet for the **Master's** use" (II Timothy 2:21) and when Peter mentions "false teachers ... even denying the Lord that bought them" (II Peter 2:1). The word means an owner of slaves, one who has bought another and owns him completely. Christ has redeemed us with His blood, and we are His. He is our Despot. Jude speaks of those who deny "our only Master (Despot) and Lord, Jesus Christ." (verse 4 ASV).

We do not like the word despot, but it has been well said that the only perfect government is an absolute monarchy where the monarch is absolutely perfect ... Christ Jesus is our perfect Despot.

Then our Lord is addressed as "Rabbi" by both His disciples and others, a word which occurs seventeen times in the New Testament, eight times translated "rabbi" and nine times translated "master." It means "highly honored" or "respected," used generally in addressing a teacher. The word *rabboni* is used twice; this is still a stronger term meaning "prince" or "chief." Once it is used by Mary (John 20:16) and once by a blind beggar (Mark 10:51).

The sum of all this is that the Lordship of Christ and His Saviorhood are always linked together. He is Savior because He is Lord. If He is not Lord, He is not Savior. When we make Him our Savior, we make Him our Lord; and if we do not make Him our Lord we cannot make Him our Savior. The Lordship of Christ is proclaimed, shall we say, more than His Saviorhood. He is King of kings and Lord of lords - Lord of all!

In our Lord's earthly ministry, while He proclaimed His saving mission, telling us that He came to seek and to save that which was lost, He always laid down the strictest conditions if one were to come and partake of His salvation. "So likewise," He says, "whosoever he be of you that forsakest not all that he hath, he cannot be my disciple." (Luke 14:33). In other words, His followers are those who make Him their Lord, their Despot. This is the taking up of one's cross daily (Luke 9:23), the denial of self.

This does not mean that one must forsake his position and go about as a beggar (unless his position dishonors the Lord). It means that he must bring all things into the captivity of Christ (II Corinthians 10:5). In doing this our acceptance by Him and then forgiveness of our sins are taken for granted. It is those who endeavor to accept Jesus as Savior and not as Lord (alas, there are so many) who wonder why they have not assurance. The answer is simply that they have no Savior. Christ Jesus is our Lord and Savior. It has been well said that a religion which costs nothing is worth nothing.

What, then, is saving faith? It is not a mere intellectual acknowledgment or confession that Jesus is the Christ. The demons believe that much (James 2:19). It is the casting of ourselves upon Him and making Him our personal Lord. No one can do this if he does not put his whole trust in Him.

If you want to go into the heart of Africa, you may be introduced to a guide who is able to take you there. You may know his name and believe that he is able, but you will never get there until you follow him. Jesus says, "Follow me." Following Christ is proof of genuine trust, trust that brings a full surrender whereby we make

Him our Lord - the Lord of our time, our money, our occupation, our entire life.

We cannot trust one we do not love. If we love Him, it will be our joy to keep His commandments; and we love Him because He first loved us, while we were yet sinners, and died for us. There are gods many and lords many, everyone having his own. But what god or lord is there like unto the King of kings and Lord of lords?

What we are is in proportion to the worth of our god or lord. It may be only self. Come into the fullness of life and make Jesus Christ Lord of all. Give your heart fully to Him, and then take for granted, on the basis of His Word alone, your acceptance by Him and full pardon from Him.

It is written, "If thou shalt confess with thy mouth Jesus as Lord, thou shalt be saved" (Romans 10:9, 10 ASV). The Early Church turned the world upside down because the people made Christ Lord. Let those who call themselves His followers do so today. We may have many martyrs, but we shall have a great revival - and that is what we say we want.

Reach hither thy hand with Thomas to touch the scars of our risen, living Savior and cry out with him, "My Lord and my God." (George Wells Armin, Tract, **Can Christ Be Savior Yet Not Lord?**, Bible Research Fellowship, Inc. Chicago, IL 60666)

WHAT IS YOUR WILL?

Your will is your decision-making faculty. Often it is caught between your thoughts and your desires. Your emotions express how you feel: your mind says what you know, but your will tells what you want.

Before you can bring your will into harmony with God's purposes, you need adequate goals for your life.

When you surrender your will to God, you finally discover the resources to do what God requires. As you give yourself to Him, you receive His power. The power of the Word of God is unleashed when you bring yourself under its authority.

WHAT IT MEANS TO ACKNOWLEDGE CHRIST AS LORD

As I have already said, Lordship has to do with your will. It involves surrendering it to Jesus Christ. It means that Jesus is Lord of all of you, not just part of you. Someone has said, "Lord of all, or not Lord at all." When Christ is Lord, we are filled with the Holy Spirit. The Spirit-filled life is simply a life that is empty of self and yielded to the leading and the enabling of God's indwelling Spirit. The more you yield, the more He fills and the greater becomes your capacity for the things of God. You will begin to reach out to other people in active efforts to win them to Christ. People will see Christ in you and will be attracted to Him.

WHY DOES JESUS WANT TO BE OUR LORD?

I sometimes wonder, but He does want to get involved. He does want to be Lord of our lives. When I look at my own sinfulness, my own propensity for evil, I must confess that this is a staggering thought.

As we are on the move in this great adventure called life, we cannot see around the bend into tomorrow or over the hill into next week. Consequently, we are not sure when it is safe to pass. Because Jesus Christ is Lord of all, seeing the end from the beginning, He does know.

His willingness to be our Lord reveals His desire to get involved in our lives so He can tell us when it is safe to move ahead and when it is best not to move. Would we not be extremely foolish to turn down such a gracious offer?

JESUS AS LORD
JESUS IS LORD WHETHER WE WANT HIM TO BE OR NOT

Jesus Christ is the Creator of all things and "by the word of His power" He holds everything together. "For by Him were all things created, that are in heaven, and that are in earth, visible and invisible, whether they be thrones, or dominions, or principalities, or powers; all things were created by Him, and for Him, and He is before all things, and by Him all things consist; and He is the Head of the Body, the church; who is the beginning, the firstborn from the dead; that in all things He might have the preeminence." (Colossians 1:16-18)

Have you ever considered how little of your life you control? Did you decide when you would be born? Or who your parents would be? Or in what country you would be born? Did you decide the color of your skin? Your eyes? Your hair? Did you decide your intelligence or your gifts and talents? How about your height - did you determine that? Or your appearance, whether you would be good looking or rather plain? The answer to all these questions is, "no." In every one of these areas and in many more, you have no say in the matter. Your vote counts for absolutely nothing!

Then at what point do you exercise control? The Bible suggests that you control a small but important part of your life, namely your will. Lordship has to do with your will. It involves surrendering it to Jesus Christ. It means that Jesus is Lord of all of you, not just part of you. In making this decision of the will, remember that He has control over most things that concern you, whether you like it or not.

"It is your will God is interested in. If you say with full conviction, 'I *will* ask Christ to take over my life. I *will* obey what He tells me in the Bible. I *will* start specific actions right now to bring myself into line with what I know He wants. I *will* yield my body to Him.' If you say all that, then no matter how lost you may feel, no matter how defeated you may feel, He'll be working in you, bringing you to full maturity."

REASONS WHY WE DO NOT WANT TO ACKNOWLEDGE CHRIST AS LORD

Though every person has his own reasons not to acknowledge Jesus as Lord, some reasons come up with remarkable frequency.

1. He may ask us to do something that we do not want to do.

Of course, He will. If this were not so, there would be no issue involved. When you make Jesus Christ Lord of your life, you can count on Him asking you to do things you would rather not do.

Abraham did not want to offer up Isaac as a sacrifice. Moses did not want to go before Pharaoh. Joseph did not want to spend all those years in prison. Jesus Christ did not want to go to the Cross.

Nobody likes to deny himself. But this is what Lordship is all about. A disciple is a disciplined one. He is one who says no to what he wants in deference to what his Lord wants. The disciple does not pamper himself by satisfying his wants and desires in a self-gratifying fashion.

When Jesus Christ is Lord of your life, every area is under His jurisdiction - your thoughts, your actions, your plans, your vocation, your leisure time, and your life's goal. All of these are under His Lordship.

2. We think we know what is best for us.

Nothing could be farther from the truth. A child left alone would kill himself. He might eat the wrong things, or run out in the street, or grab hold of a sharp knife, or play with something equally dangerous. The parent must keep constant watch over his child. That is, the parent must be lord of the child's life. In fact, the law requires that this be so; and when the parent refuses to exercise such lordship, the courts hold him accountable.

When we reach physical maturity, however, we think that things suddenly change. This is where we make our mistake. A child left to himself will probably hurt himself. As mature adults, left to ourselves, we do hurt ourselves. Statistics reveal that more people die each year in automobile accidents than by cancer and heart disease combined.

A group of scientists have warned that the United States has enough atomic warheads to destroy every human being on the face of the earth - the equivalent of one railroad boxcar load of dynamite for every man, woman, and child in the world. And this is to say nothing about the atomic warheads that other nations of the world have.

Have you ever thought about the fact that we hire policemen to watch over us to make sure that we don't do anything wrong. Yet, we have the audacity to say that we know what is best for our lives.

3. We are not sure that God has our best interests at heart.

If God wanted to make it hard on us, can you imagine what He could do? If He wanted to make us miserable and plague us with difficulties, He could make life absolutely intolerable. What is your concept of God? God is our wonderful, loving Heavenly Father and He loves us and wants only that which is best for us. (Romans 8:28)

The New You
By; Harold Myra

VII-D: DEATH TO SELF

The Self Life

In some ways I have already dealt with this subject, but I would like to be more specific at this point.

When we receive Christ as our personal Savior, the Holy Spirit comes to put God's seal of ownership on us. He washes us from our sins and gives us new life, but He wants to do more than that. He comes to make his abode within us so He can deal with our old sinful nature. It is God's desire that we be like Jesus. It is that old sinful nature that hinders the image of Christ from shining forth in our lies. The Holy Spirit goes to the root of the problem, the root that produces sin.

The Bible uses several words or terms to describe the self-life. It will help us to understand better if we look at some of these. Galatians 5:17 calls it the sinful nature. Romans 6:19 calls it "natural self." Ephesians 4:22 calls it the "old self."

We can see from these verses that the self-life is our old defective human nature. A crisis must take place in the believer's life. We must answer the question, "What am I going to do with the self-life?"

We can let it limp along causing continual conflict. There will be a constant tug-of-war. We may try to make a truce with it. We may try to train it, or improve it. We may deceive ourselves into believing we can do better. Galatians 3:3 says, "Are you so foolish? Having begun in the Spirit, are ye now made perfect by the flesh?" Colossians 3:5 tells us to "put to death, therefore, whatever belongs to your earthly nature."

If Christ is to be seen in us, we must deal with that old nature. We can't train it to do what we know is right. We may try to deal with it in every way but the right way. The only right way to deal with it is to go to the cross and have it crucified. We are thereafter to reckon ourselves dead to sin but alive to God. Paul said, "I am crucified with Christ, nevertheless I live, yet not I but Christ liveth in me, and the life which I now live I live by the faith of the Son of God who loved me and gave Himself for me." (Galatians 2:20)

To refuse to have the self-life crucified is to lose out on the fullness of life that Jesus died to give us. I must offer my self-life up to death. I must surrender it to the death of the cross. Rev. Douglas Miller, The Alliance Witness, 1982

"There is where I own up to the reality of the conflict. There is where the battle between self and the Holy Spirit, both craving for the use of my life, ends. It ends with the Holy Spirit being given unconditional control of the temple bought with the blood of Jesus. How do I put the crucifixion process into motion? First, 'count yourselves dead to sin but alive to God in Christ Jesus.' (Romans 6:11) 'Count' is a bookkeeper's word. Here it means the ledger shows indisputably that in my position with Christ I died back there on the cross to this evil self-life within me.

"Self's place is on the cross, not on the throne of our lives. It is in this experience of crucifying the real you that you discover how badly you want God and want to be holy like He is. Here, too, you find out how deeply you love self and sin and depend on them.

"When you have offered the self-life to the death of the cross, then in faith you offer the empty clay that remains to the full control of the Holy Spirit." (Rev. Douglas Miller, "The Self-life and How to Deal with It," *The Alliance Witness,* Aug. 1982-Nov. 1982.)

Once we have done this does not mean we will never again have a problem with the old self-life. It does not eradicate the sinful nature. Self remains crucified only as long as we, in the power of the Spirit, keep it on the cross. It is daily counting ourselves to be dead to sin. Sin is not dead, but we are to be dead to it. I must die to sin whenever I see it in my members, so that the fruit of holiness may progressively grow in my life.

As I reckon myself dead to sin, the Holy Spirit begins to weave a new thread of desire into the fabric of my life. As I obey God, power comes from the Holy Spirit to strengthen the action of my will in that obedience. From this point on, in a sense, the struggle is gone because I know what is going on and I know how to handle it. There is a certain rest to it all because I know I cannot do any better, but I know the One who can – the Holy Spirit – and I turn it all over to Him.

Remember: the continuing experience is based on the law of reckoning myself dead to sin but alive to God, and it is realized through the change wrought in my responses to life's situations by the power of the Holy Spirit. As we daily apply this principle to our lives in the power of the Spirit, we will attain the goal of being conformed to the likeness of Jesus Christ.

I would like to share with you now F.B. Meyer's experience of dying with Jesus:

"On the cross Jesus Christ offered a substitutionary sacrifice for the sins of the whole world. God sent His Son in the likeness of sinful flesh and for sin. 'For sin' is substitutionary. 'In the likeness of sinful flesh' is the reference of the cross to sanctification. On the cross God nailed, in the person of Christ, the likeness of our sinful flesh. I cannot explain it to you more than that, but I know this – that next to seeing Jesus as my Sacrifice, nothing has revolutionized my life like seeing the effigy of my sinful SELF in the sinless, dying Savior. I say to myself ... God has nailed the likeness of my SELF-LIFE to the cross ... If, then, God has treated the likeness of my sinful SELF, when borne by the sinless Christ, as worthy of HIS curse, how terrible in God's sight it must be for myself to hug it, and embrace it, and live in it!

"Christ and I are one. In Him I hung there. I came to an end of myself in Christ, and kneeling at His Cross, I took the position of union with Him in His death, and I consigned my SELF-LIFE with its passions, its choices, its yearnings after perfection, its fickleness, its judgment of others, its uncharity – I took it as a felon and said: 'Thou art cursed: thou shalt die. My God nailed thee to that cross. Come, thou shalt come. I put thee there by my choice, by my will, by my faith. Hang there.'

"After that moment, that decisive moment in my life, I have ever reckoned that myself is on the cross, and that the death of Christ lies between me and it.

"O man and woman, forgive me! It is a very broken way of putting the deepest mystery of the Bible, but I can only ask that the Holy Spirit may make you know what it is to have Jesus as the center and origin of your life."

F.B. Meyer
The Christ-Life for the Self-Life
Moody Press
Chicago, IL
Pg. 39-40

THE SELF-LIFE AND HOW TO DEAL WITH IT

To be like Jesus Christ is the prayer of every believer truly born of the Spirit of God. But how can anyone ever come close to realizing this? Jesus Christ was very God joining His Deity to a sinless humanity.

And yet the Bible says, "Those God foreknew he also predestined to be conformed to the likeness of his son ..." (Romans 8:29)

The how of being conformed to Jesus Christ is answered in the next chapter: "Through Christ Jesus the law of the Spirit of life set me free from the law of sin and death" (8:2)

Do you see it? As the Holy Spirit comes to rule in our lives, we actually experience God's purpose of conforming us to the likeness of His son.

Too often people stop short in their understanding of the work of the Holy Spirit in a believer. He comes to do more than put God's seal of ownership on us as we trust in Christ, more than wash us from our sins and renew us.

He comes to take up residence in us so that He Himself may deal with our sinful nature – this nature that hinders the expression of Christ's life in ours.

In the born-again experience God removes our sins from us as far as the east is from the west. In the sanctifying process that our salvation sets in motion, God the Holy Spirit comes to deal with sin's nature in us. He goes to the sin root that produces sins.

It is subsequent to the saving experience that the Holy Spirit begins to show us what we really are. We must first see what we really are before we will give up trying to be Christians and let Jesus Christ live His life through us.

So let us examine the real you – your natural self.

Aliases of the Self-Life

Several terms are used in the Bible to describe the self-life. They help us to see more clearly what it is that we wrestle with.

It is called "sinful nature" in Galatians 5:17; "The sinful nature desires what is contrary to the Spirit, and the Spirit what is contrary to the sinful nature."

It is called "natural self" in Romans 6:19; "You are weak in your natural selves."

It is called the "old self" in Ephesians 4:22; "You were taught, with regard to your former way of life, to put off your old self, which is being corrupted by its deceitful desires."

Thus we can see that the self-life is our defective human nature. Its whole inclination, and purpose is to live in the pursuit of that which is temporal and unregenerate.

If that to which God has predestined us – conformity to the likeness of His Son – is to be realized, we must do something about our natural selves. As I said before, the temptation is to try to train this hostile thing within us. But that we do not want to do.

DEATH TO SELF

When we realize what the self-life in us really is, we do not want to do anything with it but what Scripture teaches us to do. If we do not deal with the self-life by crucifying it, we risk living in a tug-of-war with the flesh that may erupt at any time.

The believer is in a spiritual tug-of-war. Self until now has been the undisputed ruler. According to Ephesians 2:1-3, it is the devil who energized self to live according to the cravings of our sinful natures.

At the moment of the born-again experience, self is confronted by a new Resident with a life-altering claim. The identity of this new Resident is made clear in I Corinthians 6:19: "Do you not know that your body is a temple of the Holy Spirit, who is in you, whom you have received from God? You are not your own."

This new Resident, the Holy Spirit, claims ownership over what the self-life previously claimed without challenge. The Spirit enters the life to create a desire for holy things. But self resists.

GOD'S PURPOSE

God reveals all this to us about ourselves for a purpose. He knows that we need to be shocked out of the subtle complacency that often develops from the security there is in Christ. He knows that we must be so totally disappointed in what we are in our natural selves that we will never again try to make ourselves what we cannot be.

He knows that our pride of life must be so deeply hurt that we will no longer linger in the struggles of the flesh but will instead hurry on to the fullness of Christ's life in us.

In the sanctified or Spirit-filled life, God teaches us to take sides with Him against sin's nature in us.

It is this approach that enables us, by the power of the Spirit over the self-life, to free our personalities from the bends and twists that sin has put on them. It is this approach that makes us transparently honest. We recognize and deal with what we know ourselves to be, so that Christ's likeness can be more perfectly seen in us.

What a difference He makes! I can stop trying to be something I cannot be and let Christ be in me what He already has proven Himself to be.

He lives His life through me. Paul says, "I have been crucified with Christ and I no longer live, but Christ lives in me. The life I live in the body, I live by faith in the Son of God, who loved me and gave himself for me" (Galatians 2:20).

If only you can see it as God says it, you can come out of the frustrations of the self-life into the perfect rest of Christ's fullness in your life.

RESOLUTION: CRUCIFIXION

Can you not see from this summary how a crisis should arise in Christian experience? The issue is apparent: What are we going to do with the self-life?

Shall we let it limp along causing us continual conflict? Shall we try to make a truce with it? Shall we try to train it, improve it?

No! None of these. Paul says in Galatians 3:3: "Are you so foolish? After beginning with the Spirit, are you now trying to attain your goal by human effort?"

There is only one Scriptural way to deal with this hostile, wretched thing deep within every one of us. Self is to be kept in a state of death through crucifixion.

God deals with self when we are saved. Romans 6:1-7 makes this clear. In the crisis experience that follows, we come to deal with self ourselves. That is, by an act of our will, we put our self-life on the cross. Note in Romans 6:11, 13, 19 and Ephesians 4:22 such verbs as "count (yourselves)" "offer (... your body)," "put off (your old self)." This is something the believer does subsequent to his being born again.

But when this is done, Someone must take self's position as ruling authority. That Someone is the Holy Spirit.

THE REAL YOU CRUCIFIED

Often overlooked by Christians are the passages of Scripture that reveal what is involved in becoming personally holy in daily practice. At the heart of effective Christian living there is a crucifixion principle that must be applied in our daily lives.

The Bible says, "I have been crucified with Christ and I no longer live, but Christ lives in me" (Galatians 2:20). And again, "Those who belong to Christ Jesus have crucified the sinful nature with its passions and desires" (5:24). And still again, "Put to death, therefore, whatever belongs to your earthly nature" (Colossians 3:5).

Our acquaintance with and practice of this principle determines the quality of our walk with God.

It was this that Jesus spoke of when He said, "If anyone would come after me, he must deny himself and take up his cross daily and follow me" (Luke 9:23).

It is obvious from this statement that the self-life is a threat to the expression of Christ's lordship in our lives. Self must be dealt with at the cross.

If Jesus is to be supreme in our lives, self cannot be supreme.

THE NEED FOR CRUCIFIXION

We see then that the self-life is our defective human nature. It belongs to that era before we were identified with Christ Jesus. We were slaves to the principle of sin – so much so that sin in us created a deep spiritual crisis soon after we were born again.

The craving of self to use the body for unholy pursuits was in constant conflict with the Holy Spirit's craving to use that same body for godliness. And the Scriptures tell us that as long as that state of war persists, we cannot live as we should.

Jesus said that self must be denied (Luke 9:23). He made the statement in conjunction with another: His disciple daily carries a cross. It was Jesus who first indicated that self would have to be dealt with through a cross.

THE CONTINUING EXPERIENCE

It is quite possible that in the course of our study, you took the three steps outlined: (1) reckoning yourself dead to sin, (2) offering yourself to God and (3) offering the parts of your body to God as instruments of righteousness.

If so, you may have found new and glorious liberty in Christ and a new awareness of the dynamic of the Christian life that is filled with the Holy Spirit. You have an intense desire to keep going on and ever higher with God.

On the other hand, you may have found yourself sliding and tumbling back into the dark valley of your old self. You may feel unsure of what you did – even hypocritical and disappointed. You may wonder if it was one of those emotional experiences not well-founded on Scripture.

A Bible study such as this on death to self and the filling of the Holy Spirit can create a dangerous illusion. We can imagine that once filled with the Holy Spirit, we will have no further struggles in living for the Lord.

Nothing could be further from the truth. Sanctification is also a continuing experience. We must "live by the Spirit" (Galatians 5:16), we must "keep in step with the Spirit" (5:25).

RESHAPED LIVES

To come to an understanding of what is involved in the continuing experience, we need to review briefly what happens when we crucify self and ask the Holy Spirit to fill us.

First, crucifying self allows the Holy Spirit to have control of our lives. He is at liberty to begin the deeper work of reshaping us.

Here is where we become intensely aware of the Person of Jesus. We begin to desire to know Him rather than just to have His blessings and gifts.

We are also aware of liberty that we never experienced before. There is a new restfulness that comes from relying not on ourselves but on Christ Himself.

There is an excitement and anticipation of what life is now to become under the control of the Spirit.

Second, crucifying self does not eradicate the sinful nature. Self remains crucified only as long as we, in the power of the Spirit, keep it on the cross. This is why Jesus spoke of a person's need to "take up his cross daily" (Luke 9:23). Crucifixion of self must be a perpetual thing.

The continuing experience of sanctification is maintaining in daily practice what we did with self when we initially nailed it to the cross.

Only the believer who has been to the cross to crucify self can understand the value of this law to reckoning. It is a daily counting of ourselves to be dead to sin. Sin is not dead, but we are to be dead to it.

Reckoning by faith that I am dead to sin is the action of my Spirit-empowered will to keep self on the cross so that the positive side of Romans 6:11 – "Alive to God in Christ Jesus" – becomes a daily reality.

It is not enough to reckon daily with the crucifixion principle: I must also reckon by faith that the Holy Spirit energizes my union with Christ with power for holiness to all departments of my life.

In the continuing experience of sanctification I must die to sin whenever I see it in my members, so that the fruit of holiness may progressively grow in my life.

Dying to self and being filled with the Holy Spirit may cause a greater awareness of sin in our lives. This is understandable, for the Holy Spirit is holy, and sensitive to sin.

He will invade the gray areas of our lives where sins can sap us of power and holiness. He wants to thoroughly houseclean; He wants to rearrange our furniture. And he will do it in such a way that we will never again want self to be in control of our lies. Where there was once defeat and discouragement, there is now going to be spiritual growth and victory.

To accomplish this, God has to reprogram our responses. Self caused us to respond to things in a corrupting way if the situation was evil, or in a self-glorifying way if the situation was morally good. Either way, we gratified self rather than brought pleasure to God, for whom we were created.

As I reckon myself dead to sin, the Holy Spirit begins to weave a new thread of desire into the fabric of my life. As I obey God, power comes from the Holy Spirit to strengthen the action of my will in that obedience.

Suppose, for example, that hate and bitterness are a natural expression of my self-life. When I offer up self to that the cross, I am bidding good-bye to that old way of life. But the next day I see a person for whom I have never had any real love. As I see this person, I feel that old hatred.

Am I going to respond to the feeling, or will I obey the Holy Spirit and walk in His power to overcome?

Here is where I yield my body to the Spirit and not to self. At that very instant, I pray something like this: "Lord, there is that person I can't tolerate. But in Your name I deny the feeling of hatred springing from my old self. I yield to the power of Your spirit to keep self on the cross. Now I obey You, Lord, by doing a deed of kindness and love for this one I formerly hated."

This is how the continuing experience of the walk in the Spirit conditions our responses so that we deny self and express the life of Jesus. This is how the fruit of the Spirit is going to begin to grow in my life.

From this point on, in a sense, the struggle is gone because I know what is going on and I know how to handle it. There is a certain rest to it all because I know I cannot do any better, but I know the One who can – the Holy Spirit – and I turn it all over to Him.

Remember, the continuing experience is based on the law of reckoning myself dead to sin but alive to God, and it is realized through the change wrought in my responses to life's situations by the power of the Holy Spirit.

Walk daily in this reckoning and by the power of the Spirit over self. Then you will attain the goal of being conformed to the likeness of Jesus Christ!

Death to self – initially and then daily from that point on – is a mark of the disciple of Jesus Christ. To spare our self-life from crucifixion is to lose the fullness of life that Jesus died to give us.

CRUCIFIXION: HOW IT HAPPENS

OUR POSITION

The mechanics of the crucifixion principle – the way it operates – begins with an understanding of our position in Christ. By position I mean the state in which God has placed us by His sovereign action in our lives when we believed on the Lord Jesus Christ and were saved.

Our position with regard to the crucifixion of the self-life is described in these texts:

"I have been crucified with Christ" (Galatians 2:20)

"If we have been united with him in his death, we will certainly also be united with him in his resurrection. For we know that our old self was crucified with him so that the body of sin might be rendered powerless, that we should no longer be slaves to sin – because anyone who has died has been freed from sin" (Romans 6:5-6)

"You died and your life is now hidden with Christ in God" (Colossians 3:3).

The truth of those verses is this: when by faith I trusted Christ to save me, God saw me as having entered with Christ into the death of the cross. When in faith I trusted Christ to save me, God brought my spirit to life, releasing it from the power of the sinful self-life.

In that moment of being born again, God dealt with my self-life through the crucifixion principle so that from that moment on I am with Christ in my spirit in the heavenly realms.

This is the position given me over sin and its power.

Do you see it? In my spirit I am in and with Christ seated over everything that is contrary to God and His purposes.

The Bible says, "God raised us up with Christ and seated us with him in the heavenly realms" (Ephesians 2:6). That is where I am in my spirit. That is my position granted by a sovereign act of God the Father.

What my spirit experiences in its position, God wants to become the practice of my body and soul in everyday life. In actual experience, then, I must go back to the cross and there deal with my self-life in the way that God dealt with it.

I must offer my self-life up to death. I must surrender it to the death of the cross.

That is the burden of Paul in Romans 12:1-2. "I urge you, brothers, in view of God's mercy, to offer your bodies as living sacrifices, holy and pleasing to God – which is your spiritual worship. Do not conform any longer to the pattern of this world, but be transformed by the renewing of your mind. Then you will be able to test and approve what God's will is – his good, pleasing and perfect will."

There is where I own up to the reality of the conflict. There is where the battle between self and the Holy Spirit, both craving for the use of my life, ends. It ends with the Holy Spirit being given unconditional control of the temple bought with the blood of Jesus.

This glorious, liberating truth can be implemented because of the power of our position.

This crucifixion process deals initially with self. Crucifixion is the solution to coping effectively with whatever belongs to the self-life. But how? How do I put the crucifixion process into motion?

FIRST: "count yourselves dead to sin but alive to God in Christ Jesus (Romans 6:11). "Count" is a bookkeeper's word. Here it means the ledger shows indisputably that in my position with Christ I died back there on the cross to this evil self-life within me.

Now faith in Christ and in my standing He has granted me gives me the power to offer up my self-life to the death of the cross.

It is this offering of self to the death of the cross that is referred to in the admonition "Offer yourselves to God" (Romans 6:13). And that is the SECOND step: Offer yourself to God.

Jesus offered Himself to the death of the cross through the eternal Spirit (see Hebrews 9:14). The Holy Spirit within us enables us to come to the cross and offer ourselves. "If by the Spirit you put to death the misdeeds of the body you will live" (Romans 8:13).

Ours is an offering not to save souls from eternal death but to save ourselves from the self-life.

Self's place is on the cross, not on the throne of our lives. It is in this experience of crucifying the real you that you discover how badly you want God and want to be holy like He is. Here, too, you find out how deeply you love self and sin and depend on them.

When you have offered the self-life to the death of the cross, then in faith you offer the empty clay that remains to the full control of the Holy Spirit. This THIRD step is expressed in Romans 6:13: "Offer the parts of your body to him as instruments of righteousness."

At that point Ephesians 5:18 becomes reality and a constant experience: "Ever be filled with the Spirit" (Williams).

Now all that remains is for me to invite you to crucify the real you, if you have never done so. Be assured this is not the end of all good living. Rather, it is the step that ends the tyranny of self and begins your unhindered maturing in the life of the Holy Spirit. You were saved for this!

Will you voluntarily come to the cross and nail self there? This is not a compulsory, enforced surrender. It is a voluntary surrender prompted by love.

But while it is a voluntary act, is it to be complete and final. You do not come back from the cross. Jesus, in His Lordship, takes over your life from that point on, and "the life (you) live in the body, (you) live by faith in the Son of God, who loved (you) and gave himself for (you)." (Galatians 2:20).

Die now so that you may live!

By Rev. Doug Miller
The Alliance Witness – Aug. 1982 - Nov. 1982

GREATEST NEED IN CHURCH
Spiritual Helps For The New Member
By: Homer G, Lindsay, Jr.

The greatest need of the Church is to love Jesus more.

My decision to love Jesus more did not create any more love in my heart for Jesus. I desired to love Jesus more but I did not love Him more. I sought to love Him and in seeking to love Him more I decided to be more faithful in serving Him. But this did not create love for Christ and I found that my own will power was of no value and I found that it was impossible to discipline one's self into loving Christ more. And that this shallow love that I had for Christ did not mature. There seemed to be a coldness in my heart and my heart did not respond. And this led me to great perplexity. I was led by the Holy Spirit to John's writing in I John, seeking to discover what was this cold resistance I had toward loving Christ. I was shocked. I became disgusted with myself. I was amazed because I knew that all of Christianity and everything that I believe and everything that I sought to live for in all the years in school and all the years of pastoring and teaching and preaching all centered around the person of Jesus Christ and what Christ had done for me. I knew that the Bible taught that God so loved the world that He gave His only begotten Son and that God proved His love toward us in dying for us while we were yet sinners; why couldn't I love Him like I desired to? Then I read from this little epistle of John. John who loved Jesus more than anyone. John said, "that which we have seen and heard declare we unto you that ye also may have fellowship with us and truly our fellowship is with the Father and His Son Jesus Christ. These things write we unto you that your joy may be full." And I said, "Dear Lord, how may my joy be full when I want to love you and I can't?" This was the most pathetic thing that had ever happened to me, wanting to love Jesus and not being able to. "This, then, is the message which we have heard of Him and declare unto you, that God is light and in Him is no darkness at all. If we say we have fellowship with Him and walk in darkness, we lie and do not the truth, but if we walk in the light as He is in the light, we have fellowship one with another and the blood of Jesus Christ His Son cleanseth us from all sin. If we say that we have no sin, we deceive ourselves and the truth is not in us." So I was led to realize that my problem was sin. Then the Holy Spirit led me to Matthew, and in Matthew, studying the words of Jesus and the teachings of Jesus, I discovered that this particular sin was self sin. That self was ruling my life; that self was reigning; that self was on the throne; that everything that I did sought to bring glory to my self. Self wanted the credit for everything that I did for God and everything I did for Jesus. If I tithed, self wanted the credit; if I witnessed, self wanted the credit. If I was faithful, self wanted the credit. So I worked seventy or eighty hours a week; self wanted the credit for it. He didn't want anything to go to Jesus and he wasn't willing to move over and make room for Jesus. I read where Jesus said that self must be crucified and so I decided to crucify my self. To my utter amazement, I found I couldn't crucify self; that self was more powerful than I was, that he was ruling me, I wasn't ruling him. That he was running the show and even though I had a desire somewhere that Jesus should be first in my life and be most important, He wasn't; self was. And I had to come back to John again. John said, "If we confess our sins," and I said, "Oh Jesus, my sin is self, self-rule, self-reign, self-desire, self-centeredness, self-pride, self-ishness, self-joy, self-pleasure, self..." all these sins of self that were destroying my testimony and my witness and was destroying me, destroying my ability to love my Lord. "If we confess our sins, He is faithful and just to forgive us our sins and to cleanse us from all unrighteousness." So I began to confess. I began to confess and to ask Him to remove these sins. Oh, what a major operation it was. What a major thing it was to get these self-sins out of my life. They were so big; they were so important, I had no idea they were so powerful. One by one self-sins began to crumble beneath the hammer - like blows of the power of Jesus Christ my Lord. One by one He began to remove them and to cleanse me and as self was removed there was made room for Christ. Oh, what a thrilling, day. Oh, how wonderful to be able to love Jesus and I found each day as Jesus removed a little bit more of self there was a little bit more room for Him. And each day it has become my prayer: "Jesus, a little bit less of self and a little bit more of you." I join my heart with

John the Baptist that I must decrease and He must increase. This was the most thrilling discovery of my life.

In the second chapter of I John we read, "And hereby we do know that we know Him if we keep His commandments. He that sayeth I know Him and keepeth not His commandments is a liar and the truth is not in him. But whoso keepeth his word, in Him verily is the love of God perfected." The love perfected... "Hereby know we that we are in Him. He that sayeth he abideth in Him ought to himself also so to walk, even as He walked." This is the perfection, the perfecting of the love of Christ, to be able to walk as Jesus walked. Oh, this is the greatest need that we have, the greatest need of the church, for when the love of Christ is perfected then we walk as Jesus walked.

VII-E: THE FILLING OF THE SPIRIT

THE SPIRIT FILLED LIFE
Learning To Live
By: Keith M. Bailey

The Holy Spirit comes to each believer to make him alive in Christ. The Spirit gives life and He sustains spiritual life daily. A Christian is to have the Holy Spirit not only as Lifegiver, but he is to be filled with the Spirit.

The new believer may question, "How can I be filled with the Spirit?" To be filled with the Spirit is every believer's privilege. The Scriptures give the following conditions for being filled with the Holy Spirit. The first condition is consecrating oneself to God: *"I beseech you therefore, brethren, by the mercies of God, that ye present your bodies a living sacrifice, holy, acceptable to God, which is your reasonable service."* (Romans 12:1). The second condition is being willing to forsake all known sin and have a desire to be pure in heart. (Acts 5:32). The third condition is having an attitude of ready obedience to the known will of God. (Acts 5:32). The Scripture says, *"Blessed are they who hunger and thirst after righteousness..."* (Matthew 5:6) Jesus is teaching in this passage the value of spiritual desire. It is a necessary attitude for being filled with the Spirit.

When the believer understands, according to the Scriptures, the provision of the filling of the Spirit and has prepared his heart by meeting the above mentioned conditions, he is ready to pray. Jesus said, *"If you then, being evil, know how to give good gifts to your children: how much more shall your heavenly Father give the Holy Spirit to them that ask him?"* (Luke 11:13). The believer comes to the Father in faith and simply asks that he be filled with the Spirit.

Jesus pictures the Spirit-filled life as a river of living water overflowing with blessing: *"In the last day, that great day of the feast, Jesus stood and cried, saying, 'If any man thirst, let him come unto me, as the scripture hath said, out of his belly shall flow rivers of living water.'"* (John 7:37) The fullness of the Spirit brings abundance, completeness, power and victory.

The Holy Spirit not only fills the heart, but He sanctifies the whole spirit, soul and body of the believer. The word "sanctify" means to separate from sin and dedicate to God for His holy purpose. **God's purpose, according to the Scriptures, is to make the believer Christ-like.** After the Christian is filled with the Spirit and wholly sanctified, the growth process is accelerated. Being filled with the Spirit is not an end in itself, but the introduction of an ongoing growth and development of holy living. Maturity comes by a process of growth in the grace and the knowledge of the Lord Jesus Christ. It is futile to seek such growth apart from total consecration and the filling of the Holy Spirit.

The believer is not able to overcome weakness and sin in his own strength. The life of victory is assured by Christ living in the believer; Victorious living is made possible through the Holy Spirit. Christ is personal representative to each individual Christian. It is by the Holy Spirit that Christ lives in you.

I believe that as soon as possible after a person has been born again, he should be introduced to the Spirit-filled life. I believe it is God's desire for each one of us, but many do not understand or feel the need for this until they have failed God a number of times and realize they are unable to live above sin in their own strength.

The Holy Spirit comes to us to make us alive in Christ. He also sustains our daily spiritual life.

The Christian will no doubt ask, "How can I be filled with the Holy Spirit?" God's word sets forth the following conditions for being filled with the Holy Spirit. I would like to say first that a person is not ready to be filled with the Spirit until he has been to the cross and had self crucified. We must be emptied before we can be filled. In Ephesians 5:18, we are commanded to be filled with the Spirit. It is not a one-time experience, but we are told to continue being filled.

Once we have been emptied of self, we must give ourselves totally to God. (Romans 12:1) The second condition is that we must be willing to forsake all known sin. There is no sense asking to be filled with the Spirit if we allow known sin to remain in our lives. "Whoever would be filled and indwelt by the Spirit should first judge his life for any hidden iniquities: he should courageously expel from his heart everything which is out of accord with the character of God as revealed by the Holy Scriptures. The true Christian ideal is not to be happy, but to be holy. The holy heart alone can be the habitation of the Holy Ghost." (A. W. Tozer, *The Divine Conquest,* Christian Publications, Inc. Harrisburg, PA, p. 99-100)

The third condition is that we must be willing to obey the known will of God. Acts 5:32: *"And we are his witnesses of these things; and so is also the Holy Ghost, whom God hath given to them that obey him."* We must remember that Christ is now our Lord and we should obey Him without question.

The fourth condition is that the Spirit-filled life is a life that is emptied of self and yielded to the leading and the enabling of God's indwelling Spirit. The more we yield, the more He fills and the greater becomes our capacity for the things of God.

"The Holy Spirit not only fills the heart, but He sanctifies the whole spirit, soul and body of the believer. The word *sanctify* means to separate from sin and dedicate to God for His holy purpose. *God's purpose according to the Scriptures, is to make the believer Christlike*. After the Christian is filled with the Spirit and wholly sanctified, the growth process is accelerated. Being filled with the Spirit is not an end in itself, but the introduction of an ongoing growth and development of holy living. Maturity comes by a process of growth in the grace and the knowledge of the Lord Jesus Christ. It is futile to seek such growth apart from total consecration and the filling of the Holy Spirit.

"The believer is not able to overcome weakness and sin in his own strength. The life of victory is assured by Christ living in the believer. Victorious living is mainly possible through the Holy Spirit. Christ is personal representative to each individual Christian. It is by the Holy Spirit that Christ lives in you." (Herb Wander Lugt, ***Filled With the Holy Spirit***, Radio Bible Pub., Grand Rapids, Ml, 1986.)

Once these conditions have been met, the seeker comes to the Father in prayer and in faith asks to be filled with the Holy Spirit.

For many there has been confusion and frustration when it comes to the evidences of the fullness of the Spirit in their lives. How can one know that self has truly been crucified and that the Holy Spirit has unconditional control of one's life? What are the evidences of the Spirit-filled life?

We should not look for physical manifestation or for verbal expression as evidence of the Spirit's fullness. The true test is the fruit of the Spirit. There are listed in Galatians 5:22-23.

1. Love - an attitude that moves us to put God and others ahead of ourselves; a spirit that impels us to give, to serve, and to forgive.
2. Joy - a spirit of gladness rooted in our faith, expressed through song, and accompanied by an optimistic spirit.
3. Peace - inner serenity derived from God and based on the reality of our peace with God through Christ's sacrifice.
4. Longsuffering - patience in the midst of difficult circumstances, and in our relationships with difficult people.
5. Kindnesses - practicing the golden rule of treating others as we expect them to treat us.
6. Goodness - Open, honest, pure, and generous behavior.
7. Faithfulness - we can be trusted and depended on in all our relationships.

8. Gentleness - a tenderness of spirit that enables us to discipline others properly, to endure persecution graciously, and to witness to others sensitively.
9. Self-control - the quality that gives us control over our desires, especially those that relate to the body.

When a person's life is marked by these nine moral qualities the demands of the law are being fulfilled. When they are present, they provide evidence that you are filled with the Holy Spirit. (Herb Wander Lugt, *Filled With the Holy Spirit*, Radio Bible Pub., Grand Rapids, Ml, 1986.)

The fruit of the Spirit is the life of Christ growing in us. Fruit doesn't appear all of a sudden. It takes time for it to grow. The New Testament indicates that the evidence of death to self and the fullness of the Holy Spirit is consistent obedience. It is also evidenced by a desire to share Christ with those who do not know Him.

I'll Take The High Road. Milestones In Christian Living
By: Christian Direction Inc., Canada

1. THE PRACTICE OF THE SPIRIT-FILLED LIFE.

Be sure to read carefully Ephesians 5:18-19. Paul tells us that we are not to be drunk with wine, but we are to be filled with the Spirit. The verb he uses is in the present continuous tense and could be translated "Be ye being filled." In other words, the filling of the Spirit is not a once-for-all experience but is something which needs to be continually repeated. Nor is it a sovereign, unconditional gift of God but, on the contrary, is the one ministry of the Spirit which depends, to a large extent, upon the cooperation of the Christian.

The illustration of being drunk is startling and significant. When a person becomes drunk, he deliberately hands himself over to a filling with an alcoholic spirit. Under the influence of that spirit he is **diabolically transformed.** Often his character radically changes so that his tongue is loosed or his temper is aroused or his tears flow, as the case may be. That he is drunk is evident in his walk and in his talk. But the next morning he is likely to be sober and will require a fresh intoxication if he is to show the effects of drunkenness again.

A person who is filled with the Spirit of God is **divinely transformed.** His nature and his personality reflect the character of the Lord Jesus Christ. It is evident in his walk and in his talk. The Christian life is not a matter of our trying to imitate Christ; it is a matter of the Holy Spirit filling the life and making us like Christ. The filling is conditional however for the Holy Spirit can be grieved by our sin and disobedience (Ephesians 4:30). When this happens we need to confess our failure to the Lord, ask for cleansing and request a fresh filling of the Spirit. The Holy Spirit is grieved by anything in the Christian's life which is contrary to the known mind and will of God.

2. THE PROCESS OF THE SPIRIT-FILLED LIFE.

How does a person become filled with the Spirit? First, examine Colossians 3:16 and Ephesians 5:18-19. Look these verses up in your Bible right now. Observe that the results of a life filled with the word of God can be equated in some measure with the results of a life filled with the Spirit.

A. You begin by determining before God that Jesus is to be Lord, i.e., to obey in your life in all things (Acts 2:36; 9:5; 16:6-10; James 4:15). Therefore in prayer, tell God the Holy Spirit that you acknowledge His right to control your life (Romans 12:1-2). All impressions we receive and all impulses we express are through the channel of the body and the senses. The yielding of the body to the Holy Spirit is therefore a key requirement.

B. Having determined that Jesus is to be Lord in your life, you begin to read the Word of God in a new way in your daily quiet time, expecting God to speak to you as you read. As you thus read God's Word, the Spirit of God speaks to you and shows you things in your life that need to be given up or things which need to be said or done. Because Jesus has become your Lord you yield to the authority of the Word of God, determined that you are going to obey. Many people have trouble at this point, because they are afraid to trust

God fully. Perhaps they feel that God is not fully dependable, or fear that His commands might be capricious, arbitrary or too difficult to obey. God assures us that His will is good and perfect and acceptable (Romans 12:2), and that He Himself is utterly dependable.

C. (Romans 4:20-23). Moreover, He will never ask us to do things for which He does not give the needed grace and power (II Corinthians 2:8-10). Settle these facts firmly in your mind. Then, as you give in to God, the Spirit of God will fill you and enable you to do what God says. This process is repeated continually, day after day as long as the Lord leaves you here on earth.

The Spirit-filled life is simply a life that is empty of self and yielded to the leading and the enabling of God's indwelling Spirit. The more you yield, the more He fills and the greater becomes your capacity for the things of God. This process is not a drudgery; it is a delight. As the Spirit of God makes the Word of God a living part of your life, you will be filled with song. You will praise God again and again for who He is and for His wisdom, love and power. Moreover, you will begin to reach out to other people in active efforts to win them to Christ. People will see Christ in you and will be attracted to Him.

3. THE PRECAUTION OF THE SPIRIT-FILLED LIFE

Supposing you fail. Does this mean that the whole process needs to be begun all over again? Perhaps an illustration will help. A friend who is an avid collector of antique books visits your home and notices on your shelf an old book that has been there for years gathering dust. He expresses an interest in the book so you give it to him, handling it carefully because many of the pages are loose. He accepts your gift and promises to take good care of it. A few days later, you are cleaning up the bookshelf and you notice some pages that evidently had fallen out of the antique book. Now what do you do? Do you start all over again and re-present the book to your friend? Of course not! You simply give him the missing pages and explain that you have come across them since you gave him the book at his last visit. The loose pages were really all part of the original gift.

It is the same with the filling of the Spirit of God, As you see fresh areas of your life, which are un-surrendered, you simply hand those over to the Holy Spirit too. They were all part of the original yielding.

4- THE PROOFS OF THE SPIRIT-FILLED LIFE

The results of the fullness of the Spirit will be quite evident in a radiant and joyful life (Ephesians 5:19) and in an effective testimony for the Lord Jesus. (Acts 8:17-22; 6:3, 5, 8-10; 13:52-14:1) It is the filling of the Spirit which makes the Christian life worthwhile and which, indeed, makes it possible at all.

WHY SHOULD I BE FILLED WITH THE HOLY SPIRIT?
By: Joe C. Humrichous

A discussion of the Holy Spirit often leaves us dry because we fail to relate the filling of the Holy Spirit to practical areas in our lives. However, even a quick glance at Ephesians 5:17-6:17,18) shows that control of the Holy Spirit directly affects every major area of life. Let's see seven reasons why believers should be filled with (appropriately translated "controlled by") the Holy Spirit.

1. Because it is a command and affects my relationship to God (5:17,18). Spirit control is not an option. It is a command. It is not just for church leaders or the spiritually elite but for all believers every day (continuous action). The only part of our lives God has promised to bless is that which is lived in the will of God, by the power of God, and for the glory of God. Living under the control of the Spirit is to live under the authority of God.
2. Because it affects my personal walk and inner joy (5:19-21). Every believer is controlled by something. If he is not controlled by the Holy Spirit, he will be controlled by such things as worldly philosophies, emotions, or a selfish nature.

Only a life controlled by God's Spirit will produce joy, thankfulness, and submission in the inner man. In essence, we lose our song if we are not Spirit controlled.
3. Because it affects my relationship with the body of Christ (5:21). How easily we are offended or how quickly we rise up in a domineering spirit when our lives are not under the Spirit's control. We lose our sense of teamwork and the body of Christ becomes a collection of "lone rangers" or celebrities rather than a body of members serving one another in love.
4. Because it affects my relationship with my mate (5:22-23). As a result of "the fall" of our first parents, we now have corrupted leadership and corrupted fellowship. The only solution to the paralyzing effects of this disaster is for each partner to willingly submit himself to the Spirit's control in his respective role. Marriage seminars can help, but the "good advice" of information will fall short without the "good news" of divine intervention through the work of God's Spirit.
5. Because it affects my relationship with my children (6:1-4). In his book **Generation at Risk,** Fran Sciacca says, "Today's youth are at risk simply because they have no satisfactory reason to live. This is just as true of Christian young people as of those outside the influence of Christianity." Servant parents on duty for the King are God's solution for this dilemma. The hearts of the parents must be controlled by God's Spirit and turned toward their children in order for a God-centered life to be in their vision (Malachi 4:5,6).
6. Because it affects my witness in the marketplace (6:5-9). If there is not control of the Spirit, people will not see the fruit of the Spirit. Lack of Spirit control dilutes our testimony in the workplace, No one is sure if the believer is a transformer or a conformer. The salt has lost its savor and the light is under a bushel.
7. Because of the aggressive nature of Satan (6:10-18). Our final reason for spirit control is found in our need to be able to stand against the wiles (strategies/methods) of the devil.

He is both organized and energized and without the Holy Spirit's direction and protection, our fleshly weapons will fail.

We are to be reminded that the question is not IF Satan is working but WHERE is he working, for he is at work and only the Spirit-filled believer will stand.

Friend, may I suggest you review the list and be convinced that the Spirit's control is an absolute for the victorious, God-honored believer. If we are honest, we must admit we cannot afford to live one hour without being Spirit filled. Welcome His presence, enthrone Him by choice, and walk in obedience to His instructions through God's Word,

THE SPIRIT-FILLED LIFE
The Divine Conquest
By: A.W. Tozer
Christian Publications, Inc.
Harrisburg, PA

"... the man who would know God must give time to Him. He must count no time wasted which is spent in the cultivation of His acquaintance. He must give himself to meditation and prayer hours on end." (p. 22)

"Whoever would be filled and indwelt by the Spirit should first judge his life for any hidden iniquities; he should courageously expel from his heart everything which is out of accord with the character of God as revealed by the Holy Scriptures." (p. 99)

"The true Christian ideal is not to be happy but to be holy. The holy heart alone can be the habitation of the Holy Ghost." (p. 100)

Before a man can be filled with the Spirit he must be sure he wants to be. And let this be taken seriously. Many Christians want to be filled, but their desire is a vague romantic kind of thing hardly worthy to be called desire. They have almost no knowledge of what it will cost them to realize it.

Let us imagine that we are talking to an inquirer, some eager young Christian, let us say, who has sought us out to learn about the Spirit-filled life. As gently as possible considering the pointed nature of the questions, we would probe his soul somewhat as follows: "Are you sure you want to be filled with a Spirit who, though He is like Jesus in His gentleness and love, will nevertheless demand to be Lord of your life? Are you willing to let your personality be taken over by another, even if that other be the Spirit of God Himself? If the Spirit takes charge of your life He will not tolerate in you the self-sins even though they are permitted and excused by most Christians. By the self-sins I mean self-love, self-pity, self-seeking, self-confidence, self-righteousness, self-aggrandizement, self-defense. You will find the Spirit to be in sharp opposition to the easy ways of the world and of the mixed multitude within the precincts of religion. He will be jealous over you for good. He will not allow you to boast or swagger or show off. He will take the direction of your life away from you. He will reserve the right to test you, to discipline you, to chasten you for your soul's sake. He may strip you of many of those borderline pleasures which other Christians enjoy but which are to you a source of refined evil. Through it all He will enfold you in a love so vast, so mighty, so all-embracing, so wondrous that your very losses will seem like gains and your small pains like pleasures. Yet the flesh will whimper under His Yoke and cry out against it as a burden too great to bear. And you will be permitted to enjoy the solemn privilege of suffering to 'fill up that which is behind of the afflictions of Christ' in your flesh for His body's sake, which is the Church. Now, with the conditions before you, do you still want to be filled with the Holy Spirit?"

Before we can be filled with the Spirit, the desire to be filled must be all-consuming. It must be for the time the biggest thing in the life, so acute, so intrusive as to crowd out everything else. The degree of fullness in any life accords perfectly with the intensity of true desire. We have as much of God as we actually want.

The Christian who is seeking better things and who has to his consternation found himself in a state of complete self-despair need not be discouraged. Despair with self, where it is accompanied by faith, is a good friend, for it destroys one of the heart's most potent enemies and prepares the soul for the ministration of the Comforter. A sense of utter emptiness, of disappointment and darkness can (if we are alert and wise to what is going on) be the shadow in the valley of shadows that leads on to those fruitful fields that lie further in. If we misunderstand it and resist this visitation of God, we may miss entirely every benefit a kind heavenly Father has in mind for us. If we cooperate with God, He will take away the natural comforts which have served us as mother and nurse for so long and put us where we can receive no help except from the Comforter Himself. He will tear away that false thing the Chinese call "face" and show us how painfully small we really are. When He is finished with us, we will know what our Lord meant when He said, "Blessed are the poor in spirit."

Be sure, however, that in these painful chastenings we shall not be deserted by our God. He will never leave us nor forsake us, nor will he be wroth with us nor rebuke us. He will not break His covenant nor alter that which has gone out of His mouth. He will keep us as the apple of His eye and watch over us as a mother watches over her child. His love will not fail even while He is taking us through this experience of self-crucifixion so real, so terrible, that we can express it only by crying, "My God, my God, why hast Thou forsaken me?"

Now let us keep our theology straight about all this. There is not in this painful stripping one remote thought of human merit. The "dark night of the soul" knows not one dim ray of the treacherous light of self-righteousness. We do not by suffering earn the anointing for which we yearn, nor does this devastation of soul make us dear to God nor give us additional favor in His eyes. The value of the stripping experience lies in its power to detach us from life's passing interests and to throw us back upon eternity. It serves to empty our earthly vessels and prepare us for the in-pouring of the Holy Spirit.

The filling with the Spirit, then, requires that we give up our all, that we undergo an inward death, that we rid our hearts of that centuries-old accumulation of Adamic trash and open all rooms to the heavenly Guest.

The Holy Spirit is a living Person and should be treated as a person. We must never think of Him as a blind energy nor as an impersonal force. He hears and sees and feels as any person does. He speaks and hears us speak. We can please Him or grieve Him or silence Him as we can any other person. He will respond to our timid effort to know Him and will ever meet us over half the way.

However wonderful the crisis-experience of being filled with the Spirit, we should remember that it is only a means toward something greater: that greater thing is the life-long walk in the Spirit, indwelt, directed, taught and empowered by His mighty Person. And to continue thus to walk in the Spirit requires that we meet certain conditions. These are laid down for us in the sacred Scriptures and are there for all to see.

The Spirit-filled walk demands, for instance, that we live in the Word of God as a fish lives in the sea. By this I do not mean that we study the Bible merely, nor that we take a "course" in Bible doctrine. I mean that we should "meditate day and night" in the sacred Word, that we should love and feast upon it and digest it every hour of the day and night. When the business of life compels our attention we may yet, by a kind of blessed mental reflex, keep the Word of Truth ever before our minds.

> "Then if we would please the in-dwelling Spirit, we must be all taken up with Christ. The Spirit's present work is to honor Him, and everything He does has this for its ultimate purpose. And we must make our thoughts a clean sanctuary for His holy habitation. He dwells in our thoughts, and soiled thoughts are as repugnant to Him as soiled linen to a king. Above all, we must have a cheerful faith that will keep on believing however radical the fluctuation in our emotional states may be." (p. 122-127)

The Essentials of the Spirit-Filled Life Are:
1. Be Christ-Centered - The first essential for being Spirit-filled is to center our lives on Jesus Christ. He must be the

focal point of our thoughts and aspirations. In all we do, we must be conscious of following His example and doing His will. When we are Christ-centered, we are pleasing the Holy Spirit because that's what He wants us to do. In fact, Jesus said, "He (the Holy Spirit) will glorify Me, for He will take of what is Mine and declare it to you." (John 16:14) In a good marriage, the wife or husband enjoys seeing the other receive honor. Similarly, the Holy Spirit derives great pleasure from seeing us cooperate with Him in glorifying Christ. He Himself wants to remain hidden, so that nothing diverts our gaze from the Lord Jesus.

When we focus our attention on Christ, the Holy Spirit is in close partnership with us. The Spirit is blessed when we are glorifying the Lord. We can do this by:

a. Observing the Lord's Supper to remember Christ in His suffering and death for our sins. (I Corinthians 11:23-26)
b. Making Jesus our example. (John 13:15, Philippians 2:5-11, I Peter 2:21-24)
c. Longing to know Christ better, so that we may be more like Him. (Philippians 3:10-14)
d. Not being afraid of dying because we're looking forward to being with Christ. (II Corinthians 5:8, Philippians 1:21-23, II Timothy 4:6-8)
e. Living in anticipation of the day we will appear at the "judgment seat of Christ." (II Corinthians 5:10)
f. Being comforted by the fact that Christ is our intercessor in heaven.
(Hebrews 4:14-18)
g. Purifying ourselves from sin as we're living in the light of Christ's return.
(I John 3:2,3)
h. Looking forward to Christ's rule over the earth. (Isaiah 2:1-4, Jeremiah 23:5,6, Revelation 20:1-4)

i. Rejoicing in the assurance that every mortal being in God's universe will bow before Jesus Christ and confess Him as Lord. (Philippians 2:9-11)

The Holy Spirit keeps Himself out of the limelight so that Christ may be honored. He is pleased when we praise and adore the Lord Jesus. He views us as partners with Him in glorifying Christ. Being Christ-centered, therefore, is an essential in being filled with the Spirit.

2. Be in the Word - The Christian who wants to be Spirit-filled should be spending time in God's Word. His mind must be so filled with its truths that Bible passages automatically come to his mind when he encounters the situations of life. Just before Paul gave the command, "And do not be drunk with wine, in which is dissipation; but be filled with the Spirit" he wrote, "Therefore do not be unwise, but understand what the will of the Lord is." (Ephesians 5:17) How do we know God's will? Primarily through the Scriptures, which came into existence when "holy men of God spoke as they were moved by the Holy Spirit." (II Peter 1:21)

The importance of the Bible in the Spirit-filled life was demonstrated by the Lord Jesus in His encounter with Satan at the beginning of His public ministry. Luke told us that Jesus was "filled with the Holy Spirit" when He entered into the wilderness for testing. (Luke 4:1,2) In response to each of Satan's temptations, our Lord answered by quoting the Scriptures - specifically Deuteronomy 8:3, 6:13, and 6:16. Since Jesus took on our genuine humanity, He "increased in wisdom and stature" (Luke 2:52) like other boys. So we can be sure that He had to study to know the Scriptures. Christ's familiarity with the Bible, therefore, was an important element in His being "filled with the Holy Spirit."

As noted earlier, Paul pointed out the close relationship between "knowing what the will of the Lord is" and being "filled with the Holy Spirit" when he wrote Ephesians 5:17, 18. He made the same connection in Colossians 3:16, which says, "Let the word of Christ dwell in you richly in all wisdom, teaching and admonishing one another in psalms and hymns and spiritual songs, singing with grace in your hearts to the Lord."

The last part of this verse is almost identical to Ephesians 5:19,20 where Paul described the characteristics of a Spirit-filled Christian. In other words, letting the Word of Christ dwell in us richly is an essential in letting the Holy Spirit keep filling us.

If you want to be a Sprit-filled Christian, then, you must be in the Word of God. Give the Bible ample room in your life by reading it, studying it, and reflecting on it. The Scriptures were inspired by the Holy Spirit and are "profitable for doctrine, for reproof, for correction, for instruction in righteousness, that the man of God may be complete, thoroughly equipped for every good work." (II Timothy 3:16,17)

Read the Bible! Study it! Be instructed by it! Obey its commands! Let it correct you! The Word of God has been given to make you a complete, well-equipped Christian. You cannot be Spirit-filled without it.

3. Be Submissive - The third essential for a Spirit-filled life is to be submissive to God and His Word. Paul indicated this attitude of submission by the language he used when he wrote Ephesians 5:16. Translated literally, the latter part of this verse reads, "Keep letting the Holy Spirit fill you." We must continuously allow the Holy Spirit to fill us. We can do this only when we possess a submissive attitude toward Him.

The analogy Paul used of being drunk with wine carries the idea of submission. Paul wrote, "And do not get drunk with wine...but keep letting the Holy Spirit fill you" (literal translation). A person who is drunk is under the influence of alcohol. If he is very drunk, he is under its control. A person who keeps letting the Holy Spirit fill him consciously, continuously, and voluntarily places himself under God's influence or control. No, he doesn't lose self-control. In fact, he exercises far more self-control than a person who does not possess the Holy Spirit. When a Christian consciously, continuously, and voluntarily submits to God, he is freed from slavery to the sinful habits and drives that once controlled him.

This attitude of submission is also present in Colossians 3:15-4:10, a passage that parallels Ephesians 5:18-6:9. When Paul told the believers in Colosse to place themselves under the rule of Christ's peace, and to give the Word of Christ a dominant place in their lives (3:16), he was calling for a submissive attitude. You place yourself under God's influence and control when you do these things. The result of letting the Holy Spirit keep filling you (Ephesians 5:18) and letting the peace of Christ and the Word of Christ have dominance in your life (Colossians 3:15,16) is the same: joy, mutual encouragement, praise, and gratitude.

When you have a submissive attitude toward God and His Word, the Holy Spirit can keep filling you. This is because:

1. You place yourself under the authority of the Bible when it tells you to "put off" and "put to death" the sins of the flesh and to "put on" Christian virtues (Ephesians 4:17-5:7, Colossians 3:5-17)
2. You humbly confess your sins so that you will experience God's fellowship and cleansing. (I John 1:9)
3. You submit to others as an expression of your love for God, thus becoming a good marriage partner, a good citizen, and a good representative of Christ. (Ephesians 5:2-33, I Peter 2:11-3:17)
4. Be Confident - The fourth essential in being filled with the Spirit is to be confident. When you have centered your life on Jesus Christ, when you are in the Word, and it is in you, and when you have submitted to the Holy Spirit's leading, you can know that you have done your part. And, having done that, you can be absolutely certain that God has done His part. He has responded to you by filling you with His Spirit. Because of that:

1. You don't need to wonder if you are spiritual enough to be filled with the Spirit.
2. You don't need to compare yourself with other believers.

3. You don't need to keep looking for some spectacular sign from Heaven.
4. You don't need to wait for a great feeling of tingling excitement to sweep over you.

Rather, you can know with absolute certainty that because you are doing your part, God is doing His part. And this confidence will help you live day-by-day in the assurance that you are filled with the Holy Spirit.

But if you live with a defeatist attitude, it is probably because you feel that you are losing your battle with sin. Your lack of confidence, though, shows a failure to trust in the Lord's provision for you and in His power to keep His part of the bargain.

Look at the Apostle Paul. Although he was very much aware of the power of the old nature and of the ongoing battle with the flesh, he was brimming with confidence. In Romans 7, for example, he was painfully honest in describing the battle between his old nature (the "law of sin") and his new nature (the "law of my mind"). But he then went right on to point out that the way of victory is through "Jesus Christ our Lord." He then said:

There is therefore now no condemnation to those who are in Christ Jesus ... For the law of the Spirit of life in Christ Jesus has made me free from the law of sin and death. For what the law could not do in that it was weak through the flesh, God did by sending His own Son in the likeness of sinful flesh, on account of sin: He condemned sin in the flesh, that the righteous requirement of the law might be fulfilled in us who do not walk according to the flesh but according to the Spirit (Romans 8:1-4).

This walking "in the Spirit" occurs when we are filled with the Spirit. It includes the four essentials we've just looked at in a blend of divine and human activity to overcome sin.

The walk in the Spirit is a walk of confidence in God. And this confidence produces spiritual victory because of:

1. A continual awareness of the Spirit's presence (I Corinthians 8:19, 20).
2. A conscious dependence on the Spirit's power (Ephesians 5:18).
3. An acceptance of the Spirit's help in fulfilling the law of God. (Romans 8:4).
4. A deliberate "putting off" of the flesh (Ephesians 4:22).
5. A willful rejection of sin (Romans 6:1, 2).
6. A determined pursuit of what is right (Ephesians 4:24).

The fourth essential in a Spirit-filled life, then, is confidence. This is especially true in our battle against sin. But when you have done your part – when you have repented of all known sin, confessed it, and replaced it with obedience to Christ – you can be certain that God has done His part in forgiving you and in giving you the power for spiritual victory. You can move ahead with your heart filled with confidence and the knowledge that you are filled with the Holy Spirit.

How Can I Tell When I'm Spirit-Filled?

There are four evidences:
1. Joyful Fellowship
2. Heartfelt Praise
3. Abounding Gratitude
4. Reverent Submission

NINE FRUIT

1. Love – an attitude that moves us to put God and others ahead of ourselves. A spirit that impels us to give, to serve, and to forgive.
2. Joy – a spirit of gladness rooted in our faith, expressed through song, and accompanied by an optimistic spirit.
3. Peace – inner serenity derived from God and based on the reality of our peace with God through Christ's sacrifice.
4. Longsuffering – patience in the midst of difficult circumstances and in our relationships with difficult people.

5. Kindness – practicing the golden rule of treating others as we expect them to treat us.
6. Goodness – open, honest, pure, and generous behavior.
7. Faithfulness – we can be trusted and depended on in all our relationships.
8. Gentleness – a tenderness of spirit that enables us to discipline others properly, to endure persecution graciously, and to witness to others sensitively.
9. Self-control – the quality that gives us control over our desires, especially those that relate to the body.

When a person's life is marked by the four evidences of Ephesians 5:18-21 and the nine moral qualities of Galatians 5:22, 23, the demands of the law are being fulfilled. When they are present, they provide evidence that you are filled with the Holy Spirit.

By: Herb Vander Lugt
Radio Bible Class Publications
Grand Rapids, MI, 1986

TEN MARKS OF THE SPIRIT-FILLED CHRISTIAN

The Bible likens itself to a mirror into which the Christian may look to check on himself. Likewise, the Word of God clearly says we are to be "doers of the word, not hearers only"; otherwise we deceive ourselves (James 1:22).

Thus, from time to time, it is important for us to check our spiritual state with the Word of God and with the degree to which God, through us, is able to meet the need of the world about us.

This study provides a good opportunity for evaluating our spiritual status. So here are ten major checkpoints from the Scriptures. I hope they remind you, as they do me, of the tremendous possibilities open to us through the truly Spirit-filled life.

1. The truly spiritual Christian lives a life of **fruitfulness**. Through the indwelling Holy Spirit, the life of the Lord Jesus is made manifest in the Christian, thus fulfilling our Lord's promise: "He that abideth in me, and I in him, the same bringeth forth much fruit, for without me ye can do nothing."

This fruit is the spontaneous expression of the new life within, and not an addition made by human effort. Abiding in Christ is essentially obedience to Him, doing His bidding in the light of His Word. "Hereby we know that he abideth in us, by the Spirit which he hath given us," declares I John 3:24. Abiding is obedience — and the spontaneous consequence is a fruitful life.

That fruit is spelled out in Galatians 5:22-23. Therein we find nine characteristics of fruitfulness which should be obvious to anyone observing a Spirit-filled Christian. These characteristics are produced by the Holy Spirit.

2. He demonstrates the **love** of God. The affection, sympathy, the tenderness of heart and devotion of the Spirit-filled Christian is directed toward the Savior and also toward his fellowmen. Declared by the Lord Jesus, the great commandment is to love God with all the heart and soul and mind (Matthew 22:37-38). The new commandment of the Savior is that we love one another as He has loved us. By that characteristic, others know that we are His disciples (John 13:34-35). The love of God wrought in the heart by the Holy Spirit is further elaborated in I Corinthians 13.

3. He exhibits **joy**, the gladness, delight, enjoyment, cheer which fills to overflowing the heart of the believer. The Savior promised: "These things have I spoken unto you, that my joy might remain in you, and that your joy might be full," (John 15:11). He added: "Ask, and ye shall receive, that your joy may be full." (John 16:24).

The joy of the Spirit-filled Christian is best seen in time of deep testing and trial. "Count it all joy when ye fall into divers temptations," admonishes James 1:2. During the trial of our faith we are to "rejoice with joy unspeakable and full of glory" (I Peter 1:8). When passing through fiery trials, we are assured that we can rejoice as partakers of Christ's sufferings, and be glad "with exceeding joy" (I Peter 4:13).

4. He reflects the **peace**, the calmness, composure, cool-headedness and restfulness of God Himself. Promised the Savior: "Peace I leave with you, my peace I give unto you ... Let not your heart be troubled, neither let it be afraid" (John 14:27). Through the Holy Spirit the believer, justified by faith in the Savior, has "peace with

God through our Lord Jesus Christ" (Romans 5:1). By casting all his care upon the Lord, and making known the petitions of his heart, he experiences "the peace of God which passeth all understanding" (Philippians 4:7).

The Old Testament saints, as well as the New, experienced this peace. Testified David: "I will both lay me down in peace, and sleep; for thou, Lord only makest me dwell in safety: (Psalm 4:8). Isaiah added the promise of the Almighty: "Thou will keep him in perfect peace, whose mind is stayed on thee, because he trusteth in thee" (26:3).

Because of the peaceful heart by the Holy Spirit the Spirit-filled Christian is to be a peacemaker, thereby sharing the beatitude, "Blessed are the peacemakers; for they shall be called the children of God" (Matthew 5:9). By the indwelling Spirit is fulfilled the exhortation of Hebrews 12:14 — "Follow peace with all men, and holiness..."

5. He is **longsuffering.** This patience, forbearance, persistence, hopefulness, expectation and even temper marks a Spirit-filled Christian.

Like the other characteristics of the Spirit-filled life, this one is especially apparent in times of pressure and perplexity. We can be sure that "tribulation worketh patience; and patience, experience; and experience, hope," which hope is not put to shame, "because the love of God is shed abroad in our hearts by the Holy Ghost which is given unto us" (Romans 5:3-5). Answer to prayer may not come immediately; and therefore we are taught, "Cast not away your confidence, which hath great recompense of reward; for ye have need of patience, that, after ye have done the will of God, ye might receive the promise" (Hebrews 10:35-36). By looking unto the Lord Jesus, the Spirit-filled Christian is enabled to run "with patience the race that is set before us" (Hebrews 12:1).

We are admonished strongly to let "patience have her perfect work" (James 1:17); thus evidencing maturity in the spiritual life.

6. **Gentleness.** The kindliness, graciousness, gentility, courtesy, consideration for others is the expression of the indwelling Spirit. Gentleness is the outworking of one's birth. On the human plane we speak of gentlemen and their old-fashioned counterpart,

gentlewomen. Originally that concept referred to those who were of noble birth, that is, of nobility. By the new birth, "born again by the Spirit of God," the Spirit-filled Christian is to be God's gentleman, God's gentlewoman.

We are to be taught gentleness by the Lord Jesus who said, "I am meek and lowly in heart..." (Matthew 11:29).

Declares II Timothy 2:24-25: "The servant of the Lord must not strive; but be gentle unto all men, apt to teach, patient, in meekness instructing those that oppose themselves,,," Paul reminded the Thessalonians that when he was with them he was gentle, as a nurse with children (I Thessalonians 2:7).

From the Old Testament record we would gather that David's secret of greatness was his courage or his fearlessness; but he himself declares: "Thy gentleness hath made me great" (Psalm 18:35). We have the proverb that "Cleanliness is next to godliness." However, Scripture says that brotherly kindness is next to godliness (II Peter 1:7).

7. **Goodness,** the benevolence, good will, eagerness to be helpful to others is also the natural outworking of the indwelling Holy Spirit. Of the Lord Jesus it is said: "God anointed Jesus of Nazareth with the Holy Ghost and with power; who went about doing good..." (Acts 10:38). Of Barnabas, that son of consolation, the Bible states: "He was a good man, and full of the Holy Ghost and of faith" (Acts 11:24). The fruitfulness of the Spirit-filled Christian is underlined in Colossians 1:10 - "Being fruitful in every good work, and increasing in the knowledge of God." By the Spirit, young women are taught to be "discreet, chaste, keepers at home, good, obedient to their own husbands..." and young men to be "a pattern of good works..." (Titus 2:5-7).

The Spirit-filled Christian may not be a wise man, a rich man, a busy man, a prominent person, he should and can be by the Spirit a good man. As the Amplified New Testament puts it, speaking of Barnabas, "good in himself and also at once for the good and the advantage of other people..." (Acts 11:24).

8. **Faithfulness** — loyalty, trustworthiness, probity, integrity, uprightness and honesty of heart-characterizes the Spirit-filled Christian. Throughout the Scriptures we read that God is faithful (Deuteronomy

7:9; I Corinthians 1:9; I Peter 4:19 and elsewhere), Jeremiah in his deep distress learned that "great is thy faithfulness" (Lamentations 3:23).

On our part we are to show forth, by the Holy Spirit, a faithfulness corresponding to that of the Most High. Faithfulness, in addition to meekness, was the outstanding characteristic of Moses (Numbers 12:3, Hebrews 3:5). Every servant is to be faithful (I Corinthians 4:2). The Lord Jesus taught that faithfulness in little things would mean faithfulness in larger responsibilities (Luke 18:10).

9. **Meekness**, the humility, modesty, submissiveness and the abasement of the Lord Jesus, is made real by the Holy Spirit. It is by the "meekness and gentleness of Christ" that we are exhorted to be consistent Christians (II Corinthians 10:1). By separation from worldliness we are to follow after meekness as well as righteousness, godliness, faithfulness, love, and patience (I Timothy 6:11). It is with meekness that we are to restore a fellow Christian overtaken in a fault (Galatians 6:1). By the transforming power of the indwelling Spirit we are in honor to prefer one another (Romans 12:10). It is "with all lowliness and meekness, with longsuffering, forbearing one another in love" that we are to keep "the unity of the Spirit in the bond of peace" (Ephesians 4:2-3).

10. **Temperance** — self-control, self-restraint, continence, equanimity and unruffled tranquility — is evidence of the indwelling Holy Spirit. To knowledge whereby we understand the truth of God, we are to add this composure (II Peter 1:6). The athlete knows the necessity of self-discipline; how much more the Christian who runs the Christian race by the power of the Spirit (I Corinthians 9: 24-27). The tongue is the highest test of self-control. It is "out of the abundance of the heart the mouth speaketh" (Matthew 12:34). If one is able to bridle his tongue he is able "also to bridle the whole body" (James 3:2). The spiritually minded Christian is to "show out a good conversation (behavior) his works with meekness of wisdom"; with warning against bitterness, envy, and strife (James 3:13-14).

Fruitfulness, love, joy, peace, patience, gentleness, goodness, faithfulness, meekness, and self-control, these are evidence of the Spirit-filled life. They cannot be imitated. There is no artificial substitute. An acid test of the Spirit-filled life is whether the Christian battles within himself to achieve the fruit - or senses the Spirit of God gently removing strain and fretfulness of trial.

Looking into the mirror, am I a Spirit-filled Christian?

By: Br, V. Raymond Edman
Christian Life Pub., Inc.
33 S. Wacker Dr., Chicago, IL

EXAMINE YOURSELF

1. Am I abiding in Christ because of implicit obedience to Him, and therefore a fruit-bearing Christian?
2. Do I show the love and loveliness of the indwelling Savior according to the standard of I Corinthians 13?
3. Do I have joy that is spontaneous and serene by the indwelling Spirit - irrespective of outward circumstances?
4. Deep within do I know the unperturbed peace that passes understanding - and misunderstanding?
5. Am I patient, persistent, even-tempered under heavy trials?
6. Am I kind, considerate, polite, gentle to all?
7. Am I genuinely good (helpful) at heart and glad to do good for others?
8. In the smallest duties, as well as the largest, can others count on my faithfulness, loyalty, singleness of heart?
9. Am I content to be unnoticed, unappreciated, humbled, and even humiliated, without retort or retaliation?
10. Do I have the unruffled tranquility, equanimity and composure that come from control by the Holy Spirit?

By: Dr. V. Raymond Edman
Christian Life Pub., Inc.
33 S. Wacker Dr., Chicago, Il.

VII-F: SPIRITUAL GIFTS

When a person is saved, God gives him a gift or gifts to use in serving Him. Many Christians go through life never knowing what their gifts are. These gifts are not material gifts, but are special abilities which the Holy Spirit will use as we are channels for His work.

Do you know what your gift is? Each Christian is given a motivational gift from God when they are saved. It is one's frame of reference through which he speaks or acts as a Christian. We need to discover and develop that gift, because it is the channel of your life through which God will show His power and love. If a Christian fails to know and use his gift, he is an unfulfilled Christian. It is the basis of our joy and fulfillment.

Each gift is designed to bring the body of Christ to maturity. They are for the well being of the church. (Ephesians 5:11-13) When we are open to the Holy Spirit, He will enable us to discover where our greatest motivation lies.

There is no clear teaching in Scripture on how to determine what gift(s) you have. Answering the following questions may be helpful.

1. What do you enjoy doing?
2. What do you do well?
3. What do you do which brings pleasure to others?
4. In what area do others say you are talented?

"Understanding the gifts helps us to develop skill in our ministry: Through our gift, the love of Christ is being expressed to the perfecting of the body." (I Peter 4:10) If we fail to know and exercise our gifts, there will be weakness in the church of Christ

THE GIFTS OF THE HOLY SPIRIT

WORDS OF WISDOM AND KNOWLEDGE

The first gift mentioned is "the word of wisdom." This is the power to speak with wisdom, to give the message with discretion and understanding. Then there is the word of knowledge," another gift given to some people. This is the power to speak with knowledge, or intelligence. For instance, words of wisdom are the deep things of God; whereas, words of knowledge are to help make clear and intelligible the deep things of God.

THE GIFT OF FAITH

Then we have the gift of "faith." This is not speaking of faith in salvation. That, too, is a gift, for we read in Ephesians 2:8-9, "For by grace are ye saved through faith; and that not of yourselves; it is the gift of God." But in this particular chapter of I Corinthians 12, the gift of faith refers to faith by which great exploits for God may be accomplished.

This has been illustrated by such men as Moses; who was able, by faith to bring about great miracles in Egypt, at the Red Sea, in the desert, etc. It was illustrated by Joshua at the Jordan River and at the city of Jericho, as well as by Jehoshaphat, who broke his alliance with Ahab and went on his own with God, vanquishing the enemy. (II Corinthians 19:20)

It was also illustrated by David, when he went out after Goliath and overcame him by his faith in God. It was illustrated by Gideon, who with three hundred men drove out great armies. It was illustrated by Peter when he walked out on the sea to Jesus. It was illustrated by Paul in his Christian walk. It was illustrated by such men as Hudson Taylor, who went to China by faith, and George Mueller, who was able, by faith in God, to do great things for a large number of orphans in England. Even today we have men who are accomplishing great things for God because they are willing to believe Him. Faith is a wonderful gift of the Holy Spirit.

GIFTS OF HEALING AND MIRACLES

Then Paul mentions the "gifts of healing." This is power to cure diseases. But please note that it may be by means of medicines, by means of surgery, or by means of prayer and faith. We cannot limit it to one of these. It is the ability to heal, and the method is not the important question.

Another gift, mentioned in verse 10, is "the working of miracles," a supernatural power given to some men to do great deeds or work wonders.

THE GIFT OF PROPHECY

Next is the gift of "prophecy," which is really the gift of preaching, prophetic utterance, or prophetic insight. Some people have a special gift to see things as they are happening and to understand how they harmonize with Scripture, This is prophetic insight. Speaking to the edification and exhortation and comfort of people is preaching. Some men are great orators, but they may not necessarily have anything to do with the gift of prophecy at all. One who is a prophet is one who speaks so that people are moved under the impact of his speaking.

DISCERNING OF SPIRITS

Another gift of the Spirit is that of "discerning of spirits," which means distinguishing between true and false inspiration. This was very necessary at the time when Paul was writing, because the Word of God was then being given. Some of the writing was by inspiration, but some was not and was not to be part of God's Word. Someone had to have the gift of discerning which was inspired and which was not. Thank God for that gift!

It is still necessary today, because of the many cults and doctrines of devils that are springing up everywhere. We need to have people with this gift who are able to discern whether or not something is of God. Of course, the Spirit will enlighten us by His Word, and we need the ability to discriminate in spiritual matters, to distinguish between imitation gifts and those that are real. Satan often comes as an angel of light, and he may imitate some of the gifts.

This gift of discernment is lacking in so many churches today. The fact that a preacher names the Name of Jesus Christ does not mean that he is a gospel preacher. He may even be a Modernist, or he may be able to leave out the gospel altogether and fool many people. We need to discern whether or not men are preaching the Word of God,

GIFT OF TONGUES AND INTERPRETING

Another of the gifts mentioned is the gift of "tongues." This means a variety of tongues, or languages, or various utterances that are for edification. Then we have the gift of interpreting these tongues, or explaining what was said in another language. These gifts were distributed to each individual as God willed. Some people think we all must speak in tongues, but God says that the gift is given to whom the Spirit desires and wills it.

THE PURPOSE OF THE GIFTS

The purpose is "for the perfecting of the saints, for the work of the ministry, for the edifying of the body of Christ," until we all come into the unity of the Spirit of God.

CONTRIBUTING THROUGH SPIRITUAL GIFTS

Spiritual gifts do not come wrapped in colorful paper and bright bows. They come wrapped in flesh. God has gifted His children for special purposes.

Having gifts
1. Which Christians have spiritual gifts? I Corinthians 12:7
2. How do you "get" a spiritual gift? I Corinthians 12:11 (K.J. - "severally"-"individually")
3. Complete the chart near the end of the chapter by listing the gifts from each passage.
4. What significance do you attach to the fact that these lists of gifts are all slightly different?
5. What conclusion do you draw from the fact that the Bible contains no definite statement about how to know your spiritual gift(s)?

Determining Gifts
6. What do you think may be your gift(s)?
7. How do you presently use your gift(s) to contribute to the well-being of your church? What are additional ways you can use your gift(s)?

Using Gifts
8. Why has God gifted you? I Corinthians 12:7
9. How should you view yourself and your gift(s)? Romans 12:3
10. How should you use your gift(s)? I Peter 4:10,11

11. What truths about spiritual gifts are illustrated by the human body in the following verses?
    I Corinthians   12:14-16
    I Corinthians   12:21-22
    I Corinthians   12:23,24
    I Corinthians   12:25,26

12. What benefits to the church result from the proper use of God's gifts? Ephesians 4:11-16
13. Compare the fruit of the Spirit listed in Galatians 5:22,23 with your lists of gifts of the Spirit in question 3. What difference do you see between the fruit of the Spirit and gifts of the Spirit?
14. Complete the following sentences:
    I am important to the growth and well-being of our church because...
    I cannot be boastful or proud of the contribution I am making because...

Key Concept
God has given every believer a spiritual gift that is to be used for the well-being of the church.

Memory Verse - I Corinthians 12:7 - But to each one is given the manifestation of the Spirit for the common good.

HOW CAN I RECOGNIZE MY SPIRITUAL GIFTS?

1. Be connected to and active in a local body of believers. You can start by responding to needs in the congregation for teachers, ushers, nursery workers, coffee servers, etc. Whether you feel "gifted" or not, get involved. As you step out in faith and obedience with a servant's heart, the Holy Spirit will show you the areas for which He has gifted you. This often occurs through positive feedback from people who are experiencing God's grace through your acts of service.

2. Invite the filling of the Holy Spirit. Your spiritual gifts are a manifestation of the Holy Spirit in you (1Corinthians 12:7,11).

As you are surrendered to and filled by the Spirit, you give Him the opportunity to release and empower your spiritual gifts. Paul's admonition in Ephesians 5:18 to "be filled with the Spirit," implies a continuous action, rather than a one-time event. It literally means "keep on being filled."

The Holy Spirit wants to be invited to fill you. He wants to demonstrate God's grace through you! But just as He can be welcomed into your life. He can also be grieved (Ephesians 4:30) and quenched (I Thessalonians 5:19). If you desire Him to fill you and release His gifts in you, you cannot at the same time be grieving Him through unbelief or sinful attitudes, thoughts, or actions.

3. **Ask.** James says, "If any of you lacks wisdom, he should ask God, who gives generously to all without finding fault, and it will be given to him" (James 1:5). Asking God for wisdom about our spiritual gifts is a good place to start. Since it's God's will for you to exercise your spiritual gifts, you can ask with confidence that He will respond and give you direction,

4. **Seek prayer, discernment, and blessing from your spiritual leaders.** In the early church, leaders commissioned individuals into ministry. Paul and Barnabas were sent out in this way:

In the church at Antioch there were prophets and teachers... While they were worshiping the Lord and fasting, the Holy Spirit said, "Set apart for me Barnabas and Saul for the work to which I have called them." So after they had fasted and prayed, they placed their hands on them and sent them off. — Acts 13:1-3

Paul, in turn, repeated this process with Timothy: "I remind you to fan into flame the gift of God, which is in you through the laying on of hands" (II Timothy 1:6).

The prayers of our spiritual leaders are one way of releasing the Holy Spirit's gifts. In Romans 1:11 Paul says, "I long to see you so that I may impart to you some spiritual gift to make you strong." (The word for spiritual gift in this passage is charisma, the same word used in the spiritual-gift passages in I Corinthians).

When you are embarking on a ministry — or if you are already involved in a ministry and have never done this — it is valuable (and biblical) to ask your church or ministry leaders to lay hands on you and to pray for the Holy Spirit's empowering. If you are a leader, you can do this for the people who serve in your ministry.

5. **Look for fruit.** Because it's the Holy Spirit who empowers spiritual gifts, we should expect evidence of His presence, power, and work when we serve in our areas of gifting (I Corinthians 2:4-5). I call this the "fruit test." For example, if I think I have the gift of evangelism, I can ask, Are people being saved as a result of my ministry? Or if I think I have the gift of mercy, I can ask, Do people feel Jesus' love and compassion through me?

6. **Use a spiritual-gifts inventory.** Though this option can be helpful, it also has its pitfalls. Even an unbeliever can take a spiritual-gifts test and come away with a list of gifts. So a pen-and-paper test is best evaluated alongside the trial and error of hands-on ministry and the feedback of others.

A spiritual-gifts inventory can help you pinpoint your strengths and weaknesses and reveal patterns in how the Holy Spirit seems to use you. It may also help you identify what fulfills you when you serve — what gives you that I-just-gave someone a gift feeling.

By: Arlyn Lawrence

SCRIPTURAL GUIDELINES FOR SPIRITUAL GIFTS

I. Romans 1:11. Gifts are to confirm, strengthen or establish the "believer.

A Christian without the knowledge of his own spiritual gift(s) is an unfulfilled Christian. We have a desire for meaningful achievement. The ultimate of this is having a significant part in a divine plan.

II. Romans 11:29. God will not take away our gifts in this earthly life.

III. Romans 12:6. We differ in gifts.

IV. I Corinthians 7:7. Whatever your gift(s) are, they are proper for you.

V.	I Corinthians 12:1. There is no excuse for ignorance on this subject,
VI.	I Corinthians 12:4. There are different gifts.
VII.	I Corinthians 12:7. Gifts are given for the profit of the church.
VIII.	I Corinthians 12:7. All Christians are given at least one gift. (Romans 12:5,6)
IX.	I Corinthians 12:11. Gifts are given on an individual basis.
X.	I Corinthians 12:11. Gifts are given as the Spirit of God wills. (Hebrews 2:4)
XI.	I Corinthians 12:14-21. Every gift has its place in the church.
XII.	I Corinthians 12:28-30. God has set an order of importance concerning the gifts.
XIII.	I Corinthians 13:1,2. Spiritual gifts are to be exercised with love as their basis.
XIV.	I Corinthians 14:12. Gifts are for the edification of the church. (I Peter 4:10).
XV.	Joy comes in exercising our gift(s). The root word for gift is CHARISMA. This comes from the word CHAR which means joy.
XVI.	I Timothy 4:14. We are not to neglect our gifts. (II Timothy 1:6)
XVII.	I Timothy 4:12,14. Young people are not excused from gifts.
XVIII.	Matthew 25:14-30. We shall be held accountable for either the use or neglect of our gifts,

* Use your gifts with I Corinthians 13 in mind!

By: John Gilliom

An Overview: In I Corinthians 12:4-7 and 11, there are four distinct categories dealing with Spiritual Gifts. In the chart list the categories, who gave them, and the gifts.

Scripture	I Corinthians 12:4	I Corinthians 12:5	I Corinthians 12:6	I Corinthians 12:7
Categories				
Given By				
Scriptures: Where they are found	Romans 12:6-8	Ephesians 4:11	I Corinthians 12:28	I Corinthians 12:7-10
G I F T S	1. 2. 3. 4. 5. 6. 7.	1. (sent ones) 2. (proclaiming of the Word) 3. 4. 5.	1. 2. 3. 4. 5. 6. 7. 8.	1. 2. 3. 4. 5. 6. 7. 8. 9.
	Personal Gifts To the Individual Believer	To Edify the Total Body of Christ	In the Local Church	To Profit Everyone

Through our gifts the love of Christ is being expressed to the perfecting of the body (I Peter 4:10). If we fail to know and exercise our gifts, there will be weakness and imbalance in the body.

The following is a list of the various kinds of gifts and their main purpose,

Ministry Gifts	Motivational Gifts	Manifestation Gifts
Opportunities to serve I Corinthians 12:28 Ephesians 4:11 1. Apostles (sent out by church) 2. Prophets (proclaiming truth) 3. Teacher (clarifying and guarding truth) 4. Workers of Power (Natural & supernatural deeds with precise timing to God's glory) 5. Healings (making whole) 6. Helps (to assist) 7. Governments (control of the gifts) 8, Tongues (other languages)	Power to serve Romans 12:6:8 a) Prophecy (revealing truth) b) Serving (meeting practical needs) c) Teaching (checking out truth) d) Exhortation (guiding to spiritual maturity) e) Giving (entrusting assets) f) Organization (coordinating others) g) Mercy (identifying with inner needs)	Results of serving I Corinthians 12:7-11 a) A word of wisdom (seeing as God sees) b) Word of knowledge (responding wisely) e) Faith (visualizing what God will do) d) Gifts of Healing (restoring health) e) Working miracles (what only God can do) f) Prophecy (bringing to light) g) Discerning of spirits (spiritual perception) h) Tongues (needing interpretation)

Do you see yourself in any of these gifts? Then ask the Lord to use you. Get involved in your church and help it bring the unity and the power back to the church which is so desperately needed today.

CHAPTER VIII

OVERCOMING TEMPTATION

If You Fail

"Does becoming a Christian mean that all your struggles are over? Not according to the Bible or the experiences of the best Christians. The truth is that temptation is a universal experience. The Devil does not leave you alone because you were converted. So don't be surprised when you are tempted. It happens to all Christians. Be ready for it. The Christian life is a spiritual warfare, a life-long battle with temptation. But, now you can win by God's help. A few things to remember about temptations are:

1. **Temptation is not sin.** Jesus was without sin, yet He was tempted throughout His life. It is yielding to temptation that is sin. The test of a person's character is how he resists temptation. So don't feel condemned because you feel tempted.

2. **Guard against temptation.** It is not something to toy with. Avoid situations that expose you to temptation. Remember how Jesus taught us to pray? He said, "Lead us not into temptation, but deliver us from evil." (Matthew 6:13) Don't go where the danger is. Watch what you read. Be careful where you go. Some friends may not be good company unless you can help them spiritually. No Christian can afford to get careless.

3. **God will help you overcome.** Victory over temptation and sin can be had by anyone, anywhere, if he is fully surrendered to Christ. When in actual practice Christ is Lord of your life, sin can no longer be in the saddle. But you will not be able to overcome all temptations in your own strength. Learn to use the Bible to help you to victory. You will remember that it was the weapon that Jesus used to overcome the tempter. (Matthew 4:4) "When temptation comes - and it will come - you will find your escape in the Word of God. Christ gained victory over Satan in the wilderness by quoting the Scriptures. He answered all three temptations with, "it is written..." (I Corinthians 10:13) Prayer is a positive way of handling temptation. Plan to replace evil to which you are tempted with its opposite, good. For example, if your besetting tendency is to dislike some person who has wronged you, the first step is to put that person on your daily prayer list. Pray for his needs and problems. Also, go out and do some positive good for that person. You will find that you gained a friend. You also won a battle with yourself.

Beginning with Christ was wonderful, but overcoming with Him day by day is even better. You'll get to see His faithfulness demonstrated continually.

4. **Final outcome of the battle**. I John 3:8

Satan has made large gains in our world. Many people follow him. He is more powerful than any person and has the assistance of a vast army of highly intelligent evil spirit beings. But, he is already defeated. Jesus came to earth to destroy Satan's work. When He took the penalty for sin by dying on the cross, Jesus broke Satan's power.

That doesn't mean that Satan is completely powerless. He still wins some battles. He succeeds in keeping some people captive. But he will be destroyed in the end. His days are numbered. What will happen to him when his time is up? He will be cast into hell.

Christians can defeat Satan now. Because of Jesus' death and resurrection, Satan has no power over us. If we resist him in the strength of the Lord, we can have victory over each of his attacks. We don't have to give in to him, because the One who lives in us is greater than the one (Satan) who lives in the world. (I John 4:4) (Except what we allow him.)

James 4:7 gives us a great two-part battle plan for defeating Satan: submit and resist. What does it mean to submit? (To place ourselves under God's command.) How can we resist Satan? (By saying no to every kind of sin.) What will happen when we resist Satan? (He will "flee.") What does that mean? (He will run away and leave us alone.) Do you think that means that Satan will never bother us again? (No, he will try again to tempt us to do wrong.) Defeating Satan is a matter of resisting him every day if necessary, and staying close to the Lord at all times. Victory is not automatic. (Ephesians 6:10-17)

What should you do if you fail?
The Devil would want you to think that God writes you off when you fail. But that is a lie. God never gives up on us. God has made provision for this need in the lives of His children. We read it in I John 2:1. Isn't that tremendous? Even our sins do not turn away His grace. But we must repent sincerely. A Christian simply cannot make a practice of sin. (I John 3:9) Keep "current" accounts with God. Receive His cleansing every day. Trust Him with all your heart.

Now That You're A Christian
By: Michael P. Horban

SIX STEPS TO SUCCESSFUL CHRISTIAN LIVING

When temptation comes - and it will come - you will find your escape in the Word of God. Christ gained victory over Satan in the wilderness by quoting the Scriptures. He answered all three temptations with, "It is written..." I Corinthians 10:13.

By: Bobby Jackson

Pitfalls To Avoid
1. Do not keep your eyes on men. (Psalm 118:8)
2. Do not place too much importance on material things. (I Timothy 6:10)
3. Do not become too friendly with unspiritual people.
4. Do not participate in gossip and criticism.

5. Beware of pride, conceit and self-confidence. (Romans 12:3, James 4:10, Proverbs 16:18, 21:4, I Corinthians 10:12, James 4:6-7)

WHEN A CHRISTIAN SINS

All Christians sin. And no Christian can have day-by-day victory over sin and live the happy, joyful, triumphant life, until he faces the true facts about sin in his own nature, sin in his own life, what sin will do and what to do about it.

WHAT CONFESSION INVOLVES
It is a blessed promise, that wonderful promise in I John 1:9. We can have the clear-cut assurance that "If we confess our sins, he is faithful and just to forgive us our sins, and to cleanse us from all unrighteousness." The very moment one confesses sin, and thus judges sin and takes sides with God against sin, that sin is blotted out, both forgiven and cleansed. Thus, upon simple confession of sin, the child of God has peace with God about sin, and he has victory over the sin.

Of course, when God says confession, He means honest confession. So let every Christian solemnly consider what is involved in honest confession of sin.

First, confession means not only that you admit you did the thing, but you admit that it was a sin. Make sure that your wicked heart does not deceive you here. To say, "Lord, I did it, but I couldn't help myself; it was not really my fault," is not confession of sin but is excusing sin, taking sides with sin. If you want peace and forgiveness and cleansing, face sin honestly, call it by its right name, admit your guilt.

Many times Christian people say, "If I have done wrong, I want God to forgive me." That is no confession. As long as you put an **if** about your confession of sin, God puts an **if** about His forgiveness of that sin! I beg of you, if you want mercy, face sin for the black thing it is, recognize it, admit it, take sides against it, judge it!

It is no honest confession that leaves the sin half-covered, half-excused, and still loved and defended. Do not trifle with sin, do not call it a nice name, do not look on it with allowance and with regard. Call it the sin that it is, hate it, turn from it in your heart.

Second, of course, any honest confession means forsaking sin. For your mouth to say, "Lord, this is a sin, I am sorry," while the heart says, "But I still love it and I still plan to hold on to it," is no honest confession of sin. It is hypocrisy. Watch that deceitful heart of yours and make sure that it releases its grip on the sin that it pretends to confess. Sin that is not forsaken is not honestly confessed. Any straightforward confession of sin that will please God and gain His forgiveness and cleansing must involve the will. Does your will give up the sin? Do you want to be rid of it? Do you beg for cleansing? Does your mind cry out with broken-hearted David: "I acknowledge my transgressions; and my sin is ever before me...Create in me a clean heart, O God; and renew a right spirit within me...The sacrifices of God are a broken spirit; a broken and a contrite heart, O God, thou wilt not despise" (Psalm 51:3, 10, 17). The honest confession of sin ought to mean that you are sick of it, that you despise it, that you long to be cleansed from it. If you truly lament your sin and turn from it in your heart, judge it honestly; in the very moment of your confession your sin will be forgiven and cleansed away and God will smile into your heart in sweet fellowship. Honest confession means honest repentance.

Third, an honest confession of sin, an honest judging of sin, when you ask for forgiveness, often means restitution.

Fourth, now, believe God. Accept and rejoice in the forgiveness that He freely gives.

Have you confessed your sin to God? Have you turned away from it? Have you done all you can do to stop the evil effect of the sin? Then I beg you, dear troubled soul, believe what God has said and take the forgiveness.

I trust you will set out to make this a daily matter; every day confessing any known sin that has come up to mar your fellowship with God; every day instantly claiming forgiveness for it when you judge it and forsake it. That way you can live the happy, joyful life of fellowship.

When A Christian Sins
By: John R. Rice

In order to have continual victory over sin, we need to know what to do when temptation comes and how to put on the armor of God. We will be studying that next.

OVERCOMING TEMPTATION

"At the cross Jesus won over the devil and crushed his power. This same victorious Christ will stand by your side in the hour of temptation and give you His strength. Revelation 12:11 says that the believers overcame Satan by the blood of the Lamb. Trust in the power of the blood and the devil will flee." (Keith M. Bailey, *Learning to Live,* Christian Pub. Inc., Harrisburg, PA 17101, p. 31, 32.)

We need to remember, too, that there are three things the devil hates: the Word, the name of Jesus and the blood. How can we use these in our time of need? We can quote Scripture as Jesus did when He was tempted. This is one reason why we need to memorize Scripture. There is power in the Word. We also can sing and praise the name of Jesus. Satan doesn't like that and won't stay around long if we are consistent in praising our Lord. There is also power in the blood. We can pray and ask Jesus to cover us with His blood. Satan hates that also, and it was because of Jesus shedding His blood for us on Calvary that we can be free from our sin.

Another precious promise is found in James 4:7. "Submit yourselves therefore to God. Resist the devil, and he will flee from you." In times of temptation, we need to give ourselves afresh to God. We need to tell the devil to leave us alone, and quote Scripture that fits the temptation. God's promise is that the devil will run from us.

Praise God there is a way of escape and it is ours as we appropriate God's provision.

In the next chapter, we will discuss each piece of armor God has provided for our protection against Satan.

CHAPTER IX

PUTTING ON
THE ARMOR OF GOD

1. If Satan wanted to destroy you – and he does – how would he do it? What sin in your life is the most likely place for him to attack?
2. Here are the seven pieces of armor listed in Ephesians 6:12-17. Included is a brief description of what each piece ought to mean to us personally.

    a. The belt of truthfulness: an attitude of complete honesty.
    b. The breastplate of righteousness: all sin must be confessed and we must constantly look to Christ who is our righteousness.
    c. The feet shod with the preparation of the Gospel of peace: an eagerness to present the Gospel whenever possible.
    d. The shield of faith: a life lived with implicit trust in God's Word.
    e. The helmet of salvation: confidence in the hope of salvation and the sufficiency of the Cross.
    f. The sword of the Spirit: knowing the specific statements of God to apply at the point of temptation.
    g. Pray always: a prayerful attitude of thankfulness and dependence.

What steps do you plan to take to put on any missing pieces?
3. In addition to using Scripture, we must learn to pray against demonic activity in our families, church, and also in specific individuals. We can do this best by putting on the armor of God daily and rebuking satanic activity by the use of Scripture.

Notice this armor carefully, for you too, must wear it if you would live victoriously.

First there is the garment of truth; next the breastplate of righteousness; then the shoes of peace, the shield of faith, the helmet of salvation; and finally the sword of the Spirit, "which is the word of God."

Obviously this armor is not material but spiritual. It has to do with the mind and the heart rather than the body. But, once donned, it will preserve the whole being from "all the flaming darts of the evil one."

Truth will give us certainty and keep our thoughts balanced and reasonable.

Righteousness will give us confidence and free us from fear of criticism.

Peace will give us gentleness and enable us to ignore all slights and slurs upon our character and way of life.

Faith will give us courage and buoyancy and place all disappointments and hardships in their true perspective.

The Word of God will supply every weapon we need in our warfare with the powers of darkness. Like the flaming sword over the gates of Eden, it will turn "every way" in the battle with evil.

Notice particularly that last piece of equipment suggested by the apostle – "the word of God.' That, of course, is the Bible. Your Bible!

This means that the very Book you have in your home can help you to triumph over every difficulty, every sorrow, every setback, and to live victoriously here and hereafter.

I add one more to the list that is found in verse 18. That is Prayer. We are to pray always. As we put on the armor of God we need to have a prayerful attitude of thankfulness. We need to realize that our total dependence is on God. We cannot fight the devil in our own strength.

> Ephesians 6:11-12 tells us why we need to put on the whole armor of God . "… that ye may stand against the wiles of the devil. For we wrestle not against principalities, against powers, against the rulers of the darkness of this world, against spiritual wickedness in high places."

We are in a spiritual warfare. We can see the works of Satan on every hand, especially in these last days. Let us, by faith, put on each piece with prayer, and let us be faithful soldiers of the cross. Take whatever steps are necessary to put on any missing pieces.

As well as using Scripture, we must learn to pray against demonic activity in our families, church, and also in specific individuals. We can do this only as we put on the armor of God daily and rebuke satanic activity by the use of Scripture.

If we are to be victorious over temptation, we need to understand the armor of God, and to be able to apply it to our lives.

Paul tells us about the armor in Ephesians 6:10-18. "Finally, my brethren, be strong in the Lord, and in the power of his might. Put on the whole armor of God, that ye may be able to stand against the wiles of the devil. For we wrestle not against flesh and blood, but against principalities, against powers, against the rulers of the darkness of this world, against spiritual wickedness in high places. Wherefore take unto you the whole armor of God, that ye may be able to withstand in the evil day, and having done all, to stand. Stand therefore, having your lions girt about with truth, and having on the breastplate of righteousness; And your feet shod with the preparation of the gospel of peace; Above all, taking the shield of faith, wherewith ye shall be able to quench all the fiery darts of the wicked. And take the helmet of salvation, and the sword of the Spirit, which is the Word of God; Praying always with all prayer and supplication in the Spirit, and watching thereunto with all perseverance and supplication for all saints."

Obviously this armor is not made of material but it is spiritual. It has to do with our mind and heart rather than our body. But, when we by faith put it on, it will protect the whole being from "all the fiery darts of the wicked one."

Here are the pieces of armor which we see listed.

TAKING THE SHIELD OF FAITH

Two analogies can be drawn from the shield referred to: The first is, the Christian "soldier," who is in spiritual warfare, needs to utilize a shield. Logically, it should be the largest one. He must have total protection from his archenemy, Satan. The shield of faith can accomplish this.

Second, the shield of faith is effectual since it is God who provides the protection – not the soldier. The Christian has no need to worry because his security does not stem from his own ability in maneuvering the small shield for protection, but, rather, he is wholly dependent upon God who never fails. God, not the Christian, is the only One able to withstand Satan.

Faith then is a belief and a trust in God and His inspired word, the Holy Bible. Faith is the reality or the assurance which one can and should have concerning the spiritual realm which operates in the invisible rather than the visible – the immaterial rather than the material arena of life. Faith manifests the protection necessary in the invisible world in the same way a shield defends one in the physical world.

Israel My Glory
By: Stan Rosenthal

THE SWORD OF THE SPIRIT

The Greek word used here is *hrema*, which refers to a specific statement or utterance. The "Sword of the Spirit" refers to the specific statements of God. It is not enough to say "I believe the Bible" when we encounter Satan in spiritual combat. We need to know the specific principles of Scripture to deal with the specific temptations of Satan.

The entire message of Ephesians 6:10-17 is that we are in a spiritual battle with Satanic forces, and battles are not won by retreating!

When we fight Satan's temptations, however, we can't contend with our own strength, wisdom and human reasoning. We must employ the sword – the Word of God – if we are to put him to flight. It is, therefore, absolutely necessary that believers know the Word. It is indispensable for spiritual victory in our lives. We are to hide the Word in our hearts (Psalm 119:11); heed the Word in our lives (James 1:22); handle the Word in our struggle (Ephesians 6:17); and hold forth the Word in our witness (Philippians 2:16)!

Israel My Glory
By: Will Varner

THE BREASTPLATE OF RIGHTEOUSNESS

Putting on the breastplate of righteousness is the believer simply applying to his own life the very character of Christ, made available to him by virtue of his being in union with Christ, and living that life. Since a believer has no righteousness of his own, he must rely on that provided by the Lord Jesus Christ. He is only wearing the breastplate of righteousness when the righteousness of Christ is able to be manifested through his life.

To put on the breastplate of righteousness is a little like getting dressed in the morning. There is more than one step involved. The starting point is to be under the controlling influence of the Holy Spirit, who will begin to produce the fruit of the Spirit and the righteousness of Christ in our lives.

The second step is to be living daily in the Word of God. This gives direction to the Spirit-filled life. Without this, we soon would flounder and go nowhere.

The third step for the believer to put on the breastplate of righteousness comes when he yields his members to the Lord. It is simply giving every part of our bodies over to the Lord, so that He can produce the righteousness of Christ through us.

The child of God, controlled by the Spirit, living in the Word, and with his members yielded to the Lord, has on the breastplate of righteousness.

Israel My Glory
By: Fred Hartman

YOUR FEET SHOD WITH THE GOSPEL OF PEACE

Here we can easily see that our readiness for action and our firm-footed stability are a direct result of the goodness of peace. This peace, or act of being bound, must be in relation to the Almighty God and is accomplished through the shed blood of Jesus Christ. We simply cannot be at enmity with God and stand united with Him against the devil.

The key to having our feet shod with "the preparation of the gospel of peace" remains in our having daily, growing confidence (trust) in God. Those who have been redeemed can have confidence and are able to stand firm. How great your confidence is, is dependent on how well you know your Redeemer. Your ability to be perpetually prepared and withstand the devil is in direct proportion to your confidence and trust in God.

Israel My Glory
By: Ron Weinbaum

THE HELMET OF SALVATION

When Paul commands the Christian soldier to put on the helmet (Ephesians 6:17a), he uses one of the richest words in all of the Bible to describe that piece of armor - the helmet of salvation. The figure of a helmet immediately suggests that this is something designed to protect the head, seat of the mind and intellect. This helmet can keep our thinking straight and preserve us from mental confusion and darkness.

Paul is not speaking of the salvation decision made in the past, which we call regeneration. Neither is he talking about salvation as a present experience which we call sanctification. Paul is looking on into the future and is talking about a salvation which will be a future event. This is confirmed by two references. The first is Romans 13:11: "And that, knowing the time, that now it is high time to awake out of sleep; for now is our salvation nearer than when we believed." The second reference defines this helmet further, "But let us, who are of the day, be sober, putting on the breastplate of faith and love, and, for an helmet, the hope of salvation" (I Thessalonians 5:8).

Israel My Glory
By: Ben Alpert

YOUR LOINS GIRDED WITH TRUTH

The God-Man was truth personified. "For the law was given by Moses, but grace and truth came by Jesus Christ" (John 1:17). He was God's absolute truth embodied in human form for men to see, receive and follow,

The words "Put on" in verse 11 mean literally to "envelope oneself" or "hide in" the armor of God. Herein is the clear conception of our weakness made available to His strength. Hiding in His armor is not a craven exhibition of cowardice; it is, rather the prudent appropriation of God's provision for our immediate and ultimate victory.

The word "truth" in Ephesians 6:14 is best understood as meaning sincerity, openness and truthfulness. It is a truthfulness of thought and life that is neither deceitful nor self-serving. It is a life void of hypocrisy. In short, it is a truth-dominated life that exhibits the qualities of Christian character essential to a consistent witness for Christ. It is this kind of character that establishes and maintains the effectiveness of a Christian soldier's efforts. No matter how shiny our armor may seem to be in our own eyes, it is irreparably tarnished before the world and fellow believers if we are not, in fact, sincere doers of the truth.

Israel My Glory
By: Elwood McQuaid

THE ARMOR OF GOD
(An Exercise)

Ephesians 6:10-17
Define Clearly Each Piece Of Armor.

1. Put on the Helmet of Salvation.
2. Gird your Loins with Truth.
3. Take the Shield of Faith.
4. Use the Sword of the Spirit.
5. Put on the Breastplate of Righteousness.

6. Shod your feet with the Gospel of Peace.

Why should we put on the Armor of God? (Vs. 11-13)

Resist Satan
James 4:7
Give yourself afresh to God.
Resist Satan in the name of Jesus.
Quote Scripture concerning the temptation you are facing.
Claim the victory that is yours in Christ.

THE WHOLE ARMOR OF GOD
Sermon Series by E.S. Caldwell
Pastor, Glad Tidings Assembly, Springfield, MO

All a Soldier Needs
Ephesians 6:10-13
  Introduction:
God never intended His children continually to "take it on the chin." He has provided armament, both defensive and offensive, to enable us to fight the powers of hell and win.

1. All the strength you need
   a. Spiritual strength for a spiritual battle. "Be strong – not in yourselves but in the Lord: (Ephesians 6:10, Phillips).
   b. Strength to avoid fainting (Isaiah 40:29).
   c. Strength to do all things through Christ (Philippians 4:13).
2. All the armor you need
   a. The armor is complete. "Put on the whole armor of God" (Ephesians 6:11).
   b. The armor is strong. "The weapons of our warfare are ... mighty through God" (II Corinthians 10:4).
   c. The armor is indispensable. "The day is at hand ... let us put on the armor of light" (Romans 13:12).
3. All Christians need this armor.

a. The battle is spiritual. "We wrestle not against flesh and blood" (Ephesians 6:12).
   b. The enemy is clever. We are up "against the wiles of the devil" (Ephesians 6:11, KJV); "all the strategies of and the deceits of the devil" (Amplified); "the devil's methods of attack" (Phillips); "tricks" (Living Bible). He has over 6,000 years' experience!
   c. The armor is effective. "Draw your strength from the Lord – from the mastery His power supplies. You must wear all the weapons in God's armory against those who have the mastery of the world, in these dark days" (Ephesians 6:10-12, Knox).

Conclusion:
Remember – you never fight alone (Deuteronomy 20:4). With God's help and the equipment He provides you can win. "Therefore, take up God's armor, then you will be able to stand your ground when things are at their worst to complete every task and still to stand" (Ephesians 6:13, NEB).

Protection for the Loins
Ephesians 6:14; II Samuel 11:1-7.
Introduction:
The first piece of armor Paul lists is for the loins. In the Bible, the loins usually represent a person's procreative powers – his or her sex life. Roman soldiers protected their loins by wearing a leather belt with armored leather straps attached, which formed a skirt-like covering. The Bible says, "Stand therefore, having your loins girt about with truth."

It is written of Christ, "Righteousness shall be the girdle of his loins, and faithfulness the girdle of his reins" (Isaiah 11:5). Christians should be true to God and faithful to righteousness in their sex life.

1. Four reasons for refusing to commit sexual sins.
   a. Because immorality brings God's judgment (Hebrews 12:4)

      b. Because immorality leads to other sins (James 1:14, 15). In David's case, adultery led to murder (II Samuel 11:2-5, 15).
      c. Because immorality is the way to the grave (Proverbs 5:3-5). It causes venereal disease.
      d. Because immorality is spiritual suicide. "He that doeth it destroyeth his own soul" (Proverbs 6:32).
2. Five ways to guard against sexual sins.
      a. Accept the fact that sexual purity is God's will for you. (I Thessalonians 4:3-7).
      b. Control your eyes. "I made a covenant with my eyes not to look with lust upon a girl. I know full well that Almighty God above sends calamity on those who do" (Job 31:1, 2, Living Bible).
      c. Discipline your physical passions (Romans 6:12-14).
      d. Avoid situations which might lead to temptation. "Flee fornication" (I Corinthians 6:18, KJV); "run away from sex sin" (Living Bible).
      e. Give sex its proper place in marriage (I Corinthians 7:2-5).

Conclusion:
Sex is a gift from God. He intends it to be a blessing, but sin can make it a curse. With our "loins girt about with truth" we can glorify God with our bodies and remain free from sexual sins.

Armor plate for the Heart
Ephesians 6:14
Matthew 15:10, 11, 15-20
    Introduction:
"Having on the breastplate of righteousness" (Ephesians 6:14). This piece of armor protects the heart. It suggests a life of righteousness is necessary to preserve the heart.

1. The heart is vital
      a. It is a vulnerable target. "Above all that you guard" watch your heart (Proverbs 4:23, Amplified).

b. It is the source of all your actions. "A good man produces good deeds from a good heart. And an evil man produces evil deeds from his hidden wickedness" (Luke 6:45, Living Bible).
   c. Righteousness should control his heart. Wear "the breastplate of integrity and of moral rectitude" (Amplified).
   Integrity is the quality of being of sound moral principle. *Rectitude* means conduct according to sound moral principle.
2. The breastplate is indispensable.
   a. Christ "put on righteousness as a breastplate" (Isaiah 59:17). No one could accuse Him of sin (John 8:40, Living Bible).
   b. Every Christian needs this breastplate. "When a man is clothed in righteousness, he is impregnable" (Barclay). See I John 3:4-8.
   c. It will defeat the devil. "Resist the devil" (James 4:7). The following verse (v. 8) shows this requires clean hands and a pure heart.
   d. It will make your witness effective. Love springs from the heart and without love we cannot win others for Christ.

Conclusion:
This Epistle was addressed to the church at Ephesus. In later years these people failed to fully protect their hearts, so the Lord warned them again: "Thou hast left thy first love" (Revelation 2:4).

Gospel Shoes
Introduction:
A few years ago there was a popular joke about some fainthearted soldiers who, in the midst of battle, took off their shoes and smelled "defeat." All joking aside, any soldier who fights a modern war without proper footwear are doomed to lose.

In spiritual warfare, it is just as essential that our feet be "shod with the preparation of the gospel of peace" (Ephesians 6:15).

1. Gospel shoes for standing firm.
"Stand therefore ... having shod your feet with the equipment of the gospel of peace" (RSV).

   a. Sure footing to withstand the enemy. Roman soldiers wore either heavy sandals or boots with hobnail-studded soles to ensure a foothold. An understanding of the Word prevents slipping (Psalm 73:2, 17; Matthew 13:19).
   b. Sure footing to complete the journey. Even though our way be rugged as a mountain path, God can keep us from slipping. "He gives me the surefootedness of a mountain goat:" (Psalm 18:33, Living Bible).
2. Gospel shoes for marching
   a. Soles that are not touchy. As bare feet are sensitive to rocks, nails and other objects on a path, so our spirits in the natural are touchy and easily hurt; but when shod with 'the gospel of peace," we will not stumble over personal offenses. We will go forward in spite of these (Hebrews 13:6).
   b. Soles that are tough. Nothing can trip God's soldiers if they master the Word (II Timothy 2:15).
3. Gospel shoes for carrying a message.
   a. God's messengers should be ready when opportunities arise (I Peter 3:15).
   b. God's messengers carry something precious. "Every teacher and interpreter of the Sacred Writings ... is like a householder who brings forth out of his storehouse treasure ..." (Matthew 13:59. Amplified).
   c. God enables His messengers to deliver their message (II Corinthians 3:5-6). The Romans built fine roads. They knew communication was the cement to hold their empire together, so they built 50,000 miles of roads for messengers (as well as for transporting goods and armies).
4. Gospel shoes for winning souls.
A Spanish version reads: "Having your feet shod with a joyful readiness to propagate the gospel of peace."

    a. There are people waiting the messengers of God. How shall they hear without a preacher? (Romans 10:14).
    b. There are believers who should become messengers of God. "Though by this time you ought to be teachers, you need someone to teach you" (Hebrews 5:12, NEB).

Conclusion:
The Father tell us to do something for the repentant sinners: "Put ... shoes on his feet" (Luke 15:22). Why? Because He wants every convert to stand firm, march forward, carry the message, and win souls. "Let the shoes on your feet be the gospel of peace" (NEB). "Stand therefore ... shod as ready messengers of the glad tidings of peace" (Conybeare).

Like the Christmas angels, each Christian is to echo the message of "peace on earth for all those pleasing him." (Luke 2:14, Living Bible).

The Shield of Faith
Ephesians 6:18; Luke 4:1-13
Introduction:
The word *faith* appears only twice in the Old Testament but 242 times in the new. Paul says, "Above all, be sure to take faith as your shield" (Ephesians 6:16, Phillips).

The Roman infantryman's shield was a large, oblong object carved from wood and covered with hide. In spiritual warfare there is no other part of the "armor of God" more important than the shield.

1. How to obtain it.
    a. Carve it from God's promises. "Faith cometh by hearing, and hearing by the Word of God." (Romans 10:17); "His faithful promises are your armor" (Psalm 91:4, Living Bible).
    b. Cover it with God's presence. See Psalm 5:12. Remember the Lord first protected man by His presence only; coverings made from skins came later (Genesis 3:21).
2. How to use it

a. Carry it with you at all times. "In every battle you will need faith as your shield to stop the fiery arrows aimed at you by Satan" (Living Bible). With this shield you are safe night and day. (Psalm 91:4-6).
b. Depend on it for protection. Never trust in yourself alone. "Live by faith, trusting Him in everything" (Hebrews 10:38, Living Bible). Let it protect your head (thought life; intellectual doubts), your heart (emotions, passions), your knees (prayer life), and your feet (daily walk).
c. Develop skill in using it. Memorize the Word; study its doctrine; put it to work when you encounter the devil. Each encounter will make you more skillful if you profit from past experiences.
d. Use it with boldness. With faith you can "quench all the fiery darts of the wicked." Whether the enemy be Satan or wicked men or sin in your own wicked self, faith can win. "This is the victory that overcometh the world, even our faith" (I John 5:4).

Conclusion:
Unbelief weakens us, dishonors us, saddens us, and makes us useless to God. Faith makes us happy, useful, and able to bring glory to our Lord. So hold onto your faith, Christian! Carry it confidently as your constant shield.

The Helmet of Salvation
Ephesians 6:17
I Thessalonians 5:1-9, 23
Introduction:
Since only a saved person can qualify to wear the armor of God, why is salvation listed as part of that armor? The answer may be found by understanding some of the ways the Bible uses the word *salvation*.

1. What is it?
The word appears about 45 times in the New Testament.

a. Sometimes it denotes deliverance from God's condemnation (Acts 4:12). This salvation is something a sinner receives instantly when he confesses his sin, repents, and accepts Jesus.
   b. Sometimes it denotes deliverance from sinful behavior (Philippians 2:12, 13). This is an ongoing process as shown in the Amplified: "Cultivate, carry out to the goal and full complete your own salvation."
   c. Sometimes it denotes deliverance from God's wrath (Hebrews 9:28) as in the Rapture. It is in this sense Paul uses the metaphor of the helmet. "And for a helmet, the hope of salvation" (I Thessalonians 5:8). He is saying, "Always protect yourself by living as though Jesus might return at any moment."
2. How is it worn?
   a. Wear it in honesty. "Let us then drop (fling away) the works and deeds of darkness and put on the (full) armor of light. Let us live and conduct ourselves honorably and becomingly" (Romans 12:12, 13, Amplified).
   b. Wear it in peaceableness and contentment. "Not in immorality and debauchery (sensuality and licentiousness), not in quarreling and jealousy" (Romans 13:13, Amplified). "Having food and raiment let us be therewith content" (I Timothy 6:8).

Conclusion:
Wear the helmet of salvation or you may lose your head! (He who misses the Rapture through careless living may literally lose his head).) The apostle's prayer for the believers is that their whole spirit and soul and body be preserved blameless unto the coming of our Lord Jesus Christ (I Thessalonians 5:23).

The Sword of the Spirit
Ephesians 6:17
II Corinthians 10:3-5
   Introduction:

John Wesley said: "We are to attack Satan, as well as secure ourselves; the shield in one hand and the sword in the other. Whoever fights with the powers of hell will need both."

1. What this weapon is

Roman soldiers carried short, two-edged swords called *macharia*. Christians are told to take "the sword of the Spirit, which is the word of God" (Ephesians 6:17). This Word is sharper than any two-edged sword (Hebrews 4:12).
   a. It is not a literal sword (Matthew 26:52), for that only leads to death.
   b. It is a sword that leads to life (Philippians 2:16).
   c. It is not a book but the message in the Book. In wielding the sword of the Spirit against the tempter, Jesus did not use the whole Bible. He wielded that particular saying of God which was appropriate to overcome His enemy (Matthew 4:4, 7, 10).
   d. Each individual passage of Scripture is a potential sword of the Spirit. If we store the Scriptures in our hearts and minds, the Holy Ghost will bring to our remembrance that which we need for each occasion (John 14:26).
2. What this weapon can do
   a. It can expose our true selves. "Cutting swift and deep ... exposing us for what we really are" (Hebrews 4:12, Living Bible).
   b. It can cut away all imperfections within the believer through its doctrine, reproof, correction and instruction in righteousness (II Timothy 3:16)
   c. It can capture every rebellions thought. "With these weapons I can capture rebels and bring them back to God, and change them into men whose hearts' desire is obedience to Christ" (II Corinthians 10:5, Living Bible).
3. What this weapon cannot do.
   a. It cannot help those who refuse to hear. Even Christ could not force faith on people (John 8:47).

      b. It cannot help those who refuse to believe. "It didn't do them [In the time of Moses] any good because they didn't believe it." (Hebrews 4:2, Living Bible).
4. How to use this weapon
      a. Use it as Christ did to defeat the devil (I John 2:14) and to bring life (John 6:63). Not to win arguments but to win souls.
      b. Use it in cooperation with the Holy Spirit. The Word is "the sword the Spirit wields" (Ephesians 6:17, Amplified).

Conclusion:

Jesus warned that in the last days His followers would need a word from God with which to answer their adversaries (Luke 21:12-15). In that hour the Lord "will give you power of utterance and a wisdom which no opponent will be able to resist or refute" (Luke 21:14, NEB). In the meantime, we are told to "concentrate on winning God's approval on being a workman with nothing to be ashamed of, and who knows how to use the word of truth to the best advantage" (II Timothy 2:15, Phillips).

The Weapon of Prayer
Ephesians 6:18
I Kings 8:44-50, 54
    Introduction:

"Praying always with all prayer and supplication in the Spirit, and watching threreunto all perseverance" (Ephesians 6:18). "Watching thereunto" carries the military idea of being on guard and keeping alert. Christians are to be vigilant in prayer. This is a mighty weapon. What a pity if it grows rusty!

1. When to pray
      a. Pray in the midst of conflict. Many weapons were used for Old Testament victories, including Ehud's dagger, Barak's sword, Jael's tent stake, and Shamgar's ox goad. Samson used a donkey's jawbone. But Samuel's weapon was prayer (I Samuel 7:9, 10).

    b. Pray when there is no conflict "Pray at all times – on every occasion, in every season" (Amplified). At no season is it safe not to 'watch and pray"(Matthew 26:41).
2. How to pray
    a. Use every method of prayer and supplication. Pray silently like Hannah, aloud like Elijah, alone like David, and in groups like the believers in Acts. "With all manner of prayer and entreaty" (Amplified). Don't be limited.
    b. Use every posture of prayer. Kneel with arms outstretched like Solomon, stand with head bowed like the publican; prostrate yourself like Jesus; pray when cramped into a ball like Jonah in the whale.
    c. Use all earnestness in prayer. "Supplication" means pleading. "Plead with Him, reminding Him of your needs" (Ephesians 6:18, Living Bible). "Be earnest and unwearied and steadfast in your prayer (life)" (Colossians 4:2, Amplified). "The earnest (heartfelt, continued) prayer of a righteous man makes tremendous power available" (James 5:16, Amplified). See Psalm 95:6, I Timothy 2:8, Acts 4:24; Hebrews 5:7; Jude 20.
3. Who helps us pray?
    a. The Spirit helps us pray in harmony with God's will. "The Holy Spirit helps us with our daily problems and in our praying. For we don't even know what we should pray for, nor how to pray as we should; but the Holy Spirit prays for us with such feeling that it cannot be expressed in words" (Romans 8:26, Living Bible).
    b. The Spirit enables us to pray with fervor. "With all earnestness of supplications in the Spirit" (Ephesians 6:18, Conybeare).
    c. The Spirit empowers our prayers. "Pray on every occasion in the power of the Spirit" (Ephesians 6:18, NEB). C.S. Lewis has Screwtape say to Wormwood, "Interfere at any price in any fashion when people start to pray, for real prayer is lethal to our cause."
4. For whom should we pray?

a. Pray for your fellow soldiers. We are not in this battle alone. We need one another. Therefore "keep praying earnestly for all Christians everywhere" (Ephesians 6:18, Living Bible).
b. Be alert to your fellow soldiers' needs. "Keep alert and watch with strong purpose and perseverance, interceding in behalf of all the saints (God's consecrated people)" (Ephesians 6:18, Amplified). Whenever you see a fellow Christian in danger, pray for him!
c. Intercede for spiritual leaders especially. Paul said, "Pray for me, too, and ask God to give me the right words as I boldly tell others about the Lord" (Ephesians 6:19, Living Bible).

Conclusion:
Don't worry about anything; instead pray about everything" (Philippians 4:6, Living Bible). Use the weapon of "all prayer" and you will be more than conqueror in every spiritual battle.

PRAYER TO WEAR THE ARMOR OF GOD
Author of Prayer-Unknown

Heavenly Father, I put on the armor of God with gratitude and praise. You have provided all I need to stand in victory against Satan and his kingdom.

I confidently take the belt of truth. Thank You that Satan cannot stand against the bold use of truth.

Thank You for the breastplate of righteousness which is mine by faith in Jesus Christ. I know that Satan must retreat before the righteousness of God.

You have provided the solid rock of peace. I claim the peace with God that is mine through justification. I desire the peace of God that touches my emotions and feelings through prayer and sanctification. (Philippians 4:6).

Eagerly, Lord, I lift up the shield of faith against all the blazing missiles that Satan fires at me. I know that You are my shield.

I recognize that my mind is a particular target of Satan's deceiving ways. I cover my mind with the powerful helmet of salvation.

With joy I lift the sword of the Spirit, which is the Word of God. I choose to live in its truth and power. Enable me to use Your Word to defend myself from Satan, and also to wield the sword well, to push Satan back, to defeat him.

Thank You, dear Lord, for prayer. Help me to keep this armor well oiled with prayer. All these petitions I offer You through the mighty name of our Lord Jesus Christ. Amen.

THE SHIELD

The shield, which was about two feet wide by four feet long, was used by soldiers to block thrusts of the enemy's sword as well as volleys of arrows. It was the maneuverable or moveable part of the armor that covered wherever it was needed. This moveable part of our armor is faith. Faith stands in the gap wherever defense is needed against the wiles of Satan. Faith defends us against his attacks of temptation, guilt, false doctrine, doubt, misunderstanding, and so on. The gift of faith is big enough to handle anything that Satan sends against us.

THE HELMET

The helmet protected the head. Our spiritual helmet must protect our minds from the lethal blows of Satan's vicious attacks against our salvation. One of the most important parts of our defense is our firm faith in eternal security. Our minds are the favorite area for Satan's attack. If he can plant a thought in our minds and get us to act on it, we are sunk.

Satan loves to take little known verses and passages out of context and hurl them at believers. He also uses some ministers to promote the perpetual insecurity of God's children. Many Christians are on the edge of a nervous breakdown because they are terrified that they have committed some unforgivable sin.

Many other Christians are ineffective as they work to keep themselves saved. Satan dances for joy at this kind of confusion caused by twisted Scripture. He always tries to knock off our helmets of security in our salvation. Keep yours on firmly.

THE SWORD

The sword is an offensive weapon. The Roman sword was called a *machaira* and it had a revolutionary design. Its blade was only twenty-four inches long. It was sharpened on both sides and sharply pointed on the end. This design was extremely effective because of the careful and extensive training the Roman legionnaire was given in its use. He could thrust and cut with his sword from any position so that he was never off balance or out of position.

Opposing soldiers of the day all had large swords that were usually only sharp on one side. The soldier had to bend his arm and swing at his opponent with a chopping motion. The Roman soldier would duck, catch his enemy off balance and finish him before he could get his arm back in position for another swing.

In the hands of a properly trained believer, our sword will never leave us off balance or out of position. The Sword of the Spirit is the Word of God that has been learned with combat knowledge. We must learn Scripture doctrinally to be able to use it effectively when under attack. A doctrine is simply all the Bible has to say on a given subject, organized in a logical manner so that it can be remembered and used when needed.

Our sword is the spoken word of God. Jesus used the sword of the Spirit in this manner when He was tempted by the devil in Luke 4:13. He quoted verses to Satan that exactly countered the temptations he hurled at him.

Sharpen your sword and practice using it!

PRAYER, OUR HEAVY ARTILLERY

"And pray in the Spirit on all occasions with all kinds of prayers and requests. With this in mind, be alert and always keep on praying for all the saints." (Ephesians 6:18)

We are to pray, filled with the Spirit, so that He can guide us in God's will and cause our prayers to be on target. We can also protect our flanks by praying for our fellow believers.

Having prepared, be ready to fight! We are to stand in the courage of faith on the confidence of our position in Christ when attacked by Satan.

"Resist him (Satan), standing firm in the faith …" (I Peter 5:9)

"Submit yourselves… to God. Resist the devil, and he will flee from you." (James 4:7)

THE WARRIOR'S PRAYER
Author Unknown

Heavenly Father,
Your warrior prepares for battle.
Today I claim victory over Satan by putting on
the whole armor of God!

I put on the Girdle of Truth!
May I stand firm in the truth of Your Word
so I will not be a victim of Satan's lies.

I put on the Breastplate of Righteousness!
May it guard my heart from evil
so I will remain pure and holy,
protected under the blood of Jesus Christ.

I put on the Shoes of Peace!
May I stand firm in the Good News of the Gospel
so Your peace will shine through me
And be a light to all I encounter.

I take the Shield of Faith!
May I be ready for Satan's fiery darts of
doubt, denial and deceit
so I will not be vulnerable to spiritual defeat.

I put on the Helmet of Salvation!
May I keep my mind focused on You
so Satan will not have a stronghold on my thoughts.

I take the Sword of the Spirit!
May the two-edged sword of Your Word
be ready in my hands
so I can expose the tempting words of Satan.

By faith your warrior has put on
the whole armor of God!
I am prepared to live this day in spiritual victory.
Amen!

Author of Prayer-Unknown.

X-A: SAYING "NO" TO ADDICTIONS

ADDICTIONS

In our world today, many, many people are bound by addictions. Drugs, alcohol, tobacco, prescription drugs are being consumed by people of all ages. The pressures of life seem to be overcoming not just the unsaved, but Christians as well. Many don't know which way to turn. It's important to let people know there is a way out.

I am using three different authors to present the answer.

SAYING "NO" TO ADDICTIONS
By: Duane Vander Klok

Everybody knows someone who struggles with addiction. Whether it is to alcohol, drugs, cigarettes, gambling, pornography or something as seemingly harmless as shopping, television or food, an addiction is serious business. Left unchecked, addictions have the power to ruin your life.

If you or someone you love is trapped in addiction's downward spiral, this article offers truth from God's Word that can help anyone get free and stay free from addiction.

A Vicious Cycle

Many people who are stuck in addictions have repeatedly called out to God to set them free. They've literally begged Him to take away their desire for food, drugs, cigarettes, pornography or whatever it is they are addicted to - only to find themselves still tormented by sinful desires. They want God to do it all, but there's more to it: He does His part, but we still have to say "no" to sin.

The Apostle Paul - who had a very dramatic salvation experience - wrote of his struggle in Romans 7:18-19. Anyone who has ever been addicted to anything can identify with him when he said, "I know that nothing good lives in me, that is, in my sinful nature. For I have the desire to do what is good, but I cannot carry it out. For what I do is not the good I want to do, no, the evil I do not want to do - this I keep on doing."

The Bible is clear when it talks about the conflict between the sinful nature and the Spirit. "For the sinful nature desires what is contrary to the Spirit, and the Spirit what is contrary to the sinful nature. They are in conflict with each other, so that you do not do what you want. The acts of the sinful nature are obvious; sexual immorality, impurity and debauchery; idolatry and witchcraft; hatred, discord, jealousy, fits of rage, selfish ambition, dissensions, factions and envy; drunkenness, orgies, and the like..." Galatians 5:17, 19-21.

Face it: your flesh would love to dominate your life - even after you are saved! Why? Because even though God makes you a new creation in Christ when you get saved (II Corinthians 5:17), you still have the same old body and it still leans toward doing things the old, pre-Christian way. God had done His part, but you have to do yours. You have to determine daily to walk in the Spirit and say "no" to the flesh.

Victory Begins in the Mind

Your mind is like a thermostat. Where you set it determines whether you will live hot, cold or spiritually lukewarm, and it determines whether you will say "yes" or "no" to sin. In Romans 8:5, Paul wrote, "Those who live according to the sinful nature have their minds set on what that nature desires; but those who live in accordance with the Spirit have their minds set on what the Spirit desires."

He said it even more plainly in Colossians 3:1-2, where he wrote, "If then you were raised with Christ, seek those things which are above, where Christ is sitting at the right hand of God. Set your mind on things above, not on things on the earth" (NKJV).

Every action and every behavior is determined by your mindset. It has been said that when you sow a thought, you reap an act; when you sow an act, you reap a habit; when you sow a habit, you reap a character; and when you sow a character, you reap a destiny. It all starts with where you set your mind. In I Corinthians 6:12, Paul said, "Everything is permissible for me - but not everything is beneficial. Everything is permissible for me - but I will not be mastered by anything." Paul recognized that some things have the potential to control us, to become strongholds in our lives. Just as Paul set his mind, you also have the ability to set your mind to not be controlled by anything or anyone other than the Lord,

Romans 12:2 says, "Do not conform any longer to the patterns of this world, but be transformed by the renewing of your mind. Then you will be able to test and approve what God's will is - His good, pleasing and perfect will." Renewing your mind by reading and meditating on God's Word literally sets your mind where God intends it to be. It replaces the devil's lies with God's truth so you can say "yes" to God and "no" to the pull of addiction.

Three Lies Exposed

Here are three of the devil's favorite lies:
1. You cannot change,
2. You are a prisoner of your past,
3. You are unloved and unacceptable - even to God.

The devil wants you to think that you are a poor helpless sinner who has no hope of changing. He wants to make you think that because of your past sins (whether they were 10 years ago or just 10 minutes ago) you are unworthy of receiving anything from God. And one of Satan's most effective lies is aimed at making people - even Christians - feel alone and isolated.

Here are some powerful truths from God's Word that replace the devil's lies:

1. The old person I used to be was crucified with Christ (Romans 6:4). I am a new creation (II Corinthians 5:17), who is dead to sin (Romans 6:2). I am a righteous saint (II Corinthians 5:21).
2. There is no more guilt and condemnation in Christ (Romans 8:1). God has taken care of my sins - all of them: past, present and future - at the cross.
3. God loves me and accepts me. He will never leave me or forsake me. (Hebrews 13:5, 6) and has given me everything I need for life and godliness (II Peter 1:3), every spiritual blessing (Ephesians 1:3) and victory (I Corinthians 15:57).

Receive God's Mercy

No matter how long you or someone you love has struggled with addiction, freedom is possible. It begins with God's mercy.

Paul wrote, "At one time we too were foolish, disobedient, deceived and enslaved by all kinds of passions and pleasures ... but when the kindness and love God our Savior appeared, He saved us, not because of righteous things we had done, but because of His mercy" (Titus 3:3-4).

You may fail, but God's mercy never will. I John 1:9 says, "If we confess our sins. He is faithful and just and will forgive us our sins and purify us from all unrighteousness."

To receive God's forgiveness and the freedom from addiction that accompanies it, you can pray this prayer:

Dear God,

I confess that I have been addicted to _____, I repent of this addiction and ask you to forgive me and help me to begin again. I confess that I have been in bondage to _____, and I renounce any and all involvement with it. I ask, by the blood of Jesus Christ and the power of your Holy Spirit, that You set me free. Thank You for loving me, forgiving me and setting me free.

In Jesus' Name,
Amen.

The Choice Is Yours

God will not force you to do the right things. He will love you, equip you, put people in your path to help you, and even guide you, but you still have to make the choice to say "no" to temptation. As you daily make the hard choices, it will get easier to say "no" over time.

Whatever you do, do not believe the lie that you are hopeless. With God's help and the right attitude, you can stay free from addiction,

> "For the grace of God that brings salvation has appeared to all men. It teaches us to say 'No" to ungodliness and worldly passions and to live self-controlled, upright and godly lives in this present age..." (Titus 2:11-12)

(All scriptures are from the New International Version of the Bible unless otherwise stated.)

Our prayer for you is that you would live each day totally free in Christ. If you'd like someone from our team to agree with you in prayer - and especially if you have never received Jesus Christ as your Savior - please contact us at: 800-988-5120 or at walkingbyfaith.tv.

X-B: HOW TO SAY NO TO A STUBBORN HABIT
HOW TO SAY NO TO A STUBBORN HABIT
Even When You Feel Like Saying Yes

By: Dr. Irwin Lutzer

I. Can God change His people?

Conditions:
1. You must believe God is good.
2. You are fully responsible for your behavior.
3. You must believe that deliverance is possible. (You must deal with your past before you can experience freedom in the future.)

II. Handling temptation God's way.
1. As you think of that sin you want to overcome, first thank God for this temptation and the opportunity it represents in your life.
2. Take a tour through your life, jotting down areas that need work.
3. After you have had time to reflect on your private struggles, give yourself and your problem completely to God.
4. Realize that your ultimate goal is not victory, but God Himself.

Prayer

Lord, I confess my sin, particularly my rebellion against your authority. In agreeing that I have sinned, I also agree that this sin must be forsaken. Thank You for Your forgiveness,

I am grateful for this powerful temptation which gives me the chance to prove that I love You more than any pleasure in the world. I thank You that the temptation is not greater than I can bear, and I rejoice at how You will use it in my life.

I look forward to getting to know You better, and I am glad that You have sent me this trial as a reminder of how desperately I need You. Help me to remember to give thanks at all times and in all circumstances.

In Jesus' Name
Amen.

III. Causes of repeated failures,
    1. Pride
    2. Sensuality
    3. Covetousness.

What would God want to put in the place of this habit?
A. In Christ you are already dead to your sinful passions.
B. You must admit the need for faith in your daily life. When we shift our attention to the completed work of the cross and insist on our privileges, our old self surrenders to God's authority. Through faith and faith alone we personalize our victory. Begin each day at the Cross, Take time to:
    a. Give thanks that Christ has already conquered the problems you will face that day.
    b. Accept by faith the victory Christ won at the cross - before you are tempted to sin. The most important ingredient in releasing the Spirit's power in our lives is faith. Our faith is strengthened by making the Word of God the focus of our attention, and developing the habit of praise,
C. Sinful habits cannot be broken without replacing them with righteous ones. Freedom comes by filling your mind with God's thoughts. To diffuse the power of sin, you need to have your thought patterns replaced by the Word of God. Every temptation, vice, or sinister motive comes to you by your thoughts; these must be brought under the control of the Spirit.
D. Prepare for Battle - II Corinthians 10:3-5
    1. Identify the alien thoughts that you want replaced,
    2. Be prepared for the discipline of spiritual warfare. Only a Christian who is disciplined in the Word of God can rest in the Lord.
    3. Be prepared to memorize the Word of God. Psalm 119:11.
    4. Use your artillery. Claim God's promises in the morning. (Luke 1:37, Romans 8:28, Philippians 4:13) Choose

beforehand to claim God's promises for whatever circumstances you expect to encounter.

So far you have your sins identified, you've decided to set aside 20 minutes for God each morning, and you've even got some passages of Scripture to work with. Now what? What should you do tomorrow morning? Your strategy begins the moment you awake in the morning. Those moments between waking up and getting your feet on the floor are crucial. The seeds of discouragement, anger, and lust begin here. While still in bed, thank God for the rest He has given you. Then give the new day to the Lord. Consciously commit your mind, opportunities, and time to Him. Remind yourself of God's promises. "For nothing will be impossible with God" (Luke 1:37). Reminding ourselves of God's promises gives us the perspective on life.

Then after you're out of bed and reasonably awake, read a chapter from the Bible, observing what God is saying to you. Then spend some time to prepare your mind for the particular temptation you will face that day. Let's suppose your boss habitually irritates you. An hour after you arrive at work, you wish you could scream. If you wait until your boss shouts at you before you decide how you will respond, you'll probably react in anger. Use the Word of God in anticipation. During your time with God in the morning, recite the verses you have memorized and claim Christ's victory before your boss blows his fuse.

The same principle applies whether your problem is gluttony, addiction, worry, or greed. Claim God's promises for that particular day. Tell Him that with His help you resolve to choose for Him, rather than the world.

But remember, if you wait until temptation comes to decide how you will react, you've waited too long! Choose beforehand to claim God's promises for whatever circumstances you expect to encounter.

Then, during the day, learn to obey the first promptings of the Holy Spirit. If you are tempted to enjoy a sensual fantasy, deal with those thoughts immediately. Each of us knows when we let our minds skip across that invisible line into forbidden territory. The moment we do so, we sense we are violating the purity that the Holy Spirit desires. That is the moment to say, "I reject these thoughts in the name of Jesus." And then quote the passages of Scripture you have learned for that temptation. With time, your sensitivity to the Holy Spirit will develop.

Most important, learn to switch topics on the flesh and the devil.

You can do this with any temptation you face. Simply use your temptation as an alarm system — a signal to give praise to God. If, for example, you fear cancer (since one out of four people in the U.S. will have the disease, your fears may have a statistical basis), use that fear as an opportunity to give glory to God. Quote Romans 8:35-39 or read Psalms 103, 144, or 145. Then thank God for all the blessing you have in Christ. Thank Him for forgiveness, for His sovereignty, power and love. In this way, your stumbling block will be changed into a stepping-stone. You'll be praising rather than pouting.

If your problem is gluttony, decide that your hunger pangs will be a reminder to divert your attention to God's Word. Memorize a verse of Scripture, pray for your missionary friends, sing a song. By outlining and following a specific strategy to resist temptation, you will eventually be free from its grip.

Finally, do not be discouraged by the frequency of the same temptation. If you have lived a long time with sinful thought patterns, the strongholds of your imagination will not be easily toppled. Furthermore, you must recognize the possibility that you are not merely confronting yourself, but satanic forces as well. Satan's most used weapon is discouragement. After you have rejected insidious thoughts, he delights in having them pop back into your mind. The most important insulation you have against satanic attack is personal righteousness — confessing and forsaking sin. And as you apply the above principles consistently, Satan and his forces will be weakened. Eventually they will flee.

How long does it take for your mind to be renewed? That depends. Some Christians who apply these principles recognize a noticeable difference within a week. Others, who are steeped in decades of sin, may need as long as 30 days before they can say, "I am free!" And, of course, no one reaches perfection. The more we meditate on the Word, the more clearly we see new areas of our lives that need to be changed. Subtle motives often surface only after long exposure to the light of God's Word.

I'm convinced that God intends us to be free from mental bondage. His Word is the resource by which our thoughts can become obedient to God.

Even Christ, the eternal Son of God, "learned obedience from the things which He suffered" (Hebrews 5:8). "And if He, the Son, sets you free, you shall be free indeed" (John 8:36).

12 STEPS TO AN OVERCOMING LIFE
LaVerne Trip Ministries

Step 1

We admitted we were powerless over our dependencies - that our lives had become unmanageable.

Meditation Scriptures:

Matthew 9:36; Romans 7:18-20; Psalm6:2-4; Psalm31:9,10; Psalm 38:1-9; Psalm 44:15,16; Psalm 72:12,13.

Step 2

Came to believe that a Power greater than ourselves could restore us to sanity.

Meditation Scriptures:

Matthew 12:18-21; Mark 9:23, 24; Luke 13:10-13; John 6:63; John 12:46; Psalm 18:1-3; Psalm 142.

Step 3

Made a decision to turn our will and our lives over to the care of God as we understood Him.

Meditation Scriptures:

Matthew 11: 28-30; Matthew 16:21-26; Ephesians 2:8, 9; Psalm 3:5,6; Psalm 23; Psalm 91:1-4; Proverbs 3:5, 6.

Step 4

Made a searching and fearless moral inventory of ourselves.

Meditation Scriptures:
Matthew 23:23-28; Luke 12:1-6; Romans 13:11-14; I Corinthians 4:19, 20; Galatians 6:3-5; Proverbs 5:3-6; Proverbs 16:2, 3.

Step 5
Admitted to God, to ourselves, and to another human being the exact nature of our wrongs.
Meditation Scriptures:
Luke 15:17-20; Acts 19:18; II Corinthians 10:3-5; Hebrews 4:12-16; James 5:16; I John 1:8,9; Proverbs 28:13,14.

Step 6
We are entirely ready to have God remove all these defects of character.
Meditation Scriptures:
Romans: 6,11,12; Ephesians 4:17-23; Colossians 3:5-8; I Peter 1:13-16; I John 4:18; Revelation 3:19, 20; Psalm 119:28-40.

Step 7
Humbly asked Him to remove our shortcomings.
Meditation Scriptures:
Matthew 18:4; Acts 3:19; Hebrews 12:5-11; I Peter 5; 6, 7; I John 5:14,15; Psalm 32:6-8; Psalm 37:23, 24.

Step 8
Make a list of all persons we had harmed, and became willing to make amends to them all.
Meditation Scriptures:
Matthew 18:21-35; Luke 6:37, 38; Luke 19:8; John 13:34, 35; I Corinthians 13; II Timothy 1:7; James 4:11, 12.

Step 9
Make direct amends to such people wherever possible, except when to do so would injure them or others.
Meditation Scriptures:
Matthew 5:9; Romans 15:2; Philippians 1:9-11; Colossians 4:5,6; Philemon 8-17; Psalm 51:14-17; Proverbs 16:20-24.

Step 10

Continued to take personal inventory and when we were wrong promptly admitted it.

Meditation Scriptures:

Mark 14:38; Romans 12:3; I Thessalonians 5:17-2; Hebrews 2:1-3; I Peter 2:11; Psalm 85:8, 9; Psalm 103:8-18.

Step 11

Sought through prayer and meditation to improve our conscious contact with God as we understood Him, praying only for knowledge of His will for us and the power to carry that out.

Meditation Scriptures:

John 4:13,14; Romans 8:26-28; Galatians 2:20; Philippians 4:6-9; Titus 3:1-7; Psalm 84:5-12; Psalm 127:1, 2.

Step 12

Having had a spiritual awakening as the result of these steps, we tried to carry this message to others, and to practice these principles in all our affairs.

Meditation Scriptures:

Mark 5: 18-20; 1 Corinthians 9:22-27; I Corinthians 15:10; I Timothy 1:12-16; Psalm 92:1-4; Psalm 96:1, 2; Proverbs 31:26-31.

CHAPTER X

SEPARATION

Separation is a word we don't hear preached about much anymore. Perhaps it's because we have become so much like the world that it's hard to distinguish whether a person is a Christian or not. In II Corinthians 6:14-18, God says, "Be ye not unequally yoked together with unbelievers: for what fellowship hath righteousness with unrighteousness? And what communion hath light with darkness? And what concord hath Christ with Belial? Or what part hath he that believeth with an infidel? And what agreement hath the temple of God with idols? For ye are the temple of the living God; as God hath said, I will dwell in them, and walk in them; and I will be their God, and they shall be my people. Wherefore come out from among them, and be ye separate, saith the Lord, and touch not the unclean thing: and I will receive you. And will be a Father unto you, and ye shall be my sons and daughters, saith the Lord Almighty." That pretty well speaks for itself.

Dr. George Sweeting shares four Bible guidelines for separation. (George Sweeting, *How to Begin the Christian Life,* Moody Press, Chicago, IL, 1976, pg. 121-123)

    A. Keep in mind the principle of ownership. (I Corinthians 6:19)

B. Our conduct as Christians should be governed by our awareness of responsibility for others. (I Corinthians 8:13) "How will my conduct affect others?"
C. Keep in mind the effect your choices are on yourself. (I Corinthians 9:27) "What will my involvement do to my personal effectiveness for God?"
D. Whatever we do should always be to the glory of God. (I Corinthians 10:31, I Thessalonians 5:22, Romans 12:2, Galatians 1:4) We are to be transformers not conformers. (James 4:4, I John 2:15)

If we keep these guidelines in mind, we can't go too far astray.

PRINCIPLES FOR LIVING – "SEPARATION" AND "STANDARDS"
By: Rev. Ralph Sutera
Psalm 97:10; 139:23-24; I Thessalonians 4:3

1. The desire for GODLY LIVING is the result of the work of the Holy Spirit and the LIBERATING POWER of Christ. Because this LIBERTY is in Christ, it is therefore REGULATED in the Bible. John 8:32, 36; II Corinthians 3:17.
   a. Liberty is not given to make possible self-indulgence. Galatians 5:13.
   b. Liberty is not used as an excuse for enslaving habits. I Corinthians 6:12b
   c. Liberty is not a license for hurting other Christians. I Corinthians 8:9
2. The operation of the Holy Spirit within us causes us to LONG TO BE CONFORMED TO the image of Jesus Christ. We understand this to be our MAIN PURPOSE IN LIFE. The person who does not surrender his life to the control of the Holy Spirit will NEVER UNDERSTAND and submit to God's standards. Ephesians 1:3-6; Colossians 1:27-28;
3. STANDARDS: "the *outworking* of the Spirit in our lives in the context of the culture in which we find ourselves." We are daily changed into the image of the Lord from glory to glory, beholding

His Glory through the ministry of the Holy Spirit. II Corinthians 3:17-4:7.

4. SEPARATION: NOT a process of subtraction by which something is taken away from us, leaving certain lacks in our lives. NOT a ruling out of our lives' experiences which are dear to the heart of man. Rather, it is the pulling away from something in order to GET SOMETHING IN ITS PLACE. It is the ATTACHMENT TO THE ETERNAL.

NOT A SACRIFICE TO BECOME UNWORLDLY, but rather a privilege to give our lives to more fundamental and lasting joys than the world can ever offer. It is no sacrifice to give up onions and garlic for a delicious T-bone steak! Psalm 16:11; John 15:11; Ephesians 3:19.

5. DIFFERENCE BETWEEN A BELIEF AND A CONVICTION: A belief is something a man holds, but a CONVICTION is something that holds the man! Many accept the "belief" of the Christian religion, but spiritual maturity results ONLY WHEN the CONVICTION OF WALKING WITH GOD grips us. When Christianity is merely a "belief," you will continue to live in CARNALITY AND SELF-GLORY while professing to be "saved." II Corinthians 5:14.

6. TWENTIETH CENTURY CULTURE VERSUS GOD'S PRINCIPLES!

    a. Society says everything is "RELATIVE" and there are no absolutes. Every man becomes a god to himself and does right and wrong accordingly.

THREE-FOLD SIN OF THIS CULTURE: Our culture is one of situational ethics, where the end justifies the means.

    1. Minimize sin – Why? Because we have...
    2. HUMANIZED GOD – why? Because we have ...
    3. DEIFIED MAN! Man has become a god to himself.

a. Disease from the Garden of Eden. Genesis 3:4-5.
b. Characterized humanity since. Proverbs 1:29-31; 3:5-7; 20:2a; 30:11-13; Isaiah 5:21; Hosea 10:13.

"Every man did that which was right in his own eyes." Judges 17:6. 21:25.

  c. SIGN OF LAST DAYS! II Timothy 3:1-5
  b. God ALWAYS DEALS IN ABSOLUTES as far as governing principles of life are concerned. He is the same – yesterday, today and forever. Hebrews 13:8. His Word is established in heaven and is exalted even above His Name. Blessing comes in the counsel of His Word. Psalm 1:10-2; 138:2.
  c. WALKING WITH GOD means allowing God to BREAK THE CHARM AND INFLUENCE of the cultural patterns that our society has impressed on us. Evidence of a "crucified life" is when we NO LONGER RATIONALIZE God's truth to fit OUR life-style, but we are ready for our life-patterns to be crushed and molded into conformity to Christ.

WHAT ABOUT QUESTIONABLE THINGS?

 1. Is it for the glory of God? I Corinthians 10:31
 2. Will it cause others to stumble? I Corinthians 8:13
 3. Do others have a conscience against it? Romans 14:15
 4. Will it lead to sin? James 1:13-15
 5. What effect will it have upon the unsaved? Titus 2:7-8
 6. Does it harm my body? I Corinthians 3:16-17, I Corinthians 6:9
 7. Will it hinder my testimony? Matthew 5:16, I Timothy 4:12
 8. Does it keep me from my duty? Eph 5:16, I Timothy 4:12
 9. Is it of faith? Romans 14:23
 10. Does it hurt my own conscience? I John 3:20-21, I Timothy 3:9

SIX STEPS TO SUCCESSFUL CHRISTIAN LIVING
             By: Bobby Jackson

SANCTIFICATION – Means to set apart.
 To follow Christ means to give up as well as to give. It is hard to be a pleasing servant if one is a reluctant disciple.

SPECIFIC QUESTIONS TO "ASK" ABOUT QUESTIONABLES
By: Rev. Ralph Sutera

The list below is NOT designed as legalistic "dos" and "don'ts," but as Scriptural GUIDELINES. Nor is it exhaustive. The closer we "walk with God," the more clearly we see and desire His HOLY character to be OUR life-style! The "correct" answer to any one specific question MAY NOT always in itself be the thing to do, but it is essential to consider each question prayerfully.

I. HOW DOES IT RELATE TO MY OWNER? (God)
  a. Can it be done in the Lord's Name? I Timothy 6:1; Colossians 3:17; II Corinthians 5:17-20a
  b. Will it please God or man? Colossians 3:23; I John 3:22
  c. Can it glorify God? Can He bless and use it for HIS glory? I Corinthians 6:20; I Corinthians 10:23,31; Proverbs 10:22
  d. Does it hamper my enjoyment of God? Psalm 16:11; 149
  e. Will it help me keep the first two greatest commandments? Matthew 22:37-39
  f. Am I sure it is God's will? Psalm 147:1-2,20; Ephesians 6:6; Hebrews 13:21; James 4:15
  g. Am I delighted about standing before God to give account some day of the things in question? Matthew 25:21,23; Luke 19:17; I Corinthians 3:11-14; II Corinthians 5:10
  h. Is it putting God's desires ahead of my own? Matthew 6:33
  i. Will it enable me to keep Christ preeminent? Colossians 1:18b
  j. Is it worthy of God's Kingdom? I Thessalonians 2:12; II Thessalonians 1:6; Colossians 1:10
  k. Would it be out of character for Christ Himself to do? I Peter 2:21
  l. Would it cause God to "blush"? Hebrews 2:11; 11:16
  m. Does it grieve or quench God's Spirit? Ephesians 4:30; I Thessalonians 5:19

n Does it "clip" the wings of faith or hinder my prayers being answered? Mark 11:22-26; Heb 11:1, 6; I John3:20-22; I Peter 3:7; James 1:5-6; I Timothy2:8

II HOW DOES IT RELATE TO OTHERS? (People in general)
  a. Does it involve the wrong company? II Corinthians 6:14-16
  b. Does its appearance affect my witness and take the keen edge off of my fulfilling the Great Commission? Matthew5:13-14; 28:18-20; I Thessalonians 5:22; I Peter3:15
  c. Does it indicate friendship with the world? Romans 12:2; James4:4
  d. Would I want someone else to do the SAME thing to me? Luke 6:31
  e. Can I encourage someone else to do it WITH me? Psalm148; Proverbs27:17
  f. Will it cause others to stumble? Matthew 5:16; Romans14:13, 21; 15:1; I Corinthians 8:9, 12-13; I Corinthians 9:19-23
  g. Is it wise in the sight of non-Christians? Has it the appearance of wrong or evil? Romans 14:16; Philippians 2:15; Colossians4:5; I Corinthians 8:19-23; II Corinthians 8:21; I Timothy 3:7
  h. Will it offend? Acts 24:16; Romans 15:2; I Corinthians L0:24, 32; II Corinthians 6:3; Hebrews 10:24
  i. Is it a good example? I Corinthians 11:1; I Thessaloniansl:7; I Timothy 4:12; Titus 2:7
  j. Will it help my neighbor? Matthew19:19b; 22:39; Romans 15:2; I Corinthians 10:24
  k. How does it relate to my responsibility regarding "'submission"? Does it honor my parents (Matthew 19:19; Ephesians 6:l-3; Colossians 3:20); church authority (I Thessalonians 5:12-13; Hebrews 13:7, 17); school (I Peter 5:5a); government (Titus 3:11; Matthew 22:21); employer-employee (Ephesians6:5-9); etc., etc., etc.?

III. HOW DOES IT RELATE TO MY OPPOSITION? (Satan) Ephesians6:10-18; II Corinthians 10: 3-5

    a. Is it a possible yielding to Satan? James 4:7; I Peter 5:9; I Corinthians 10:20
    b. Is it a victory or a surrender? Romans 6:13; 8:37; I Corinthians 15:57
    c. Will Satan be GLAD if I do it? Do I help or hinder his cause? Whose side am I on when doing it? John 8:44; Ephesians 6:11-12; I Peter 5:8; James 4:4
    d. Is it of the world's evil system opposed to God? I John 2:15-16; I John 5:19

IV.   HOW DOES IT RELATE TO MY ON-GOING? (Myself)
    a. Will it weaken my body? I Corinthians 6:15-20; I Timothy 5:12; I Peter 1:16
    b. How does it affect my thinking, personality, moral and spiritual nature? Philippians 4:8; 2:5; II Corinthians 10:3-4; Titus 1:15
    c. Will it enrich or impoverish my life? Psalm 84:11; Proverbs 10:22; I Corinthians 10:23
    d. Will it deepen or lessen my interest in spiritual things? Will it lead me to a holier, more separated life? Romans 8:5-6; I Peter 1:15; Hebrews 12:1-2
    e. Is it "providing" for the flesh? Romans 13:14
    f. Will it purify or cause "war" in the soul? I Peter 1:22; 2:11
    g. Is it a faithful discharge of responsibility? Titus 3:8
    h. Can it become an enslaving habit? Romans 6:16; I Corinthians 6:12
    i. Is it wise and proper stewardship of my time, talents, money, energy, etc.? Matthew 13:22; I Corinthians 4:2; Ephesians 5:15-16; Colossians 4:5
    j. Is it expedient as well as "lawful"? I Corinthians 10:23
    k. What attitude prompts me? What intentions motivate me? Proverbs 23:7
    l. What values am I about to embrace, their purposes, results? I John 2:17
    m. Am I prepared to reap all the consequences? Numbers 32:23; Galatians 6:7
    n. Do I "feel" uneasy about it? Romans 14:22; I John 3:20-22

o. Is there ANY doubt whatsoever about it? Romans 14:23
p. Does it say "amen" to the doctrine I profess? Ephesians 4:1; Philippians 1:27; Titus 2:10
q. Does it stand the test of wise counsel? Proverbs 11:14; 15:22
r. Can it be done in LOVE? Mark 12:3; John 15:12, 17; Galatians 5:22; Hebrews 10:24; James 2:8

V. HOW DOES IT RELATE TO MY ONENESS? (Body of Christ)
A. My relationship to the "Body" and "fellowship of the saints" is one of the most VITAL factors governing "QUESTIONABLES." Generally, everything else will fit right in place when THIS relationship is RIGHT!
B. I Timothy 4:12 "...be thou an EXAMPLE of the BELIEVERS in word, conversation (manner of life), in charity (love) in spirit, in faith, in purity."
C. AS MY BEING A SPIRIT-FILLED BELIEVER:
(1) Does my action cause ANY part of the "Body" to suffer? Does it alienate godly people? Does it present a "problem" for the godly to be "free" around me? I Corinthians 12:26
(2) Does my action create ANY question about where I really stand in the church? Does it allow me to be accepted in ALL situations? I Peter 3:15
(3) What influence do I have and impression do I make on younger or "weaker" Christians? Proverbs 27:17; Romans 15:1-8
(4) What does my attitude, action, or appearance do to the "good" I am seeking to accomplish for God? Is it obeying the injunction to "let not your good be EVIL spoken of" and to "AVOID the appearance of evil"? Romans 14:16; I Thessalonians 5:22
(5) Does it take the "sharpness" out of my life and hinder me from having the GREATEST possible influence in serving the "Body" through exercising my spiritual gifts properly? Does it affect the CREDIBILITY of my testimony? Romans 15:1; Galatians 6:1-2; Eph 4:11-16

(6) Will my decision tend to bring credit or discredit, to the cause of Christ in the community? Will it become more DIFFICULT for my church to do its work of reaching the world for Christ? Philippians 2:15

CHAPTER XI

RESTITUTION AND RECONCILIATION GUIDELINES

ථි

By: Rev. Ralph Sutera
Matthew 5:23-24; 6:12; 18:21 - Acts 24:16 - I Timothy 1:5, 19

1. RESTITUTION MUST ALWAYS BE A BLESSING — never a curse or burden. What God commands you to do will always end in blessing. It should not be attempted until you are certain it will "bless." TIMING is so important. DON'T RUSH IN RECKLESSLY. We are to EDIFY each other.

2. RESTITUTION RESULTS IN LOVE. It should cause more love for each other than you had before. FULL JOY comes when restitution is proper and complete.

3. RESTITUTION IS A MATTER OF OBEDIENCE. Don't sin by disobedience and expect God's blessing. Restitution evidences to man that a transaction has already been made with God. BE COMMITTED to making restitution when needed, in GOD'S TIMING.

4. RESTITUTION SHOULD WAIT FOR GOD TO PREPARE THE WAY. He provides the circumstances to bring restitution about. In some situations there is NO DOUBT or question about immediate action. In others, GOD needs to take the initiative. Begin by RESTING the case with God. Pray, "Lord, I am personally willing

to make restitution and will ALLOW THEE to take the initiative in preparing the way." When He does, ACT accordingly. It is just as important that the Lord prepares the other party to receive you as it is your being willing to go to him. As you are prayerfully "tuned" to Him, God will make it clear. Sometimes the reception may not be to YOUR LIKING, but when you move in God's way, it will be the way HE PLANNED to bring about HIS RESULTS IN HIS TIMING.

5. RESTITUTION PROVIDES AN OPPORTUNITY TO MINISTER. Often the other party is in need of a "bridge" on which to cross from his self-centeredness into positive obedience to God. Your example and making the move in his direction may free him to honestly face his own need in a way he has desired but has not been able to fulfill. In some cases merely your moving toward him "preaches" a powerful and convicting sermon to his soul, though THAT IS NOT YOUR MOTIVATION in going.

6. RESTITUTION IS ALWAYS UNILATERAL- always one-sided. Never look for the other person to take the blame or even share in the blame. Restitution is specifically a matter of settling MY WRONGNESS. It deals only with MY BLAME, MY WRONGNESS, in a given matter and MUST NEVER be related to the possibility that someone else was implicated in my wrong. It is dealing with the attitudes of my own heart that even allow the situation to remain.

By understanding MY SOLE RESPONSIBILITY to make restitution, I may move straight to the issue, avoiding the snare of thinking that I must first establish a certain kind of delicate "treaty" with the other party. God's work in another life is HIS BUSINESS, though Satan will tempt me to "share" God's responsibility. Therefore, leave the other party with God. DO YOUR PART. Be assured that if God asks you to do it, He will not only create the circumstances, but He will also PROVIDE THE RESOURCES NEEDED for you to carry it out.

7. RESTITUTION IS NEVER "IF." It is never predicated by the statement, "IF I have offended you" or "IF I have hurt you." The "Please forgive me IF I have been an offense" type restitution WILL NEVER settle anything or produce God's results. If restitution deals with MY blame, then it must be that I HAVE offended,

hurt, or allowed a bitterness to remain. It then should be "Please forgive me. I am sorry and ask your forgiveness."

8. RESTITUTION NEVER GUARANTEES OR PRECLUDES A "RIGHT" RESPONSE. At the point you ask forgiveness, you are not responsible or guaranteed a positive, "right" response. Commit that to God.

9. RESTITUTION MUST ALWAYS BE AS BROAD AS THE OFFENSE BUT NEED NEVER BE ANY BROADER THAN THE OFFENSE. Deal with GOD ALONE about PRIVATE SINS of the mind and body. These should never be included in restitution. When the other party KNOWS NOTHING about it, DEAL ONLY WITH GOD. Never say, "I have had some BAD THOUGHTS about you" or "I RESENTED YOU" or "I have had LUSTFUL THOUGHTS toward you and I want you to forgive me." Go to the other party ONLY WHEN he clearly knows about the situation. If you have shared these thoughts or feelings with a third party, go to him and let him know you have made this right with God. GO NO FURTHER UNDER ANY CIRCUMSTANCES. Some have "created" thoughts in the other party's mind that were not there previously and "created" a further problem, resulting in continued bitterness and resentment. Private lustful thoughts expressed to the other party can generate these same thoughts in his mind and precipitate a sinful immoral relationship. BE VERY CAREFUL.

Though PRIVATE SINS, some people feel strongly that they "must" say something to the person EVEN THOUGH it is not necessary and he knows nothing about it. If you are strongly compelled that this is necessary, always BE POSITIVE, SPEAK IN LOVE, EDIFY, and make TANGIBLE EXPRESSIONS that confirm your love. Never say, "I am sorry for RESENTING you, please forgive me." Say something like this: "I just want you to know that God has put so much love in my heart for you that I have never loved you more than I do right now. There have been times I SHOULD HAVE loved you more, but I thank God for giving me so much love for you now." Follow with tangible acts that confirm your love for him, build him up and bless his life in Christ.

PERSONAL SINS affecting you and another person must be dealt with at that level alone. PUBLIC SINS affecting a large group or an entire church need to be made right on whatever level of people it affects. Always be AS BROAD AS THE OFFENSE but not any broader!

10. RESTITUTION IS FOR THE GLORY OF GOD. In giving public testimony, restitution brings glory to God ONLY WHEN it exalts what Christ has done rather than MAGNIFYING the situation itself. In the light of everything else discussed, personal testimony can be given. It then is not a matter of "hanging out dirty linen in public," but rather an expression of praise to God's glory in deliverance. Others then rejoice by your testimony in that GOD has performed a MIRACLE rather than in your elaborating all the details. ONLY WHEN the glory goes to Jesus will people be blessed and the church edified.

IMPORTANT FINAL WORDS.
1. On matters of PERSONAL MORALITY (immorality), BE SURE to consult your pastor or spiritual advisor BEFORE acting in any direction.
2. Never pressure a person to respond. If he is unwilling to forgive, ask him to contact you when he is ready.
3. If the sin occurred BEFORE conversion, deal with everything the HOLY SPIRIT REVEALS.
4. Aside from matters of PERSONAL MORALITY (immorality), the general rule is to deal person-to-person. If impossible, telephone. Letters should be a "last resort."
5. If you have ANY QUESTION at all about the what, when, how OR EVEN IF restitution should be made, CONSULT YOUR PASTOR or spiritual advisor. Don't wish when it is TOO LATE you had gotten the right advice. You cannot always recover the damage.
6. FOR MORE ON THIS SUBJECT, read the tract, "CONFESSION, FORGIVENESS AND RESTITUTION" also written by Ralph Sutera, and available from CANADIAN REVIVAL FELLOWSHIP, Box 584, Regina, Sask., Canada S4P 3A3.'

CHAPTER XII

CAUSES AND CURE FOR FEAR AND ANGER
Dr. Tim LaHaye

It seems that we live in a world where fear and anger prevail. We only have to listen to the news to hear of crimes being committed hourly, which prove this.

Although we become new creatures when we are saved, we often bring a lot of "garbage" along that needs to be dealt with. Many times new Christians need a handle on how to recognize fear and anger and how to deal with them.

Tim LaHaye calls these the two universal sins of mankind. I think it is important to understand how the forms of anger and the expressions of fear are manifested.

GRIEVING THE HOLY SPIRIT THROUGH ANGER

Read Ephesians 4:29-32

Grieving the Holy Spirit through anger, bitterness, wrath or other forms of human cussedness probably ruins more Christian testimonies than any other kind of sin.

This text makes it very clear that we "grieve" the Holy Spirit of God through bitterness, wrath, anger, clamor, evil speaking and malice, which is enmity of heart. For some reason, otherwise consecrated Christians seem reluctant to face as sin these emotions that stem from anger. Instead, it is common to stop advancement in the Christian life with victory over such external habits as drinking, gambling, profanity, etc., without coming to grips with the emotions that churn within. Although unseen, anger is every bit as much a sin as these overt practices. Galatians 5:20 lists hatred, strife and wrath in the same category as murderers, drunkenness and revellings, and such like, "...of the things which I tell you before as I have also told you in the past, that they which do such things shall not inherit the Kingdom of God."

Anger - A Universal Sin

Anger is one of the two universal sins of mankind. After counseling several hundred people, I have concluded that all emotional tension can be traced to one of two things: anger or fear. I cannot think of a single case involving individuals or couples who were upset but that the basic problem stemmed from an attitude that was angry, bitter and vitriolic, or fearful, anxious, worried and depressed. I have dealt with some people who were both angry and fearful. Dr. Henry Brandt and Dr. Raymond Cramer point out that anger can cause a person to become fearful. (Ex.) At times anxiety expresses itself in anger. A tense, anxious person is much more likely to become irritable and angry. Anxiety is a form of fear; therefore, from these two Christian psychologists we can conclude that an angry person can also become a fearful person, and a fearful person can become an angry person. Anger grieves the Holy Spirit and fear quenches the Holy Spirit, as we will see.

Sanguine and choleric temperaments - angry-prone.

Melancholy and phlegmatic - fear-prone.

Since most people are a combination of temperaments, they could well have a natural predisposition to both fear and anger.

It is my personal opinion that these two emotions bring more Christians into bondage to the law of sin than any other emotions or desires.

Thank God there is a cure for these weaknesses through the Holy Spirit.

Suppressed anger and bitterness can make a person emotionally upset until he is "not himself." God has designed us to be intensely emotional creatures. If we permit anger to dominate us, it will squelch the richer emotion of love.

Anger takes many forms - (See List)
It affects us:
- A. Emotionally
- B. Socially
- C. Physically
- D. Spiritually

The Basic Cause of Anger

Although we love to excuse our weaknesses and justify them to ourselves as we nurse our grudges and indulge in anger, vengeful, bitter feelings, they are all motivated by selfishness. When I am angry, it is because someone has violated my rights and I am interested in myself. When I am bitter against someone, it is because they have done something against me, and again I come back to selfishness. Vengeance is always inspired by selfishness.

What causes a perfectly normal, likeable, congenial human being to suddenly react with heat and anger? The full realization and acceptance of the answer to that question provides the Christian with his first giant step towards its cure. Stripped of the facade and fancy excuses for condoning anger, of calling it "old nick" or "my natural Irish disposition," we are confronted with an ugly word — selfishness.

As fantastic as it may seem, I have observed this in the lives of those individuals who are willing to recognize inner anger and turmoil as the sin of selfishness and look to God for the grace, love and self-control which He promises to them who ask Him. If you are reaping a crop of anger, bitterness and hatred, a little investigation will indicate to you that you have been sowing a crop of anger, bitterness and hatred. The Bible tells us, "Whatsoever a man soweth, that shall he also reap." If you had been sowing love, you would be reaping love. If you are not reaping love, may I suggest that you change the seeds you are sowing.

The High Cost Of Anger

If man really understood the high price paid for pent-up wrath or bitterness and anger, he would seek some remedy for it.

Socially

Very simply, an angry person is not pleasant to be around; consequently, those who are angry, grumpy or disgruntled are gradually weeded out of the social lists or excluded from the fun times of life.

The social price paid for inner anger and bitterness is seen more clearly in detail as a person progresses in age. We have often heard someone ask the question, "Have you noticed how ornery and cranky Granddad is getting in his old age?" What seems to be a change is not a change at all. Granddad just loses some of his inhibitions and the desire to please others as he grows older and reverts more to the candid reactions to childhood. Children do not try to hide their feelings, but express them, and elderly people return again to this same custom. Granddad begins to act the way he has felt all his life. This bitter, resentful and often self-pitying spirit makes him unbearable to have around, which in turn makes life more difficult for him in his old age. What a tragedy if Granddad is a Christian and did not let God's Holy Spirit "mortify the deeds of the flesh" many years before.

Emotionally

Suppressed anger and bitterness can make a person emotionally upset until he is "not himself." In this state he often makes decisions that are harmful, wasteful or embarrassing. We are intensely emotional creatures, designed so by God, but if we permit anger to dominate us, it will squelch the higher emotion of love.

Dr. S.I. McMillen, a Christian medical doctor, in his book *None Of These Diseases*, says, "The moment I start hating a man, I become his slave. I can't enjoy my work anymore because he even controls my thoughts. Resentment produces too many stress hormones in my body and I become fatigued after only a few hours' work." "The emotional center produces these widespread changes by means of three principal mechanisms: by changing the amount of blood flowing to an organ; by affecting the secretions to certain glands; and by changing the tension of muscles." He then points out that the emotions of anger or hatred can cause the blood vessels to dilate, permitting an abnormal supply of blood to the head. The cranium is a rigid structure without room for expansion; consequently, anger and wrath can very easily give a person severe headaches.

A doctor friend illustrated the way in which our emotions can cause ulcers and many other stomach diseases by restricting the flow of blood to the stomach and other vital organs. He said we have a muscle over our stomach that is emotionally controlled, and in a fit of rage it will tighten down and restrict the flow of blood to the vital organs of heart, stomach, liver, intestines, lungs, gallbladder, etc.

It is easy to see from this illustration that prolonged anger, resentment, hatred, wrath or bitterness could cause severe damage to these organs of the body. Dr. McMillen lists over 51 diseases, which are caused by emotional stress. He even suggests that some very common infectious diseases are contracted when the resistance is low at the time of exposure, the reason being that prolonged emotional stress can reduce our resistance. Think of the needless sicknesses because of emotional stress of Christians who could have avoided all that heartache if they had been "filled with the Holy Spirit."

Physically

It is difficult to separate the physical price paid for anger from the financial, because anger and bitterness produce so much stress which in turn causes physical disorder so that thousands of dollars are spent needlessly by Christian people for doctors and drugs. Doctors and medical associations today have released various statistics showing that from 60 to as high as 90 percent of man's bodily illness is emotionally induced, and anger and fear are the main culprits!

How can our emotions actually cause physical illness? Very simply, for our entire physical body is intricately tied up with our nervous system. Whenever the nervous system becomes tense through anger or fear, it adversely affects one or more parts of the body. In order for any body movement to take place, a message must be conveyed from the emotional center to the member to be moved.

This message is given with lightening-like speed, and we are not conscious of the source from which it originates.

If the emotional center is normal, then the functions of the body will be normal. If, however, the emotional center is "upset" or behaves in an abnormal manner, a reaction will be generated through the nervous system to almost every part of the body.

Spiritually

The highest price of all paid for an angry, bitter disposition is in the spiritual realm. Jesus Christ came to give us not only eternal life when we die, but abundant life here and now. That life can only be experienced by "abiding in Him" or "being filled with the Spirit." No man can abide in Christ or be filled with the Spirit who grieves the Holy Spirit, and "anger, bitterness, wrath, clamor and enmity of heart" grieve the Holy Spirit of God.

Grieving the Holy Spirit limits the work of God in an individual's life, keeps him from becoming mature in Christ Jesus, and hinders him from being the glowing, effective, fruitful Christian that he wants to be. Churches are filled today with evangelical Christians just like the children of Israel, who never fully possessed their possessions. Continual grieving of the Spirit of God through anger keeps the child of God from enjoying all that Jesus Christ has for him today. This affects the believer not only in this life but in the life to come, for we should be occupying ourselves with laying up treasures in heaven, which can be done only as we walk in the Spirit. Again we say, the most important single thing to any Christian is that he walk in the Spirit, but to do so he must let God cure his natural weakness of inner anger and turmoil.

WHAT IS ANGER?

A day rarely goes by that we all don't feel some form of anger. That's why it's important to talk about our anger - what it is, what it does for us, where it comes from, and how we can learn to handle it in constructive instead of destructive ways. Only when the roots of our anger are exposed can we defuse its explosive potential.

Anger is one of the most basic human emotions. Everyone gets angry. It's a feeling of being against someone or something. It's a hostile emotion that sets people against each other, or even against themselves. By its nature, anger involves antagonism.

Anger, however, is simpler to define than it is to identify. Emotions of antagonism can take on a wide variety of faces. Expressions of anger range from the over, in-your-face brand of open hostility to the cool indifference of a silent stare.

At times, anger can feel like an inner fire. It hits you in the gut. You see red and feel hot and sweaty. Your stomach churns, your blood pressure rises, and your breathing rate increases as if you're laboring under a heavy weight. Outwardly, your body responds to the internal activity with a flushed appearance. You perspire, your nostrils may flare, and your jaw tightens. Many people describe their experience of anger as their blood boiling.

On the other hand, anger can be experienced as compliance on the outside while resentment and hostility run just beneath the surface.

Because anger is so common to human experience, and because it is such a threat to relationships, it's not surprising that the Bible has much to say about the dangers, roots, and taming of anger.

The Scriptures show the destructive potential of anger. It is not surprising, therefore, that several passages of the Bible urge us to get rid of any kind of bitterness, rage, or anger. (Ephesians 4:31; Colossians 3:8)

The Bible, however, does not always paint a negative picture of anger. The vast majority of biblical references to words like anger, rage, wrath, and fury refer to the anger and wrath of God. These passages, which speak of God's own anger with His enemies, or even with His own people, far outnumber those that tell us to avoid anger.

What the Bible shows us is that anger is neither right nor wrong *until there is a motive*. Anger can be productive and loving, just as it can be destructive and selfish. What we need is the discernment that can be developed by those who want to see their anger from the Lord's point of view.

Anger rooted in self-centered efforts to care for ourselves never works. Such anger seeks to destroy, not build.

God knows that anger is an important and necessary emotion for a healthy person living in a fallen world.

John Stott, in his commentary on Ephesians 4:26, says, the verse recognized that there is such a thing as Christian anger, and too few Christians either feel or express it. Indeed, when we fail to do so, we deny God, damage ourselves, and encourage the spread of evil.

In our anger there are three things Paul tells us to follow:
1. Don't sin.
2. Don't nurse anger.
3. Don't give Satan an edge.

We need to keep in mind, however, that there is a fine line between anger that is loving and anger that is selfish. Complete avoidance of anger is another way of giving Satan an edge.

Unfortunately, many people avoid anger at all costs because they have experienced the volatile emotion of anger that is terrifying to deal with in themselves and in others. According to Ephesians 4:26, that is not an option God gives us.

We play into the devil's hands not only when we follow our anger into sin, but when we allow sinful self-protection to keep us from obeying God's command, "In your anger do not sin." Few occasions give our enemy more freedom than when the children of God fail to love enough to be angry.

Righteous anger in a compassionate person can be very productive for the well-being of others.

John Stott reminds us that we should be angered by the things that anger God. "In the face of blatant evil we should be indignant not tolerant, angry not apathetic. If God hates sin, His people should hate it too. If evil arouses His anger, it should arouse ours also."

So, you see, the problem is not with anger as an emotion in and of itself. If it were, God couldn't get angry and still be holy. The root problem is in the source and function of our anger.

HOW CAN WE HANDLE OUR ANGER IN GODLY WAYS?

1. Acknowledge your anger to God.
2. Learn to get angry slowly.
3. Change your beliefs about God. (Our anger problem is rooted not in feelings, but in what we believe about God.) All emotions, including anger, are therefore useful to help us track down the real beliefs of our heart. Feelings of rage can be used to begin to trace the roots of that antagonism. In the process we can discern if that anger is rooted in our confidence in God or if it is a self-centered response rooted in a selfish spirit demanding that things go our way.

Whether we believe our well-being is in the hands of God, in our circumstances, or in others is a most basic factor in learning how to deal with anger.

4. Confess wrong beliefs and repent.
5. Place your anger under new management.

Placing our anger and our well-being in the hand of God will help us better understand this mind of Christ. It will also help us develop a healthy fear of the anger that God reserves for His enemies. Placing our anger under God's management will not dissolve and evaporate all anger. But it will free us to express a new and godly anger toward the kind of sin in ourselves and others that slowly anger the heart of God.

FEAR

The second Universal sin is FEAR.
There are several causes of fear.
1. Temperament traits - Some more than others. Some types of personalities are more prone to fear than others.
2. Childhood experiences - Psychologists and psychiatrists agree that the basic needs of man are love, understanding, and acceptance.

The most significant human thing that parents can do for their children, short of leading them to Christ, is to give them warmth and security of parental love. This does not exclude discipline or the teaching of submission to standards and principles. In fact, it is far better for a child to learn to adjust to rules and standards in the loving atmosphere of his home than in the cruel world outside.

There are two areas parents need to avoid:

A. Over-protection - makes a child self-centered and fearful of the very things happening to him that his parent is afraid will happen. Children quickly learn to read our emotions.

B. Dominating Children – Angry, explosive parents who dominate the lives of their children or who critically pounce upon every failure in their lives often create hesitancy, insecurity, and fear in them. Children need correction, but they need it done in the proper spirit. Whenever we have to point out our children's mistakes, we should also make it a practice to note their strengths and good points, or at least criticize them in such a way as to let them know that they are still every bit as much the object of our love as they were before.

The most devastating blow one human being can inflict upon another is disapproval.

The Spirit-filled parent is inspired through his loving, compassionate nature to build others up and to show approval whenever possible. Even in times of correction he will convey his love. To do otherwise with our children is to leave lasting fear - scars on their emotions.

C. A Traumatic Experience - Child assault or molesting leaves a lasting emotional scar that often carries over into adulthood, causing fear concerning the act of marriage. Other tragic experiences in childhood frequently set fear-patterns into motion that last throughout life.

My Personal Experience

When I was about eight or nine years old, I had a very traumatic experience. My mother's half sister had died, so Mom went to be with the family. As we were having supper that night I looked up from the table and in the doorway stood a big tall man, all wet and muddy and blood streaming down his face. He asked my Dad to call the sheriff. He said someone had beat him up. We kids were terrified. Dad took us and put us in a room and said to lock the door and not to open it until he came and knocked. The man must have heard him, because while Dad was on the phone, the man came and knocked on the door. Thinking it was Dad I opened the door quickly and threw myself into his arms. Once I realized what had happened, I almost died of fright.

As it turned out, the man happened to live a couple of miles from us. He had been drinking and wanted to take the car out. His sons didn't want him to, so they had been wrestling with him to try to keep him home. He slipped away from them and walked across fields to come to our house.

As a result of that experience, I was afraid to even walk around the house or go out to the barn, or out to the shed to get potatoes or nuts or things that Mom would need. I was afraid to even go to sleep at night. I never talked to anyone about it, and for years I was bound by fear.

After my first husband died and I moved back to Nyack, NY to live, that fear still haunted me. One night I prayed and said, "Lord, I'm not here just by my choice, but I'm here by your leading, so please take this fear away from me." He did, and I have been free of that crippling fear ever since. As I have grown older, I have learned that as I place my faith in the Lord and trust in Him, He will keep me.

D. A Negative Thinking Pattern - Or defeatist complex will cause a person to be fearful of attempting any new thing. The moment we start saying to ourselves, "I can't, I can't, I can't," we are almost certain of failure. Our mental attitude makes even ordinary tasks difficult to perform when we approach them with a negative thought. Repeated failures or refusal to do what our contemporaries are able to accomplish often causes further breakdown in self-confidence and increases fear. A Christian need never be dominated by this negative habit. By memorizing Philippians 4:13 and seeking the Spirit's power in applying it, one can gain a positive attitude toward life.

E. Anger - Anger, as pointed out earlier, can produce fear. I have counseled with individuals who had indulged bitterness and anger until they erupted in such explosive tirades that they afterward admitted, "I am afraid of what I might do to my own child."

F. Sin produces fear - "If our heart condemn us not, then have we confidence toward God." (I John 3:21) is a principle that cannot be violated without producing fear. Every time we sin, our conscience reminds us of our relationship to God. This has often been misconstrued by psychiatrists, who blame religion for creating guilt complexes in people which, they said, in turn produced fear.

A few years ago, our family doctor, who at that time was not a Christian, made the following statement to me: "You ministers, including my own saintly old father, do irreparable damage to the emotional life of men by preaching the gospel." I questioned his reason for his statement and he said, "I took my internship in a mental institution, and the overwhelming majority of those people had a religious background and were there because of fear-induced complexes."

The next day I attended a minister's meeting where Dr. Clyde Narramore, a Christian psychologist from Los Angeles, gave a lecture on pastoral counseling. During the question period, I told him of the previous day's conversation and asked his opinion. Dr. Narramore instantly replied: "That is not true. People have guilt complexes because they are guilty!" The result of sin is a consciousness of guilt, and guilt causes fear in modern man just as it did to Adam and Eve in the garden. A simple remedy for this is: "Walk in the way of the Lord."

G. Lack of Faith - Lack of faith, even in a Christian's life, can cause fear. I have noticed in counseling that fear caused by lack of faith is basically confined to two common areas.

The first is fear concerning sins of the past. Because the Christian does not know what the Bible teaches in relationship to confessed sin, he has not come to really believe that God has cleansed him from all sin. (I John 1:9) Some time ago I counseled with a lady who was in a protracted period of fear, so that she had sunk into deep depression. We found that one of her basic problems was that she was still haunted by a sin committed eleven years before. All during this time she had been a Christian but had gone through a complete emotional collapse, haunted by the fear of that past sin.

When I asked her if she had confessed that sin in the name of the Lord Jesus Christ, she replied, "Oh, yes, many times." I then gave her a spiritual prescription to make a Bible study of all scripture verses that deal with the forgiveness of sin. When she came back to my office two weeks later, she was not the same woman. For the first time in her life she really understood how God regarded her past sin, and when she began to agree with him that it was "remembered against her no more," she got over that fear.

A man I counseled that had a similar problem gave me a slightly different answer when I asked, "Have you confessed that sin to Christ?" "Over a thousand times," was his interesting reply. I told him that was 999 times too many. He should have confessed it once and thanked God 999 times that He had forgiven him for that awful sin. The Word of God is the cure for this problem, because "Faith cometh by hearing, and hearing by the Word of God." (Romans 10:17)

The second area in which men are prone to be fearful because of lack of faith concerns the future. If the devil can't get them to worry about their past sins, he will seek to get them to worry about God's provision in the future, and thus they are not able to enjoy the riches of God's blessing today. The Psalmist has said, "This is the day which the Lord hath made; we will rejoice and be glad in it." (Psalm 118:24) People who enjoy life are not "living tomorrow" nor worrying about the past; they are living today.

Anyone who thinks about the potential problems and difficulties he might encounter tomorrow will naturally become fearful unless he has a deep, abiding faith in God's ability to supply all his needs. My wife shared with me a beautiful saying she heard which bears repeating:

"Satan tries to crush our spirit by getting us to bear tomorrow's problems with only today's grace."

If you are worrying about tomorrow, you can't possibly enjoy today. The interesting thing is that you can't give God tomorrow: You can only give Him what you have, and you have today. Dr. Cramer quoted a comment by Mr. John Watson in the Houston Times, which read: "What does your anxiety do? It does not empty tomorrow of its sorrows, but it empties today of its strength. It does not make you escape the evil; it makes you unfit to cope with it when it comes." Now I think you are about to face the primary cause of fear. The above 7 causes of fear are only contributing factors. The basic cause of fear is...

H. Selfishness - the basic cause of fear - As much as we don't like to face this ugly word, it is a fact nevertheless. We are fearful because we are selfish. Why am I afraid? Because I am interested in self. Why am I embarrassed when I stand before an audience? Because I don't wish to make a fool of myself. Why am I afraid to lose my job? Because I am afraid of being a failure in the eyes of my family or not being able to provide my family and myself with the necessities of life. Excuse it if you will, but all fear can be traced basically to the sin of selfishness.

Once fear has been faced as a sin rather than excused as a behavior pattern, the person is well on the road to recovery provided he knows Jesus Christ and is willing to submit himself to the filling of the Holy Spirit.

God does not leave us in our dilemma. He always provides a way out of our problem.

Spirit-Controlled Temperaments
By: Dr. Tim LaHaye

ARE YOU AFRAID? (of what people think?)
By: Martin Bennett

The Fear of Man
The Bible says, "The fear of man brings a snare." (Proverbs 29:25) It really does! The fear of man is caring so much about what others may think, say, or do, that it keeps you from living up to your true convictions. It's wanting others to think better of you than you really are.
1. Concerned About How You Look
2. Afraid of What Others Think
3. Worried About Your Image
4. Easily Influenced By Others
5. Doing The Right Things For The Wrong Reasons

The Fear of God
Proverbs 29:25 - "But he who trusts in the Lord will be exalted." Simply stated, the fear of God is caring more about what the Lord thinks than anything else, and the source of this is a true and deep love for Him. One who fears God has a sense of the overwhelming greatness of the Lord and His constant presence. They know that what God thinks has a much greater value than what anyone thinks.

1. The Outer Man - Those who fear God don't have to have the latest in name-brand fashions...and they don't have to conform to the constantly changing standards of everyone's opinion. A godly person will give appearance its proper value and go on to more important things.

2. Committed to God's Commands - Instead of being embarrassed at every little thing, the godly man has his eyes on God, committed to His every command. (Isaiah 20 - Walk around naked)

Someone who fears God is quite defensive - of the Lord, that is. If God is slandered in any way, they will speak up, explaining that the Lord really is as good as the Scriptures testify. They trust the Lord to defend them, and devote themselves to speak out in His defense.

He is very careful to speak the truth, even if it cost him something - even if it costs him his life!

3. Built On The Rock - Unlike the man pleaser, a truly godly person can't be manipulated. The true God fearer would rather suffer anything than to shame the God he loves.

4. Clean Inside - As far as "spiritual" things go, they don't act spiritual - they are spiritual. They enjoy spending time with God, speaking and listening through prayer. And when no one's around to see them, they act just the same.

Those who are concerned about how they look to God don't spend much time polishing the outside of their cup, but you'll find the inside very clean. Since they want to please God, they have dealt with and gotten rid of the deep things of their lives that hurt Him. They're surprisingly open about their own sins and failures. They don't fear being judged by mere men or being seen as they really are. "But if we judged ourselves rightly, we should not be judged." (I Corinthians 11:31)

5. The Test of Praise - What do you do when someone really compliments you for getting your life together? Do you say, "Thank you. I've been trying much harder lately and believe I've got things under control now..."? The God-fearing man trembles at the thought of stealing from God, stealing the glory that belongs to Him. How you respond to praise can show you very well where your heart is.

Because of the wickedness of men's hearts, the more closely a person follows the Lord, the worse people tend to speak of him. So if you love God, in this world, you'll be swimming upstream.

When someone has truly given up their life, what can you take from them? This kind of totally committed person really frustrates the devil - they don't care about their social image, they don't care if they're laughed at, they don't care if you take their possessions, and they don't care if you take their life - they only care that their Father in heaven is pleased with them!

They see Christ as their only judge, and know that they will be held accountable to Him alone in the end. The opinions of people don't add up to much in comparison.

6. The Real You - What so many fail to see is that when they put up any kind of "front," whatever it is, and others accept it, they still haven't accepted you, because they haven't met you. They've only accepted the cardboard image of what you wish you were. On the other hand, when we are accepted by the Lord, we're free to serve Him without being torn in different directions. You see, the man pleaser falsely sees man as his judge, but on the last day all the opinions of all the men of all time added all together will equal... nothing! It's only what God thinks that will matter.

Ironically, those people whose ultimate goal is to please everybody in every way they can think of are, in the end, rejected by both man and God. Both Pilate and Herod bent their knees to the wishes of the people and everyone liked it - at the time. They wanted honor, but instead they became lasting examples of dishonor. Have you ever heard of a kid named "Herod" or "Pilate"?

7. Having A Single Standard - The Lord is looking for people who have set aside the cares and worries of what everybody else

is thinking, and have their hearts set on serving and pleasing Him. When you give God the honor He deserves, you will find Him to be a closer and better Friend than you had ever imagined.

Decide in your heart to yield to the urgings of the Spirit of God, no matter what it may cost you, no matter who might laugh, no matter what the temporary consequences might be before you, no matter what! And the Lord will be with you and strengthen you in every righteous deed!

OVERCOMING YOUR WEAKNESSES

1. Face your weaknesses as sin,
2. Confess your sin every time,
3. Ask your loving heavenly Father to take away this habit,
4. Believe God has given victory. Thank Him by faith.
5. Ask for the filling of the Holy Spirit, (Luke 11:13)

VICTORY OVER FEAR AND ANGER IS THE WILL OF GOD!

THERE ARE TWO UNIVERSAL SINS OF MANKIND

1. ANGER - We grieve the Holy Spirit through anger.

Forms of Anger
Bitterness; Wrath; Malice; Hatred; Clamor; Seditions; Envy; Jealousy; Resentment; Attack; Intolerance; Gossip; Criticism; Sarcasm; Revenge; Unforgiveness.

2. FEAR

Expressions of Fear
Anxiety; Worry; Doubts; Inferiority; Timidity; Cowardice; Indecision; Suspicion; Superstition; Hesitancy; Withdrawal; Depression; Loneliness; Haughtiness; Over-aggression; Social Shyness.

1: The basic cause of anger is selfishness!
2: The causes of fear:
A. Temerament
B. Childhood experience
C. A Traumatic Experience
D. A Negative Thinking Pattern
E. Anger
F. Sin
G. Lack of Faith
H. Selfishness

By: Dr. Tim LaHaye

CHAPTER XIII

DEPRESSION AND EMOTIONAL PROBLEMS

A sinful response to life's experiences is the most common cause of depression and all other emotional illness as well. Because this is true, the first step in experiencing healing is to ask God to help you identify those unbiblical responses. When these are discovered and corrected in a biblical manner, healing often comes automatically.

For instance, let's say that you have been offended by someone. What is your response? You are hurt and you are angry. Whether the hurt is real or not makes little difference so long as you think it is real. Your response is anger. Your anger in itself may not be a sinful response, because it may not be sinful anger. But if you don't channel your anger and control it and make use of it by the power of the Holy Spirit, it can turn into bitterness, which is sin. When you have been hurt, and your hurt turns into bitterness, that is a sinful response instead of a biblical response. The biblical response should have been to go to that person, speak the truth in love, deal with the problem, and forgive him.

Instead, if we don't deal with the problem, we don't speak the truth in love, we don't go to the people, we don't forgive them, then our hurt turns into bitterness. That bitterness produces self-pity, and that's one emotional reaction that leads to depression.

There is another way we can get depressed. We can come up against a situation where we are tempted to sin. Temptation is the problem, the response is yielding and committing the sin, then not confessing that sin. The Word of God says, "If we confess our sins, He is faithful and just to forgive us our sins and to cleanse us from all unrighteousness" (I John 1:9). If we are transparent, open and honest, and confess our sins, "the blood of Jesus Christ, His Son, continually keeps on cleansing us from sin" (I John 1:7-8). If we are tempted and we yield to sin and do not confess it and make it right, our emotional reaction is guilt and fear. That emotional reaction may produce depression.

We need to deal thoroughly with our sin. We need to pray, "Dear God, help me to be so honest that You can show me where the sin is in my life." It may be buried deep in the past. I don't know where it is, but God knows where it is. God can go back into your life and show you the problem.

A woman who had spent a great deal of time under psychiatric care came to me for counseling because she was very depressed. After a while I said to her, "You have done something wrong and you are not willing to admit it." She said, "I am going to tell you something I have never told any other human being." She opened her heart and told me how she had falsified some legal documents twenty years before. All this time she had covered up her sin and had never been able to get it off her mind. Not only did she have this guilt that she had to confess to God and get cleaned up before the Lord, but she also had some deep bitterness that had to be dealt with.

My friends, these are some of the major reasons for depression. These are the kinds of things that God is trying to speak to us about.

People react sinfully to some problem in their lives. Then sinful reaction produces an emotional reaction either of self-pity or guilt or fear. From that they slide into depression. When they get depressed, and everything begins to get dark, they are weighed down under this burden of depression (which is a danger signal from God, by the way, built into our systems). They lose interest in the normal activities of life, they start to neglect their responsibilities in life. As they neglect their responsibilities, they are sinning. When they sin by neglecting their responsibilities they feel more guilty. As they feel more guilty, they get more depressed. As they get more depressed, they neglect more responsibilities; and they go down, down, down, into a dark hole of despair. They don't see any way out. (See *How to Win Over Depression* by Tim LaHaye, chapter 8, "Self-pity and Depression," published by Zondervan; and *The Christian Counselor's Manual* by Jay Adams, chapter 33, "Helping Depressed Persons," published by Baker Books.)

How can you get out of your depression? The same way you got into it! You begin right where you are. Confess your sins. Make any restitution that is necessary. Then start to pick up those responsibilities you have neglected.

Now tell the truth. The truth is, you don't feel like doing it. You are living by your feelings instead of by faith. My friend, you need to go to Calvary and crucify your feelings. You are going to have to do violence to your feelings. You must do it whether you feel like it or not!

Most of us are going around with some kind of emotional pacifier in our mouths all the time. We have made awful babies out of ourselves. God needs to teach us some godly discipline. We need to start picking up our normal duties of life, regardless of how we feel. We need to get down on our knees along with that and stay on our knees until God takes us all the way back to our sin, whatever it is. We need to deal with it thoroughly, and get it cleansed. When it is cleansed and when we begin to carry out our responsibilities again, God will bless us, and marvelous healing will come.

Confession is strong medicine. Look at what happened to the Ephesians who confessed their sins:

And many that believed came, and confessed, and showed their deeds. Many of them also which used curious arts brought their books together, and burned them before all men; and they counted the price of them, and found it fifty thousand pieces of silver. So mightily grew the word of God and prevailed (Acts 19:18-20).

Have you ever been in a real revival? If you are serious about confessing your sins, you will be in one. It may be a private revival, but God will cleanse your soul and heal your emotions from one end to the other.

FREEDOM FROM EMOTIONAL BONDAGE

What is the solution to our emotional problems?

Let's be open before God, Let us get alone in the presence of the Holy Spirit, and say, "Spirit of God, please open my heart. Show me where the sin is, whatever it is, and then, Lord, give me the courage to make it right." The confession should only be to the extent of the sin. If it is a public sin, it should be a public confession. If it is a private sin, it should be a private confession. If it is a sin only against God, it should be only to God, Let us make it right. Let us forgive. Let us pick up our responsibilities before God and go back to doing the things that God wants us to do in our lives for His glory. God will heal us, totally set us free and give us healthy emotions that will honor and glorify the Lord Jesus Christ,

People with long-standing emotional problems sometimes need a thorough memory healing. To help you in this process, divide a sheet of paper into three columns: DATE, WHO WAS INVOLVED, and WHAT HAPPENED.

Now ask God to open your memory. Go back in your life as far as possible, and write down a careful record of every incident you can remember that has been hurtful in your life. Some will be things you did. Some will be things others did. Be thorough and specific no matter how painful it may be.

When you have finished, pray specifically about what you have written down. Ask Jesus Christ to take a walk with you through your personal history of pain. Stop at each incident and confess any sin of which you are guilty. Ask Christ to forgive others who are guilty. Then you forgive those who have hurt you. Do it in a final sense and close the case. If you need to confront someone while you are considering a particular incident, do so. Get the matter settled before moving on to the next incident. If it is impossible to confront a person, share the incident with a godly friend, such as your pastor or your elder, and together commit that incident to the Lord. Continue this process until your entire memory list has been thoroughly dealt with. When you are sure you are finished, burn your memory list and thank God for your healing.

Understanding Divine Healing
By: Richard M. Sipley
Victor Books
Wheaton, Illinois 60187

DEPRESSION: ITS CAUSE AND CURE

Depression is defined by **Webster's Dictionary** as "the state of being depressed... dejection, ... lowering of vitality of functional activity... an abnormal state of inactivity and unpleasant emotion." God never intended man to live like that! It has always been God's intent that man enjoy a peaceful, contented, and happy live, referred to in Scripture as the "abundant" life.

No Christian filled with the Holy Spirit is going to be depressed. Before a Spirit-filled believer can become depressed, he must first grieve the Spirit through anger or quench the Spirit through fear.

Causes

1. Hypocrisy leads to depression.

The average Christian who attends a Bible-teaching believing church soon learns the standards of the Christian life. If he attacks his weaknesses externally rather than by the control of the Holy Spirit working from within, he may become depressed.

Suppose a man has a problem with resentment, bitterness and hostility. He soon learns that this is not the standard of spirituality for the Christian. Unless he handles this matter on a personal basis with God, he will try to solve it by the power of self-control. To control anger by the force of one's will is not only futile, but it will lead to an explosion somewhere in the body -high blood pressure, heart trouble, ulcers, colitis, or a myriad of other maladies, or it may result in a belated explosion. The frustration that follows an angry reaction to a given situation leads to depression. The cure must come from within through the power of the Holy Spirit.

2. Physical Problems

Physical problems can lead to depression. Dr. LaHaye said he has observed that individuals can become depressed when there is a mineral or vitamin deficiency, Vitamin B is the nerve vitamin. If we don't get enough of it, a person will be nervous which leads to frustration and depression.

It is also apparent that some women suffer a hormone deficiency when going through the change of life, and this often produces depression. Before a person attributes all of his depression to spiritual reasons, physical causes should be investigated by his physician; however, most people are inclined to attribute their depression to physical problems rather than consider that it is spiritually and emotionally induced,

3. The Devil

Most Bible teachers remind us that the devil can oppress a Christian even if he does not indwell or possess him. It is true that some Christians have seemingly been depressed by the devil.

I do not find any place for depression as caused by the devil in the life of a Spirit-filled Christian. Keep in mind that all Christians are not Spirit-filled. We need to meet the conditions for a Spirit-filled life and walk in the Spirit to avoid being depressed by the devil.

4. Rebellion and Unbelief

If man really knew God as He is, he would believe Him implicitly. But because his faith is so weak, he has a tendency to rebel against the testings or the leading of the Lord, and rebellion and unbelief lead to depression,

5. Psychological Letdown

There is a psychological letdown whenever a great project has been completed. One can be very energetic and creative when working toward a long-range goal, But when it is reached, it is often followed by a period of depression.

The feeling of depression was eliminated when new projects and higher goals were set to replace those completed,

6. Self-pity

Self-pity is the basic cause of depression. The above mentioned elements are not primary cause for depression. They are often excuses one uses to condone depression rather than going to Almighty God for His marvelous cure. The truth of the matter is, a person becomes depressed only after a period of indulging in the sin of self-pity.

The sin of self-pity is so subtle that we do not often recognize it for what it is. The Bible clearly teaches that we do not have to be dominated by the natural man, for we are to "walk in the Spirit." (Galatians 5:16) Once we understand that self-pity produces depression, and that it is a sin, all we have to do is go to God for His cure,

THE CURE

1. Face your weakness as sin, Phil 4:13
2. Confess your sin every time. I John 1;9
3. Ask your heavenly Father to take away the habit. I John 5:14-15
4. Believe God has given the victory. Romans 14:23; I Thessalonians 5:18
5. Ask for filling of the Holy Spirit. Luke 11:13
6. Walk In the Spirit. Galatians 5:16: John 5:1-11

To be filled with the Holy Spirit means to;
a. Allow the word of God to be a regular part of your life,
b. Practice prayer daily,
c. Continually yield to the Holy Spirit,
d. Serve Christ.

We don't have to be dominated by habit!

Spirit Controlled Temperament
By: Dr. Tim LaHaye
Tyndale House Publishers, Wheaton, IL
1966

CHAPTER XIV

SICKNESS AND DIVINE HEALING

When I see all the sickness around us in the church today, I can't help but ask why more people aren't studying the word of God concerning sickness and then obeying it so they can be healed.

There are two books I want to use in studying this subject. The first is: *God, Why Am I Sick?* by Paul and Carolyn Wilde. The second is: *Understanding Divine Healing,* by Rev. Dick Sipley.

I know we live in a sinful world, but we as Christians have privileges available to us that the people of the world do not have. God does not always see fit to heal, but there are times when He will if we ask and meet His conditions.

SICKNESS

God, Why Am I Sick?
Paul and Carolyn Wilde
HC - 75, Box 350
Foley, Alabama 36535
Heartfelt Ministries 1986

"It's meaningless suffering that destroys us. If we can see a purpose, we can stand about anything." Victor Frankl discovered in the concentration camps that the human spirit can take any WHAT if it can discover WHY.

There may be one or more reasons that apply to you. The most important thing about your sickness is your attitude toward God.

Are you angry, rebellious, indifferent, losing faith and trust in Him? Are you loving and trusting in His love and care for you - even in your sickness?

First ask for a healing of your spirit, then for the body. Paul tells us to "cleanse ourselves from all filthiness of the flesh and spirit, perfecting holiness in the fear of God," (II Corinthians 7:1.)

Come before Him with a thankful heart. Praise Him for the blessings of salvation, forgiveness, cleansing, His everlasting goodness, mercy, and love, for brothers and sisters in the Lord.

Kneel before Him.

Or fall upon your face before Him and worship Him as did the prophets of old.

Wait before Him. See Him in His majesty and power. Let Him touch your spirit and cleanse and heal it.

Ask Him for His healing touch upon your body, letting your request be known to Him in a spirit of thanksgiving and praise,

For God is God.

Wait before Him, meditate upon Him, look upon Him with your spiritual eyes, and listen for His voice with your spiritual ears.

Obey the commandment of this great God to just "Be still, and know that I am God." (Psalm 4-6 1 10)

We will look at seven reasons why people are sick. Whatever the reason is, remember our God's words ring down through the ages, forever true, "I AM THE LORD THAT HEALETH THEE."

I. God wants your attention.

God wants your undivided attention. Lives are too filled with other things. Ex. 1 - Paul (Saul). Could it be that God has allowed your sickness so you would humble yourself and ask, 'Who art thou and what do you want me to do?' Ex. 2 - Nebuchadnezzar – pride. Ex. 3 – Naaman.

II. Sin.

God hates sin. That is why He went to the cross. Many people have lost sight of that. The true God demands our obedience.

Does God see our sins?

Will God bless us as we sin?

Can we hide our sins?

Can we hide from God when we sin?

Will God judge sin?

Will God punish Christians? (His own children when they do wrong)

A popular teaching today is that God only does good. His chastisement is carried out by His love for us.

God will sometimes use sickness to correct His people. Name some of the sins.

Drunkenness	Worry
Adultery and fornication	Hatred and bitterness
Homosexuality	Other addictions (medicines)
Smoking	Over-working
Drugs	Not keeping the Sabbath

Sins cause sickness!

What should we do about it?

III. To Prove Us

Man creates things and tests to see if they work. God has a proving time also to prepare His creation to be useful to Him in heaven. Is it a test of your faith? He may be proving your love for Him. (Ex. Abraham, Job)

IV. Devil Attack

One of the first things a nation in war will do is learn the tactics of their enemy. How much more do we need to learn our enemy's methods of destroying us! His full-time business is to walk about this earth, devouring men. He has no ethics or standards. He will stoop to any means to destroy a person. Jesus calls him a murderer,

If you are fully submitted to God, and the devil has attacked you spiritually, or physically, or mentally, resist him. Cast him away from you and God's Word assures us he will literally run from you. There is power in the name of Jesus.,

Use His name freely to cast away the devil and the affliction he attacks you with. Don't be passive. Don't accept defeat. Don't give him even one place! Fight him off, in the name of Jesus! Paul ended his life with the triumphant words, "I have fought a good fight!" Who was his fight with? The destroyer! Submit yourself to God! Resist the devil! Then, and only then, will he have to flee.

"Satan, in the name of JESUS CHRIST, I command you to leave my body. I do not accept this sickness you have afflicted me with. I resist your power to destroy me, in the name of the Lord Jesus Christ. I believe that Jesus Christ, the only begotten-Son of the living God, has all power and has come to destroy you. I overcome you and this sickness by the blood of the Lamb, who is my Savior, Jesus Christ."

"And they overcame him by the blood of the lamb..."
There is power, power,
Wonder-working power,
In the blood, of the Lamb,
There is power, power,
Wonder-working power,
In the precious blood of the Lamb.

V.   To Minister

Jesus gave Himself for the needs of others. Are we faithful to such a high calling? Could it be that God has put you in the hospital because it is the only way to get you there to visit the sick? You may be suffering, that you may minister healing and salvation to someone else.

Seldom do we really feel the pain another feels until we have been through that pain ourselves.

Are you as concerned about the needs of others as you should be? Are you a witness and a comfort to the sick? God is more concerned about the way you minister to others than the way you feel. If God can change you from an unfeeling self-centered person into a loving, effective, compassionate witness through your sickness, He will.

Yield to what God is doing in your life. Pray that God will remove all self-centeredness in you and replace it with the compassion that moved His body to constantly minister to those around Him - even from a cross,

Remember the words of our Master to those who would follow His steps: "Take up your cross, and follow me."

It is hard to think of the needs of others when our own needs are so great. In fact, our self-centeredness makes it impossible. But Jesus did it. And He can do it through you. His Word says, "Christ in you (is) our hope of glory,"

Your only hope of living as Jesus did is through total submission to Him. Let Him live again, on this earth, ministering love to all those around Him, this time - THROUGH YOU!

Some people are sick so God can receive glory through their miraculous healing! You may be one who is ... marked for a miracle!

VI. For The Glory Of God

Examples:
  a. Lazarus - Death could not prevent a healing miracle from taking place in Lazarus.
  b. The woman with an issue of blood. She only touched the hem of His garment.
  c. The man born blind. (Ecclesiastes 3:1-8) We don't know God's timetable. Only He does. Our responsibility is to keep faith in a God who loves us enough to heal us. "By his stripes ye *were* healed." Malachi 3:6 - "I change not." Hebrews 13:8 - Believe in the Jesus of the present whose name is "I AM."

God's healing power still flows. It may be easy to say, "God *can* heal me." But can you say, "God *will* heal me"?

VII. God is God

We have lost sight of that fact. We can't command God to do something for us. (Parents wouldn't allow that with a child - neither will God.) James 4:3. Even Jesus said, "Oh my Father ... thy will be done." He never took authority over His Father. For the one who comes for healing, the price has been paid, but God wants us to come asking for His mercy, rather than demanding His healing touch.

Let your requests ... not your demands ... be known to God. "God, why am I sick?"

Perhaps your prayers for healing have not been answered because God desires to teach you that there is a proper way and right attitude in which to approach Him! We are to approach Him with reverence and godly fear. We are told to enter into His gates with thanksgiving and into His courts with praise, and to come before His presence with singing.

Don't try to put God in a box and tell Him what He must do. Don't try to make Him conform to your will. Conform your will to His! Trust Him! Let Him have His way in your life and accomplish His will in you.

We will not understand many things that happen to us and others. But our one responsibility is to submit to Him. To trust Him. For God is God and always will be.

UNDERSTANDING DIVINE HEALING

The life of Christ is available to meet our, physical needs. This life is not received, however, by some magical means or religious rituals. This life is received "by faith when our hearts and lives are prepared in practical ways according to the instructions given in God's Word.

When we approach the question of why people are ill, and what preparations are important in seeking God for divine healing, the relationship between the spiritual man and the physical man becomes increasingly significant.

I believe this is especially true since the whole matter of divine healing is often viewed as if it were some kind of religious magic. There is nothing magical about divine healing! There is no hocus-pocus! There is nothing that remotely resembles witchcraft or black magic or the strange or the weird! Divine healing is DIVINE healing-nothing more and nothing less! It is GOD healing.

Many times our focus is unwisely on men and their gifts rather than on Jesus Christ and His will and His working. Over the years I have found that even when the focus is on anointing with oil by the elders, it is often entered into in a superficial and ritualistic way that almost completely ignores the need for those involved to deal directly with God Himself.

How am I saved? I am born again when I come to God in repentance and faith. Some dear Christians may help me understand by explaining the Gospel. There may be men and women of faith who believe God for my salvation, but I must meet God *personally* to be born into the family of God, I must come to Jesus, open my heart, and receive Jesus into my heart by faith. When Christ comes in, the new birth takes place by the power of the Holy Spirit. I am born again because of my personal relationship with Jesus Christ.

The same is true of Christian victory. I cannot enter into a life of sanctification and experience the fullness of the Holy Spirit by some kind of ritual. Certainly, there may be much help from others; there may be good advice and teaching. Some Christians may stand with me in believing prayer; they may even lay their hands on me in faith. But there must come a point, as a child of God, when I surrender everything to my Savior, when I want Him to be total Lord of my life. I must go to the cross by faith and reckon myself to be dead unto sin, but alive unto God through Jesus Christ. Then He becomes my righteousness, and He fills me with His Holy Spirit. He does the work.

It is no different with divine healing. What sad days we have fallen upon when so often the matter of divine healing is put into a form where it seems that people may be healed without dealing directly with God Himself.

At times, God in His gracious mercy and in fulfillment of Mark 16:15-20 sees fit to heal very new Christians or even non-Christians, When He does that, it is a *sign healing* that accompanies the preaching of the Gospel and the salvation of souls. That does happen just as Jesus said it would. However, this should not encourage Christians to believe that they can come to God at any time without any consideration of their spiritual condition and expect to receive His healing through a sort of magical application of the practice of anointing and prayer. Such a superstitious approach will only end in disappointment, and will bring shame on the name of Christ.

For God to continually ignore the relationship between the spiritual and the physical man, which He Himself has established in Creation, would be unrighteous in God and of no lasting benefit to the human beings involved.

Am I trying to discourage you from seeking God for physical healing? No, I wish to do the very opposite. I want to encourage you to come to God with your physical needs. I want to do it in a manner that is best calculated to bring you the healing you so earnestly desire, and to glorify God in the process. I know that the work God does in our hearts spiritually is an essential part of what He does in our bodies physically.

I believe, therefore, it is of the utmost importance that those seeking divine healing should deal thoroughly with their inner lives before God, so that spiritually they may be in harmony with what they are asking God to do for them physically. The number one key to physical healing is the inner relationship with Jesus Christ. *He* is our health! *He* is our life! *He* is the One who has come to dwell within us and to make our bodies His temple. *He* is the One who brings healing and life and strength to our mortal bodies.

In 1885, Dr. A.B. Simpson was preaching in London, England on the subject, "How to Receive Divine Healing." He said:

Be sure — if God touches you or you want Him to touch you — you use it, this new divine life, this healing for Him. It is an awfully sacred thing to have the very blood of Christ flowing through your veins! It is a solemn thing to have the life of Jesus quickening your heart, and lungs, and nerves; and it would be a dreadful thing to defile it ... it belongs to Jesus ... it is Jesus Himself! And He expects me to walk through the world as He walked, and to use every breath, thought, and power constantly for Him!

Let me introduce you to something I put together to assist the sick person in coming to God with his problem. I call it "A Personal Inventory." If you are seeking the Lord for personal physical needs, you should complete this inventory slowly and carefully. Fill in all the spaces with complete honesty. Meditate prayerfully on the Scripture passages. When you are satisfied that it is complete, take it to your church elders, or some other Christians whom you respect for their godliness and faith. Share the contents with them. Listen to their counsel. When you are confident that you have the mind of God concerning your problem, follow through in obedience as your elders or friends stand with you in prayer.

Please Answer These Questions Before Coming For Anointing And Prayer

What is my physical problem? Please make yourself be concrete and exact:

What do I want God to do for me physically? Please be exact:

What are my reasons for wanting to be healed? Please list them in order of importance in your own thinking:

Please meditate prayerfully on the following Scriptures:
I Corinthians 6:12-20; Romans 12:1-2; I Corinthians 7:3-4; II Corinthians 6:14-7:1.

Now list the changes God wants you to make in the use of your body:

Present Use

Changes God Wants

Please meditate prayerfully on the following Scriptures:
Romans 12:9-10, 14-21; Matthew 5:21-24; 18:15-35.

Now list the names of those persons with whom God wants you to make adjustments, and next to their names, what God wants you to do:

NAME	WHAT GOD WANTS ME TO DO

Write below a solemn covenant with God in which you give Him your body unreservedly to be used for His glory, by life or by death:

Please sign your name here: _____

WHERE DO I GO FROM HERE?

Are you facing a terminal illness for yourself or your loved one? Do not take death for granted! Go to God. Submit fully to His will and His ways.

Follow His Word and the guidance of His Holy Spirit in all things. Wait on God until you have a clear and definite answer.

Remember, with God *nothing* shall be impossible!

There is always a danger of making any approach to God too mechanical. God is a person and wants a personal relationship with us. God Himself has given us some instructions as to how to approach Him. I have tried to explain these instructions in the various chapters as they seemed to relate to the truths being presented.

At this point I will draw them out and state them as clearly as possible, so that there is a simple procedure that can be followed by the person seeking divine healing for himself or another. It may be that some of these steps will not apply to you. Apply the ones that do. Let God lead you. However, be diligent and thorough!

1. STUDY. Begin by making a careful study of the Word of God on the subject of healing. Get a concordance and look up all the Bible passages with words related to the concept of healing — sick, disease, weak, heal, whole, infirmity, impotent, etc. Search out all that God has to say on this matter, asking Him to enlighten you and guide you by His Holy Spirit. This first step is more important than anything else you will do. Take your time. Do it thoroughly and honestly.
2. PRAY. Go to God on a regular basis with your physical problem. Listen to what He has to say to you about it! We listen to our families or friends or various preachers, but we do not listen to God. Try to get the "mind of God" concerning your suffering. In the ordinance of healing in Exodus 15:26 we are told to "diligently hearken to the voice of the Lord thy God."
3. REPENT. Get your life in order. "Do that which is right in His sight." (Ex. 15:26). Deal thoroughly with any known sin in your life. Ask God to search you. He will deal gently but firmly with anything not right in His sight. Make restitution if God leads you to do so. Do not leave any point of controversy between you and God.
4. OBEY. The final condition in the Exodus ordinance of healing is to "give ear to His commandments, and keep all His statutes." Obey the Word of God. Make whatever adjustments are necessary to bring your life into line with the teachings of God's Word as He directs you by His Holy Spirit. Do not get entangled in legalism or asceticism at this point. Do not fall into bondage to the rules of men. Study the Word of God. Meditate devotionally in the Scriptures. Wait on God in prayer. Let God reveal His Word to you as He wants it applied to your life at this time,
5. FORGIVE. Unresolved emotional problems can affect both our emotional and physical health. One of the primary sources of these inner maladjustments is a need to completely forgive. Be honest. Ask God to search your past with you by His Spirit. If

you need to do a memory list, do it thoroughly. When your inner spirit is cleansed, released, and at rest in God, you may find that your healing will come swiftly.

6. RENEW. If your mind is out of control or enslaved by ungodly thought patterns, it needs to be set free so that it can become a channel for God's Word, God's will, and God's own faith. Make a careful study of the subjects of sickness and healing in the Bible,

7. COMMIT. You are now approaching a point of serious commitment to God, Work your way carefully through the personal inventory. Take your time. Do not write out your solemn covenant until your mind is clear and your heart is ready to mean what you say. Lay the inventory out before God. Make your commitment with all the seriousness and finality of which you are capable. Ask God to help you.

8. CALL. Now you are ready to call for the elders of the church.. If possible, have copies of your inventory made for distribution among the elders. Give them time to study it and pray over it. When they are ready, meet with them for discussion, confession, counseling, and prayer. Ask them to anoint you with oil, lay hands on you, and pray exactly as God leads them to pray. At this gathering, God may give you further guidance through the counseling or prayers of the elders.

If you experience healing, praise God and give Him all the glory. If God leads you to give public testimony, obey Him at all costs!

It may be that God will have led you by this time to accept some other form of victory over your physical problem instead of the removal of the problem. If so, accept His leading and continue to be sensitive to Him about the whole matter. He may give you further direction if He intends to remove the problem later.

EXPERIENCING DIVINE HEALING

APPLYING THE CURE - James 5:3A - Is any sick among you? Let him call for the elders of the church.

I. The Call

The one who is sick is the one who is to call and ask for prayer.

It is not the responsibility of anyone to pray for someone to be healed unless the sick person has requested that kind of prayer. If we rush in and pray for people who are sick and we are ignorant of their situation, we may be laying our hands suddenly on someone who is not ready to be healed. By doing so, we would make a mockery of divine healing.

II. The Elders

The elders are servants of Jesus Christ who are filled with the Holy Spirit; who are gifted by God and are there for a ministry. The reason the Lord says that we are to call for the elders of the church is so that they may minister to us. It may be that one of those elders has a gift of faith by the Holy Spirit. It may be that another elder has a gift of miracles by the Spirit. It may be that one of these elders has the gift of knowledge by the Holy Spirit, which may be very important in the healing of that person. It may be that one of those elders has a gift of discerning of spirits, and indeed if that person is sick because of demonic powers, someone needs to be able to discern it, so that those demonic powers may be dealt with and that person may be delivered.

What about "anointing with oil," what is the purpose'? Well, there is certainly no healing in the oil. It was used for religious purposes. What does it signify?

In the Old Testament, anointing with oil signified that someone or something was being sanctified or set apart unto God by the ministry and working of the Holy Spirit. Our bodies are the temples of the Holy Spirit. They are to be holy and are to be set apart unto God for His use and glory.

I believe God gave us the anointing oil to show that the healing would come through the Spirit of God, If God does indeed heal us, He does it by the agency of the Holy Spirit. He is there and He ministers the divine life of Jesus Christ to our physical bodies.

III. The Prayer Of Faith

The most neglected portion of this ordinance of healing is the prayer of faith. This verse doesn't say that the prayer of the elders shall save the sick, or that the prayer of the pastor will save the sick, or that the prayer of someone who has special gifts will save the sick. It says, "The prayer of faith shall save the sick and the Lord shall raise him up." The prayer of faith is a prayer offered to God in which the person who prays truly believes he will receive that for which he prays. What brings faith to the human heart? "Now faith cometh by hearing and hearing by the word of God" (Romans 10:17).

More literally, hearing comes through a *word of Christ*. If we come to God for healing and believe Him for healing, then we should believe that the Bible teaches it. Certainly, we ought to have faith through the Scriptures. It is an aid to faith to know the doctrines of the Scriptures, what the Bible has to say. It is helpful to come to God with trust and confidence in His precious word. The Word of God builds faith in our hearts.

What does God's Word say about divine healing? Many passages of the Old Testament give us clear teaching on this subject – Exodus 15:23-26; Isaiah 53:4-5; Psalm 103:3-5.

As we turn to the New Testament, we find that the Gospels abound with the healings performed by Christ, The Book of Acts continues recounting this healing ministry through the Apostles and other early Christians. In the epistles, the doctrinal aspects of divine healing are expanded in passages such as Romans 8:11; I Corinthians 6:12-14 and James 5:14-16. A good passage is found in Matthew 8;5-13.

Not only do we need to know the Word of God, but there must be a witness of the Holy Spirit in the heart of the believer. The Holy Spirit must take the Word of God, quicken it in the heart of the sinner, convict him, convince him, give him the gift of repentance, and bring him to God. We can't give another person spiritual assurance. Only the Spirit of God can quicken the Word in a person's heart and bring him to a living faith so that he can be saved.

It is the same in physical healing. The Holy Spirit must bear witness in the heart, along with the written word, so that there comes in that heart living faith. The kind of faith that produces dynamic, miraculous results.

God puts His faith in your heart and He brings faith to birth so that you believe. Faith is not something you try to make yourself believe; it is something you cannot doubt! You can't force faith.

We do need to go quietly before God, with His precious Word, humble our hearts in His presence, realize that all healing comes from Jesus, and wait in His presence until we have a word from Christ. Wait in His presence until the Holy Spirit speaks to us and tells us what God wants to say to us. Wait in His presence until our hearts are right. Wait in His presence until our will is yielded. Wait in His presence until we are cleansed, broken, and pliable in His hands — until there is no controversy left between us and God — until all the bitterness is gone — until we are totally cast upon His strength and in our helplessness we are looking only to Christ! Then a word will come from Christ by the Spirit of God that will give us an answer to our situation, whatever the answer of God might be, whether it is healing or not. If He gives us that word of assurance for our healing, we will be healed!

IV. Dealing With Sin
"'Confess your faults one to another, and pray one for another, that ye may be healed (James 5:16).

Many times sin stands in the way of healing. Not always, and in fact, not generally, but sometimes.

I am not saying that God would never heal a person if there was sin in his life. In fact, I have seen God heal people who were not even Christians. But I would say what David said, "If I regard iniquity in my heart, the Lord will not hear me" (Psalm 66:18). Christians who are coming to God to be healed should confess their faults and put every sin out of their lives. (A fault is the overall weakness in a person's life. Sin is the action that results from that weakness.) After all, if we have our hearts right with God, then we can have confidence toward God (I John 3:19-22). You see, we cannot have the witness of the Spirit in our hearts if we are willfully harboring sin against God in our hearts,

V.   The Lord
"The *Lord* shall raise him up (James 5:15)

The elders are to anoint and pray in the name of the Lord. It is to be in Jesus' name! I am astonished at how many do not pray in Jesus' name! I hear people pray all the time and they simply begin, "O God," or "Our Father In heaven," and then when they finish, they just finish! Do you know that there is no way to come to God except through Jesus? Jesus said, "I am the way, the truth, and the life; no man cometh unto the Father, but by Me" (John 14:6). The only way we have access to the throne of grace in heaven is through Jesus! This prayer for the sick is a prayer in Jesus' name.

I want to emphasize again that we are talking about divine healing, not faith healing. This verse says, "The *Lord* shall raise him up." Not the elders, but the Lord. Not the pastor, but the Lord. Not the evangelist, but the Lord — the Lord will raise up the sick.

It is the Lord we must be right with. It is the Lord who will give us the faith to believe. It is His Word that He will speak in our hearts. It is His touch and His life that will raise us up. It is the Lord!

If we really want divine life, we need to get our eyes off of men, and get our eyes on the Lord!

CHAPTER XV

THE POWER OF THE RESURRECTION

The resurrection of Jesus Christ is much more than a religious holiday or a theological truth that we celebrate once a year at Easter time. It is the crux of Christianity. It is what makes Christianity different from the religions of the world. For one to deny the resurrection of Jesus is to deny the reality of Christianity itself, the very heart of our Message.

If a neighbor who is not a Christian were to challenge you with the statement, "A resurrection from the dead is impossible. Prove to me that Jesus Christ came back to life," how would you answer? Would you be able to show your skeptical neighbor objective evidence to prove that the Son of God arose from the grave nearly twenty centuries ago?

The Bible tells us that there are many infallible proofs to prove the resurrection of Christ, Acts 1:3 says: "To whom also he shewed himself alive after his passion by many infallible proofs." Although history declares that the resurrection of Christ took place, we only need to look at the Word of God to get all the proof that is needed.

1. The first evidence I want to point to is the **empty tomb.** Joseph of Arimathea, who was a secret believer of Christ, went to Pilate, who was the Roman governor at that time, and asked to take the body of Jesus from the cross and bury Him in his own tomb.

Usually a man put to death on a Roman cross would be thrown into a pauper's grave. Joseph, a member of the powerful Sanhedrin, boldly went to Pilate and got permission to take Jesus' body and he buried Him is his own tomb,

Several **women**, who stood afar off and watched while Jesus was being crucified, followed Joseph to the sepulcher and saw where he buried Jesus. They then returned to Jerusalem to prepare spices and ointments to be put in the wrappings that Jesus' body would be wrapped in. The Sabbath day was drawing nigh, so they rested on the Sabbath day. Then, according to Luke, "upon the first day of the week, very early in the morning, they came unto the sepulcher, bringing the spices which they had prepared ... And they found **the stone rolled away.** And they entered in, and found not the body of the Lord Jesus." (Luke 24:1-3).

On the first day of the week, the ladies went very early in the morning to take the spices to the tomb. An **angel** of the Lord descended from heaven and rolled back the stone from the entrance to the tomb and sat upon it. The **soldiers** who guarded the tomb were so afraid, they fainted. The Bible says they began to shake and became as dead men. The angel spoke to Mary of Bethany and Mary Magdalene and told them not to be afraid. He said, "I know that ye seek Jesus, which was crucified. **He is Not Here: For He is Risen**, as he said. Come, see the place where the Lord lay. And go quickly, and tell his disciples that he is risen from the dead; and, behold, he goeth before you into Galilee; there shall ye see him; lo, I have told you." (Matthew 28:5-7)

Three security measures had been taken to prevent anyone from stealing the body of Jesus. The first was placing a very large stone over the entrance to the tomb by Joseph himself. Matthew 27:60 and Mark 16:4 both describe the stone as being "very great." The second security measure was to get soldiers to guard the tomb. Matthew 62-66 says, "The next day, that followed the day of preparation, the chief priests and Pharisees came together unto Pilate, saying, Sir, we remember that that deceiver said, while he was yet alive, after three days I will rise again. Command therefore that the sepulcher be made sure until the third day, lest his disciples come by night, and steal him away, and say unto the people He is risen from the dead; so the last error shall be worse than the first." Pilate gave them permission and said to make it as sure as they could. So they sealed the stone and set a watch. They thought this would prevent anyone from entering and removing the body.

With these three measures taken, who would be motivated to steal the body of Jesus? The religious authorities certainly would not because they were the ones who initiated the precautions in the first place. Pilate would not have had his men rob the tomb because he had already washed his hands of the whole matter. Joseph wouldn't because he had sealed the tomb with a very large stone. Some may say that Jesus' body was never placed in the tomb. This cannot be so because Mark 15:47 states, "Mary Magdalene and Mary the mother of Joses beheld where he was laid."

Could Jesus' disciples have stolen the body? The evidence is all against that. Not one of Jesus' disciples was willing to risk his life to save Jesus when He was being arrested. They knew they would risk certain death by stealing the dead body of the One they had earlier forsaken and even denied knowing. Furthermore, the disciples did not expect that Jesus would come back to life. They did not understand until later what Jesus had told them about His death and resurrection. When the women ran to tell them that the Lord had risen and that the tomb was empty, Luke said: "Their words seemed to them as idle tales, and they believed them not" (Luke 24:11). In fact, when Jesus appeared to His disciples, He rebuked them for their lack of belief. "Afterward he appeared unto the eleven as they sat at meat, and upbraided them with their unbelief and hardness of heart, because they believed not them which had seen Him after He was risen" (Mark 6:14).

Some of the soldiers who had guarded the tomb hurried to tell the chief priests what had happened. They were given large sums of money to keep quiet. The religious leaders were actually giving bribes for the soldiers to keep quiet. The soldiers had experienced a visitation from angels which said that Jesus had risen from the dead and yet they were willing to take the bribe. The priests instructed the soldiers to say that the disciples had come by night and stolen him away while they slept. "If the word gets back to Pilate, we will persuade him so you won't have any trouble."

Another piece of evidence that one should consider is that the graveclothes were undisturbed. John records this: "He stooping down, and looking in, saw the linen clothes lying; yet went he not in. Then cometh Simon Peter following him, and went into the sepulcher, and seeth the linen clothes lie, and the napkin, that was about his head, not lying with the linen clothes, but wrapped together in a place by itself." (John 20:5-7) Luke says the same thing, "Then arose Peter, and ran unto the sepulcher; and stooping down, he beheld the linen clothes laid by themselves. (Luke 24:12)

Attention is placed on the linen for a very good reason. The condition of the linen is one of the most conclusive proofs of the resurrected body of our Lord Jesus Christ. The way the clothes appeared convinced the disciples that Jesus had indeed risen from the dead. The custom in those days was to wrap the body in many yards of cloth for burial. This procedure was used with the body of Jesus. Yards of cloth were wound around the body and a hundred pounds of spices and ointments were poured upon the body and into the folds of the cloth. Joseph probably used spices and ointments. The women brought more spices and ointments, and also we read that "There came also Nicodemus...and brought a mixture of myrrh and aloes, about an hundred pound weight. Then took they the body of Jesus, and wound it in linen clothes with the spices, as the manner of the Jews is to bury." (John 19:39-40)

After a few days, the spices and ointments become dry, hard and crusty. They harden like the cocoon of a caterpillar into a solid coating for the body. It wouldn't be possible to remove a body in such a shell without cutting away the wrappings. On the other hand, if the person inside were not actually dead, but had merely fainted, he could not possibly break loose or get out of the wrappings. Some say that Jesus has just fainted and had not really died. If that had been true, and it isn't, there is no way that Jesus could have gotten loose because of the condition He was in. Remember how He had been beaten, how He had been nailed to the cross, how He had hung there in agony, not being able to breath, how He was pierced with a spear in His side. And then having the weight of the sin of the whole world placed on Him. No human could possibly get out of that wrapping, being in His condition.

It would be impossible to remove a body in such a shell without cutting away the wrappings. Peter and John both saw the graveclothes of Jesus lying undisturbed in the tomb just as though the body of Jesus were still encased within them. The wrappings were not cut, squashed, or torn. The only possible explanation is the divine miracle of the resurrection.

Other evidence that is often overlooked is the earthquakes that took place and the darkness that covered the land and the veil that was rent in the temple.

Another very important evidence is Christ's post-resurrection appearances. Although the tomb was empty, if no one saw the risen Lord, we could not say for sure that He was really alive. But during those forty days between the resurrection and the ascension, there were ten different times when Christ was seen. This just didn't happen in one place or to just one person, but in several locations and to different people. He met with the disciples in the upper room. He appeared to the women in the garden near the tomb. He walked with the two men on the road to Emmaus. He prepared breakfast for His disciples one morning by the sea shore. On one occasion in Galilee, He appeared to more than five hundred people at one time.

Another piece of evidence that we don't hear much about, and I think is so exciting, is the fact that many saints that had died, came out of the graves and went into the city and appeared to many. "And the graves were opened; and many bodies of the SAINTS which slept arose, and came out of the graves after his resurrection, and went into the holy city and appeared unto many." (Matthew 27:51-53) This proved that death had been conquered. The first touch of resurrection power was experienced by people who were in actual graves. When Jesus arose and brought with Him out of the grave this large company of Old Testament saints, this was the firstfruit of the resurrection of all the saints.

The Old Testament teaches us that at the beginning of the harvest in Israel, the Israelites would gather a handful of the very first ripened ears of grain and bring them to the priest as an offering of Firstfruits. It was the first handful of a harvest to come. The priest would wave this handful of ears before the Lord and thereby dedicate the entire harvest, these first ears as well as the harvest which was to follow unto the Lord. Notice, it was SAINTS that arose from the grave. There were no unsaved that arose. These were the firstfruits of the great resurrection which we all look forward to. They were the first of the great harvest to follow. The firstfruits were a promise of the great harvest which will doubtlessly come.

The cornerstone of our faith is the Message of the resurrection. "If Christ be not risen, then is our preaching vain, and your faith is also vain ... we are found false witnesses ... we are of all men most miserable. But now is Christ risen from the dead." (I Corinthians 15:14-20)

As Christ's followers, we can confidently proclaim to anyone anywhere and at any time that Jesus Christ lives. And we can back up the claim with "many infallible proofs."

There is one more piece of evidence I want to mention and that is the transformed lives. The women came fearful and dejected. They ran with great joy to share what the angel had told them. Peter, at first, didn't believe. He wondered at what he saw. He was a changed man under the fullness of the Spirit on the day of Pentecost. He preached, "This Jesus who you crucified, God hath raised up." (Acts 2:32). He was a changed man and had great boldness. The risen Christ changed Saul of Tarsus.

The message and the transforming power continues today to transform sinners into saints, defeated Christians into victorious ones, and depressed souls into happy, radiant personalities. This is our message. This is the power that is available to us and can change us into people who are like Jesus.

I remember reading a story one time of a woman who did not believe in the resurrection. Before she died, she ordered that her tomb would be securely closed and that the grave be surrounded and built of great slabs of granite and marble, cemented together and bound with steel clasps. This grave is in a cemetery in Germany. An inscription says, "This burial place must never be opened." A little seed fell into one of the crevices and started to grow. Gradually it burst the stone slabs, and is now a full grown tree. In like manner, the life of Christ dropped into any human heart may seem to be a small thing, but its almighty power bursts asunder the granite walls of death, and brings the consciousness that because He has conquered and is alive, we also shall reign with Him. "Hallelujah, Christ Arose!" He is alive!

CHAPTER XVI

THE POWER OF THE RESURRECTION

Many people do not know the privileges that are theirs because of the resurrection. We are told in the Bible, Romans 13:14, to put on the Lord Jesus Christ. What does that mean? How do we do that? We can't really answer those questions until we understand the deep meaning of the resurrection. The Christian life is not a matter of us getting better and better, trying to improve ourselves. It is completely supernatural and Divine. There are any number of passages in the Bible that tell as that when Christ died, we died with Him. And, when he was raised, we were raised also.

Because of that fact, we can see how intensely practical and glorious the resurrection life can be.

I want to talk to you about six areas that this resurrection life makes possible. This lesson is based on Dr. A.B. Simpson's book, *The Self-Life and the Christ-Life.*

I. **It has power, in the first place, to confirm our hope and assurance of salvation** because the resurrection of Jesus was the finishing work and a guarantee to men and angels that the ransom price was paid and the work of atonement complete. "That if thou shalt confess with thy mouth the Lord Jesus, and shalt believe in thine heart that God hath raised him from the dead, thou shalt be saved." (Romans 10:9).

When Jesus came forth triumphant from the grave, it was evident to the universe that the purpose for which He went there was fulfilled, the work He undertook satisfactorily done, the Father satisfied with His finished atonement. Therefore, faith can rest upon His resurrection as an everlasting foundation, says "Who is he that condemneth, it is Christ that died, yea rather that is risen again." (Romans 8:34)

II. The resurrection of Christ is the power that sanctifies us. It enables us to count our old life, our former self, nullified, so that we are no longer the same person in the eyes of God, or of ourselves; and we may with confidence repudiate ourselves and refuse either to obey or fear our former evil nature. Indeed, it is the risen Christ Himself who comes to dwell within as, and becomes in us the power of this life and victorious obedience.

"Therefore we are buried with Him by baptism into death: that like as Christ was raised up the by the glory of the Father, even so we also should walk in newness of life. For if we have been planted together in the likeness of his death, we shall be also in the likeness of his resurrection. Knowing this, that our old man is crucified with him, that the body of sin might be destroyed, that henceforth we should not serve sin. For he that is dead is freed from sin." (Romans 6:4-13)

Just think about that for a moment. He that is dead is freed from sin.

> "Now if we be dead with Christ, we believe that we shall also live with him: Knowing that Christ being raised from the dead dieth no more; death hath no more dominion over him. For in that he died, he died unto sin once; but in that he liveth, he liveth unto God. Likewise reckon ye also yourselves to be dead unto sin, but alive unto God through Jesus Christ our Lord. Let not sin therefore reign in your mortal body, that ye should obey it in the lusts thereof. Neither yield ye your members as instruments of unrighteousness unto sin; but yield yourselves unto God, as those that are alive from

the dead, and your members as instruments of righteousness unto God." (Romans 6:8-13)

It is not merely the fact of the resurrection but the fellowship of the Risen One that brings us our victory and our power. We have learned the meaning of the sublime paradox, "I am crucified with Christ; nevertheless I live; yet not I, but Christ liveth in me" (Galatians 2:20). This is the only true and lasting sanctification, the indwelling life of Christ the Risen One, in the believing and obedient soul.

III. **There is power in the resurrection to heal us.**
He who came forth from the tomb on that Easter morning was the physical Christ, and that body of His is the head of our bodies, and the foundation of our physical strength, as well as our spiritual life. If we will receive and trust Him, He will do as much for our bodies as our spirits, and we shall find a new and supernatural strength in our mortal frame and the pulses of the future resurrection in our physical being.

> "But if the Spirit of him that raised up Jesus from the dead, dwell in you, he that raised up Christ from the dead shall also quicken your mortal bodies by His Spirit that dwelleth in you." (Romans 8:11)

> "For we which live are always delivered unto death for Jesus' sake, that the life also of Jesus might be manifest in our mortal flesh ... Knowing that he which raised up the Lord shall raise up us also by Jesus, and shall present us with you." (II Corinthians 4:11)

IV. **Christ's resurrection has also a mighty power to energize our faith and encourage us to claim God's answers to our prayers, and ask difficult things from God.**
What can be too difficult or impossible after the open grave and the stone rolled away? God is trying to teach us the exceeding greatness of His power to usward "who believe according to His mighty

power which He wrought in Christ when He raised Him from the dead and set Him at His own right hand," (Ephesians 1:19-20) Christ's resurrection is a pledge of all we can ask for, and if we fully believed in the power of that resurrection we would take more than we have ever done.

V. **The resurrection of the Lord Jesus Christ is the power for true service.** The testimony of His resurrection is always peculiarly used by the Holy Spirit as the power of God unto the salvation of men. It was the chief theme of the ministry of the early apostles. They were always preaching of Jesus and the resurrection. It gives a peculiar brightness and attractiveness to Christian life and Christian work.

The message of the resurrection is the message that a sad and sinful world needs today. The more of the indwelling Christ and the resurrection life in Christian work, the more will be its living power to attract, sanctify and save the world.

> "Wherefore, my brethren, ye also are become dead to the law by the body of Christ, that ye should be married to another, even to him who is raised from the dead, that we should bring forth fruit unto God." (Romans 7:4)

VI. **Christ's resurrection will enable us to meet the hardest places in life and endure its bitter trials.** We read in Philippians that the power of His resurrection is to bring us into the fellowship of His sufferings, and make us conformable onto His death. We go into the resurrection life that we may be strong enough to suffer with Him and for Him,

His sufferings are on behalf of others and the power of resurrection will bring us to share His high and holy sorrows for His suffering church and a dying world. It is a fact that the harder our place and the lower our sphere of toil and suffering, the more do we need the elevation of His grace and glory to meet it. From the heights we must reach the depths. Therefore we find these epistles, which lift us into heavenly places, bring us back in every instance to the most commonplace duties, the most ordinary relationships and the most severe trials.

These letters to the Ephesians and the Colossians which speak about the highest altitudes of faith and power, speak also more than any other of the temptations common to men, and the duties of husbands and wives, and the need of truthfulness, sobriety, honesty and righteousness, and all the most unromantic, practical experiences of human life,

The apostle speaks of glorying in tribulation. "Glory'" expresses the highest attitude of the soul, and "tribulation" the deepest degree of suffering. And. so it would teach us that when we come to the deepest and lowest place, we must meet it in the highest and most heavenly spirit. This is going down from the Mount of Transfiguration to meet the demoniac in the plain below, and cast out the power of Satan from a suffering world,

Yes, these are the sufferings of Christ. The power of His resurrection is designed to prepare, enable us and help us to rise into all the heights of His glorious life, that like Him we may go forth to reflect it in blessing upon the lives of others, and find even sweeter joy in the ministrations of holy love than we have in the ecstasies of Divine communion.

> "And he said unto me, My grace is sufficient for thee: for my strength is made perfect in weakness. Most gladly therefore will I rather glory in my infirmities, that the power of Christ may rest upon me." (II Corinthians 12:9)

> "For unto you it is given in the behalf of Christ, not only to believe on him, but also to suffer for his sake." (Philippians 1:29)

> "For it is God which worketh in you both to will and to do of his good pleasure." (Philippians 2:13)

VII. **Christ's Resurrection was His Victory Over Death.** He had gone down into the den of the King of Terrors in single combat and come forth Conqueror, and not only had come forth alone, but brought with Him a train of rescued captives. "And the graves were opened and many bodies of the saints which slept arose and came out of the graves after His resurrection and went into the holy city and appeared unto many." (Matthew 27:52)

These were the firstfruits of the resurrection and they are pledges of that great company who at His second coming will come forth from the cemeteries of earth and will be clothed upon with glorified bodies and enter with Him into the inheritance of the Age to Come.

Henceforth death is a conquered foe, its sting is gone and to the child of God it has no terrors. It may still come to him as it came to the Master, "but it will be as a servant and not as a master, to open the gates of heaven and let us pass into the joy of our Lord: for He hath abolished death and brought life and immortality to light by the Gospel. And He Himself has told us "If a man keep My sayings, he shall never see death."

VIII. **Christ's Resurrection was His Victory over Satan.** Death was but one of Satan's dark disguises. When Jesus conquered death, He conquered "Him that had the power of death, that is the devil." His resurrection has guaranteed the final overthrow to the "prince of darkness," and. standing by that open grave we can put our feet upon his neck and triumph over him as a conquered foe.

IX. **Christ's Resurrection was His Victory over Sin.** He went down into that tomb as a person might go into a dungeon under a sentence for debt and crime. Had He remained in that prison. it would have shown that the debt was still uncancelled and the sentence still in force. But when He comes forth in victory and glory, all the officers of heaven's court of justice waiting upon Him and the Father Himself recognizing Him and taking Him to sit down by His side on the Ascension Throne, then we may know that the debt is paid, the cross is cancelled, and the power of sin destroyed. His deliverance was your deliverance for "He was delivered for our offences and raised again for our justification."

But not only does His resurrection cancel the curse that was against us, it brings the power of His life to dwell within us and purifies from the dominion of sin. Our life is just an impartation of

His resurrection life. He rose from the dead not for Himself but in union with His body, the Church, and that resurrection guarantees to each of us the power to rise above sin and into all the resources of His grace and the fullness of His life. Sanctification as well as salvation springs from the open tomb and the life of the risen Lord and the very secret of it is "Reckon ye also yourselves to be dead indeed unto sin but alive unto God through Jesus Christ, our Lord. Let not sin therefore reign in your mortal body that ye should obey it in the lusts thereof; neither yield ye your members as instruments of unrighteousness unto sin, but yield yourselves unto God as those that are alive from the dead and your members as instruments of righteousness unto God," (Romans 6:11-13)

X. The Resurrection of Jesus Christ Guarantees Victory over every Obstacle that can Obstruct our Way. It is the pattern of His kingly power over all forces and adversaries and guarantees to us that abide in Him and press on in the power of His resurrection that nothing can prevail against us but that all things shall be subdued under the victorious feet of overcoming faith ... The Lord Jesus can pass through the stones of difficulty and if we are walking with Him we can pass through them too, and so rise above them that even if they still remain they cannot impede us or imprison us but we may overleap their barriers and laugh at their resistance.

Have we spiritual difficulties, temptations and obstacles? Let us not wait for them to pass away but rise above them in resurrection life of Christ, and instead of being hindered by them, turn them into occasions of greater victory and blessing.

How do I respond to such a message? By faith I enter into the full power and authority of my Lord's resurrection. I desire to walk in the newness of life that is through my Lord's resurrection. Lead me into a deep understanding of the power of the resurrection. Help me learn to apply all the privileges that are mine as a result of the resurrection. In Jesus' name. Amen,

CHAPTER XVII

FELLOWSHIP

A: SHARING BURDENS

What is fellowship? "Fellowship has been defined as 'the close personal relationship which believers have with God and with each other by virtue of their union with Christ. This relationship is affected by the Holy Spirit who lives in every believer, uniting him with Christ and every other believer. It expresses itself in the sharing of material goods and the work of the gospel ministry, and in mutual love and unity.' Fellowship is an active relationship shown among believers." (Steve Donoghue, *Fellowship*, Rives Junction Baptist Church Paper, May, 1988.)

As Christians, our fellowship must first be with God. It is a very special friendship we have with Him. He made us for fellowship. Fellowship with God makes us happy Christians. When we don't have that kind of relationship with God, we don't experience the joy of the Lord that he desires that we have. (John 15:11; Romans 14:17; I Peter 1:8)

There are two basic reasons why we need fellowship with God. First, it is necessary if we are to live a life of victory over sin and Satan. We can't do this in our own strength. So if we fail to cultivate and maintain fellowship with God, we soon backslide and drift away from Him.

The second reason fellowship with God is so necessary is so we can bear fruit for the Lord. Jesus used the example of the vine and the branches in John 15:4-5. He points out that the branch can bear fruit only while it is firmly attached to the vine and draws its life and fruit-bearing qualities from the vine. If we fail to maintain fellowship with the Lord, our lives become barren, and we accomplish little or nothing.

Fellowship is also necessary with other believers. We have become so busy these days that it is difficult to find time for real fellowship. Yet, we all need this badly and should make it a priority in our lives to make time for it.

Fellowship is much more than Christians just getting together and talking. Fellowship means a mutual sharing of something we have in common. What we have in common is Christ and in order to have real fellowship we need to share the reality of Christ in our lives. True Christian fellowship involves the exposure of our real selves to each other. We often hear in revival meetings about "transparent honesty." Men fellowship with each other as they are mutually transparent. John 1:7 says, "If we walk in the light, as he is in the light, we have fellowship with one another, and the blood of Jesus Christ, God's son, cleanses us from all sin."

Getting together with other Christians and sharing can be encouraging, challenging, and healing.

We seem to be very slow in sharing our problems with others. We are almost made to feel that if we have a problem, it is sin. And who of us would choose to confess our sins to others? But this is exactly what God's Word encourages us to do.

I will never forget an article I read in the *Alliance Witness* in 1982. It was entitled "Confess Your Sins to One Another." (Lars Wilhelmson, Aug. 28, 1982) This is exactly what the author talks about in this article. He deals with three areas.

1. **Forgiveness** – "The result of open confession of who we are and what we have done is forgiveness, not rejection. (I John 1:9). Openness, self-disclosure, exposure and cleansing go hand in hand ...

"Although it has been taught that secret sins should be confessed secretly to God, private sins privately to the person offended, and open sins before the group offended, there are private sins that need to be confessed openly.

"Even private sin affects others. What we do or do not do affects everyone. Confession, therefore, is important."

2. The second area he deals with is **healing.** James 5:16 says, "Confess your sins one to another that ye may be healed." "The purpose of confession is the healing of both our bodies and our souls. Open confession encourages the sinner to forsake his sin and be comforted and strengthened by the knowledge and empathetic friends will be praying for him. In addition, such confession challenges others in the group to bring their own sins to light. Someone has said that people relate to our weaknesses, not to our strengths.

"In many ways another person's listening ear, understanding heart and affirmative words can be of much greater help than the expert counsel of a psychiatrist or psychologist. Healing is our need, not merely understanding. And healing comes only through forgiveness.

"The reason why so little healing is taking place today is that there is so little confession. We remain physically and spiritually incapacitated because we are too proud to confess our sins."

3. The third point deals with **Restraint**. There are dangers in confessing our sins to others. "What, how and to whom we confess is of crucial importance. Apart from the guidance and restraint of the Holy Spirit, intimate sharing might easily degenerate into exhibitionism in which we try to outdo each other in dredging up sensational sins. Paul says there are some things too shameful to talk about. (Ephesians 5:12).

> "Some things can be confessed to a large group, more personal things may be confessed in a smaller group, and certain intimate things are only properly confessed to one other person. We need to be sensitive to God's leading or our exposure will be destructive rather than constructive. (Proverbs 28:13; James 5:16; I John 1:7)"

He concludes by saying, "May those of us who have a thirst for transparent honesty and a willingness to listen and to open our heart confess our sins to one another.

"Although this may involve only a few at first, like leaves it will grow until it permeates our church family. Honest, loving fellowship becomes magnetic. We must be willing to take the first step.

"Let us unmask ourselves before God and our fellow believers so that we may live in the light, experiencing prosperity, healing and fellowship."

Fellowship is the fusion of personalities in the Person and presence of Jesus. It is more than human ... it isn't generated by zealous promotion or set up by clever organizers. It is horizontal, man with man ... and vertical, man with God.

It is men coming together like grapes ... crushed. The skins of ego are broken. The rich, fragrant, exhilarating juices of life are mingled in the wine of sharing and understanding and caring.

Fellowship is impossible when men wear masks. That is why a man must be right with God before he can enter into fellowship with man. There must be openness and transparent honesty. The man who is hiding from God cannot be open with men.

Christian Reality
By: Henry and Freda Teichrob

YOU NEED FELLOWSHIP

Fellowship is an extra special friendship. God made you for fellowship. God loves you and wants to be your friend. He wants you to love Him and be His friend. Fellowship with God makes you a happy Christian. Fellowship with other Christians will make you a stronger Christian. So go to Sunday school, church and other Christian meetings. Make friends with other Christians. Be sure that your best friend is a Christian. Do not run around with a gang who do not know the Lord. Try to attend a Christian camp or conference in the summer.

FELLOWSHIP INDISPENSABLE

Without fellowship with God, the Christian does not experience the true **joy** of the Lord. God intends that His people have joy (John 15:11; Romans 14:17; I Peter 1:8). When one does not live in fellowship with God, he loses the joy of salvation. Happy Christians experience close fellowship with God; they pray, read God's Word and obey Him.

Fellowship with God is necessary to a life of **victory over sin and Satan.** Backsliding begins when fellowship with God is not cultivated — when Bible study and prayer are neglected. If you fail to do your part in maintaining your fellowship with God, you will soon drift away from the Lord, and you will eventually fall into sin. You cannot resist Satan in your own strength; you must get strength from the Lord daily. No Christian can grow strong spiritually and triumph over sin and the world if he does not live a life of prayer and communion with the Lord.

Fellowship with God is indispensable if the Christian is **to bear fruit for the Lord.** Jesus illustrated the relationship between Himself and the Christian by the union of the vine and the branch (John 15:4-5). He pointed out that the branch can bear fruit only while it is firmly attached to the vine and draws its life and fruit-bearing qualities from the vine. If we fail to maintain fellowship with the Lord, our lives become barren, and we accomplish little or nothing.

What is fellowship? A cup of coffee and a donut? Is it a family night supper? How about getting together to sing and pray? Well, it can be these things, but actually it encompasses a lot more.

Fellowship has been defined as "the close personal relationship which believers have with God and with each other by virtue of their union with Christ. This relationship is effected by the Holy Spirit who lives in every believer, uniting Him with Christ and every other believer. It expresses itself in the sharing of material goods and the work of the gospel ministry, and in mutual love and unity." Fellowship is an active relationship shown among believers.

Probably the easiest way to learn what fellowship means for us is to study what are called the "reciprocal commands" of the New

Testament. These are specific directions given to believers. They tell us how to treat one another (reciprocal).

FORBEAR ONE ANOTHER
CONFESS YOUR SINS TO ONE ANOTHER
FORGIVE ONE ANOTHER
DO NOT JUDGE ONE ANOTHER
DO NOT SPEAK EVIL OF ONE ANOTHER

It is my prayer that God will use these to further define and refine Christian fellowship. Christian to Christian ministry is an important part of a church's life and growth. As a part of His church, will you join me in learning how to minister to, fellowship with, and love one another?

GOD'S RECIPE FOR FELIOWSHIP

How do we keep in close fellowship with others? What unites us? Is it our perfect performance? Our efficiency? Our freedom from all offences or injustices? These are all desirable virtues, but the question still remains: If we based our fellowship on efficiency and flawless performance, would the church live and prosper? We doubt it.

How did Jesus receive us into His fellowship? We ought to receive each other in the same way as Jesus Christ does,

> *He forgives and cleanses away our sins.*
> *He stoops down to serve us.*
> *He deals patiently until we get the point He is trying to teach us.*
> *He holds back disciplines that would crush or discourage us.*
> *He limits our trials according to our growth and understanding.*

His sacrificial, suffering love is the only reason we become victorious Christians. The love He has shown us is the love we must learn to give each other. Patience, making allowances for each other, gentleness, and deference are all parts of the divine recipe that unity is made of.

By: Harold J. Brokke

FELLOWSHIP. SHARING BURDENS

Simple Ways To Invest In The Lives Of People

Community doesn't just happen; community is created. Like families who want to establish a tradition of eating together, we have to practice being the body of Christ intentionally. This means building friendships, doing things together as a shared body, and being there for others in practical ways. Here are a few ways you can do that:

1. Share meals together. This doesn't have to be a big deal. Call two other families, grab sandwiches, and head to the park on Sunday afternoon.
2. Drop off food for a couple who's had a baby, but take enough for everyone so you can eat together.
3. Organize a playgroup for parents and kids in your neighborhood.
4. Ask real questions - more than "How was your day?" And take time to listen.
5. Offer to baby-sit for parents of small children so they can spend time investing in each other.
6. Call one person each week that you wouldn't otherwise talk to,
7. Take notice of what people do - and cheer them on,
8. Give away some money. Do it anonymously.
9. Pray for people. When you see them or when they come to mind, ask God to draw them to Himself.

In Home life Magazine

4 WAYS TO BE NEIGHBORLY

Follow these practices, and it will be a beautiful day in your neighborhood.

1. Ask God to help you see others through His eyes. What gifts and strengths did He create in them? In what unique ways can they bring glory to God? We're all created in His image and are all in the same need of His love, grace, and forgiveness.

2. Ask God to help you love others like He would. Pull from God's abounding love for you when you're interacting with others. Use His love to shape your words and actions toward your neighbors.

3. Take the Initiative. Truly loving your neighbors means going out of your way to meet their needs - no strings attached. It may simply be stopping long enough to smile and genuinely ask how they are, or perhaps it's dropping an encouraging word to someone for a job well done.

4. Practice the I Corinthians 13 kind of love - even when it means sacrifice or tears. This passage is full of practical ways to love others. Try meditating on one verse each day, applying it throughout your daily routine.

By: Tom Blackaby
In Homelife Magazine

BRING US TOGETHER

Oh, God, we go through life so lonely, needing what other people can give us, yet ashamed to show that need.

And other people go through life so lonely, hungering for what it would be such a joy for us to give.

Dear God, please bring us together, the people who need each other, who can help each other, and would so enjoy each other.

By: Marjorie Holmes
Guideposts
Dec. 1974

CONFESS YOUR SINS TO ONE ANOTHER

One of the most glaring deficiencies among Christians today is the lack of genuine fellowship. Much of what passes for fellowship is not that at all.

Fellowship means a mutual sharing of something in common. What Christians have in common is Christ. Therefore, Christian fellowship is the mutual sharing of our lives in Christ,

A Christian can have friendship and companionship with unbelievers, but not fellowship. Paul puts it "What fellowship can light have with darkness? ... What does a believer have in common with an unbeliever?" (II Corinthians 6:14-15).

Unfortunately what often passes for fellowship in Christian circles is our opinion about the weather or a sports event. True Christian fellowship involves the exposure of our real selves to each other.

In order for God to have fellowship with man He found it necessary to reveal Himself to man. For man to have fellowship with God, he in turn must be open before God, This is why John could write, "If we claim to have fellowship with him yet walk in darkness, we lie and do not live by the truth" (I John 1:6). To walk in darkness is to live in sin and to conceal that fact. To walk in darkness is to attempt to conceal our real self from God,

God fellowships with man as He shows Himself to man, and man in turn fellowships with God as he opens his life to God. It follows, then, that men fellowship with each other as they are mutually transparent. John said, "If we walk in the light, as he is in the light, we have fellowship with one another and the blood of Jesus, his Son, purifies us from every sin" (I John 1:7).

The apostle is saying not only that if we walk in truth and obedience (the light) we have fellowship together, but also that if we live honest lives (requiring, of necessity, self-disclosure) we experience fellowship with God and each other.

FORGIVENESS

The result of open confession of who we are and what we have done is forgiveness, not rejection. "If we confess our sins, (God) is faithful and just and will forgive us our sins and purify us from all unrighteousness" (I John 1:9). Openness, self-disclosure, exposure and cleansing go hand in hand.

It is the belief that our problems are unique that makes us think the Christian community cannot handle our sins and other burdens.

Our struggles, whatever they are, may be unique to us, but they are common to man (see I Corinthians 10:13).

Although once we have accepted Jesus Christ as Savior and Lord of our lives we are saints, in the sense that we still sin we are sinners. We all struggle with temptations and we sometimes fail in that struggle. It is at this point of failure that confession not only to God but to each other is helpful.

Open confession of sin was practiced during Bible times. David said to Nathan the prophet, "I have sinned against the Lord" (II Samuel 12:13). Saul admitted to Samuel: "I have sinned. I violated the Lord's command and your instructions. I was afraid of people and so I gave in to them" (I Samuel 15:24). Notice how specific Saul gets in his confession. He says that it was his fear of man that led to his sin.

Although it has been taught that secret sins should be confessed secretly to God, private sins privately to the person offended, and open sins before the group offended, there are private sins that need to be confessed openly.

Even private sin affects others. What we do or do not do affects everyone else. Confession, therefore, is important,

HEALING

James tells us, "Confess your sins to each other" (5:16). While open confession brings psychological relief, its main purpose should be to obtain prayer to gain healing: "Confess your sins to each other and pray for each other so that you may be healed."

The Greek word here translated "healed" is used elsewhere to denote healing of the soul as well as of the physical body. Open confession encourages the sinner to forsake his sin and be comforted and strengthened by the knowledge that empathetic friends will be praying for him.

In addition, such confession challenges others in the group to bring their own sins to light.

Confession to another person is important because it keeps us from self-deception. If we are already caught in the "cycle of self-deception" — to borrow a phrase from Dietrich Bonhoeffer — it can be broken. Other people can help us to bring to light the reality of what we are doing.

There is a danger of confessing our sins to ourselves instead of to God. Bonhoeffer suggests that this is the reason "for our countless relapses and the feebleness of our Christian obedience."

In many ways another person's listening ear, understanding heart and affirmative words can be of much greater help than the expert counsel of a psychiatrist or psychologist. Healing is our need, not merely understanding. And healing comes only through forgiveness.

This is the point that James makes: "Confess your sins ... so that you may be healed." The context is that of healing.

The purpose of confession is the healing of both our bodies and our souls.

The reason why so little healing is taking place today is that there is so little confession. We remain physically and spiritually incapacitated because we are too proud to confess our sins.

Notice that the exhortation to confess does not limit it to confession to the elders the sick person has called to pray for him. Confession is to be to "each other."

Weak, imperfect human beings though we are, we are God's vehicles of forgiveness. When confession is made to us, it is also made to God, and we have the authority to affirm God's forgiveness.

Jesus said to His followers, "If you forgive anyone his sins, they are forgiven; if you do not forgive them, they are not forgiven" (John 20:23).

RESTRAINT

There are dangers in confessing our sins to others. What, how and to whom we confess is of crucial importance. Apart from the guidance and restraint of the Holy Spirit, intimate sharing might easily degenerate into exhibitionism in which we try to outdo each other in dredging up sensational sins. Paul says there are some things too shameful to talk about (see Ephesians 5:12).

Especially in the area of sexual sins we must use restraint. As long as people know what basically we are struggling with, that is sufficient.

Some things can be confessed to a large group, more personal things may be confessed in a smaller group, and certain intimate things are only properly confessed to one other person. We need to be sensitive to God's leading or our exposure will be destructive rather than constructive.

But we should not discredit self-disclosure because of its possible abuse. Prayer, teaching, Holy Communion can also be abused, yet we carefully continue to avail ourselves of these means of grace. The same should be true of confession.

God's promises concerning confession are prosperity, healing and fellowship: "He who conceals his sins does not prosper, but whoever confesses and renounces them finds mercy ... Confess your sins to each other and pray for each other so that you may be healed ... If we walk in the light, as he is in the light, we have fellowship with one another, and the blood of Jesus, his Son, purifies us from every sin (Proverbs 28:13; James 3:16; I John 1:7).

May those of us who have a thirst for transparent honesty and a willingness to listen and to open our hearts confess our sins to one another.

Although this may involve only a few at first, like leaven it will grow until it permeates our church family. Honest, loving fellowship becomes magnetic. We must be willing to take the first step.

Let us unmask ourselves before God and our fellow believers so that we may live in the light, experiencing prosperity, healing and fellowship.

The Alliance Witness
Dr. Lars H. Wilhelmsson
April 28, 1982

XVIII-B: CHURCH MEMBERSHIP

As a new Christian you will need to become a part of a good Bible believing and Bible preaching church. You will need to gather for worship, for prayer and for being fed, and later for service. This is vital to your growth in Christ.

"A word now about the Church, It was established by Christ and has existed down through the centuries as His principal means of proclaiming and perpetuating the truth of the Gospel, and to provide an opportunity for fellowship and corporate worship.

"Pray and ask God to help you to decide where you should join and when you feel settled in your mind make an appointment with the minister of the church. He will be more than happy to talk with you. Tell him in simple terms, something of your background and your desire to live the Christian life. He will instruct you as to further steps and will tell you the conditions of membership in the church. Look upon him as a friend. He is a servant of God and is trained to understand spiritual problems. You may have confidence in him. Tell him you are anxious to be of some service in the church and offer your services in whatever way you may be useful. This is important.

"Membership is meant to be a vital and meaningful thing and you should belong to a congregation in which you can cast your influence and express your Christian life."

(*Decision, Helps For New Christians,* Churches of Christ in U.S.A., 475 Riverside Dr., NY, NY)

Some people attend a church, but fail to become a member of it. Their reasons may be because they do not fully believe in all the church teaches and stands for. It may be because they do not want to be in submission to the rules and leadership of the church. It may be because they do not want to become that involved. That is why you should ask some questions before you join any church.

CHURCH MEMBERSHIP

The Lord Jesus Christ established His church as the spiritual home of believers. His church includes all true believers — of the past and of the present. When you believed on Christ as your Savior, you were baptized by the Spirit into Christ's body, the church.

The church is both visible and invisible — part of the whole church being scattered throughout the world and part having already gone to be with the Lord in heaven. The Christian must have more than a spiritual connection with the invisible church; he must identify himself with the visible church by becoming a member of it.

A Christian needs fellowship with other believers. That fellowship may be found in a Bible-believing church which provides preaching, teaching and prayer. Meeting together with other Christians will help to strengthen your faith in the Lord Jesus Christ.

Jesus authorized the church to administer two ordinances for the spiritual good of His people — water baptism and the communion meal. The believer needs the church because only there can he partake of these ordinances commanded by Christ.

Water baptism pictures the steps of salvation. As the repentant believer is immersed in the water, it symbolized his identification with Christ in His death and burial. The baptismal candidate is saying to the world, "I stand with Christ and I believe His blood washes my sins away." As the believer is raised from the water the resurrection is in view. He is now raised to walk in newness of life through the power of the indwelling Christ (Romans 6:34).

Christ instituted communion as a reminder of His death for us and and as a reminder that He is coming again. Communion is a time of fellowship when believers break bread (symbolizing Christ's body) together and drink the cup (symbolizing Christ's blood), remembering they have been made one by the death and resurrection of Christ,

Since being baptized and becoming a member of the church is so important, ask your counselor or the pastor about enrolling in the membership class in order to prepare yourself for this step of spiritual progress.

Here, are some simple questions which you should ask concerning any church you may contemplate joining.

1. Does this church believe and proclaim the Bible to be the true Word of God and uphold it as such in all of the services?
2. Does the minister preach plainly concerning the atoning death of Christ on the cross and redemption through His shed blood?

3. Is the necessity for an experience of the new birth through personal faith in Christ emphasized?
4. Does it have a vital interest in foreign missions and an active missionary program? Are missionaries prayed for and supported? Are Christian young people challenged for missionary service?
5. Are believers urged to win souls to Christ and taught how to do it?
6. Is the literal personal return of Jesus Christ to earth believed and proclaimed?
7. Is it a praying church? Are regular weekly prayer meetings held in which the people participate in praying?

If you begin to neglect church attendance you will probably drift in your own Christian life. If you habitually stay away from the house of God, you may become a real backslider. God, realizing the necessity of Christian fellowship in the church, has urged us not to forsake "the assembling of ourselves together" (Hebrews 10:25). You need the inspiration that comes from fellowship with the other Christians in the church, so be regular in your attendance.

The church is the Christian's spiritual home while he is on earth. There he is spiritually supported, comforted and prepared for heaven, where the entire family of God will at last assemble. There he will cultivate fellowship with them. He can turn to his church for spiritual help at times. He will be instructed in the Word of God and built up in the faith. There he will worship his God each Lord's day.

On Being A Real Christian
By: G. Christian Weiss
Moody Press
Chicago, IL
1951, P. 98-99, 101

XVIII-C: THE LORD'S SUPPER
YOU AND COMMUNION

There is probably no other church service that so situates a worshipper in God's presence as does the communion observance. Like water baptism, this ordinance was given to us by our Savior during His life on earth. He instituted communion the night prior to his death on Calvary.

Christ was killed during the Passover, the great feast of the Jews. He became the ultimate "lamb," or sacrifice. In the original Passover, a lamb was slain by Jewish families and its blood sprinkled on the door of each home; thus the death angel bypassed that home. The Egyptians made no such provision, and the death visitor went to each of their homes.

Jesus showed His disciples that He was the final Lamb to be slain. The elements at the supper table were the symbols or emblems that Christ used to convey His message. The bread was Jesus' body, broken for man's sins and sicknesses. The wine represented His blood, spilled on Calvary.

Each time you partake of communion, you are graphically reminded of Christ's passion on the cross. The realization comes to you afresh that Jesus died for you.

Kyer Pearlman wrote: "The Lord's Supper is a sacred object lesson. Bread and wine are a picture of death – the separation of body and life, the separation of flesh and blood. The bread tells us that the Bread of Life must be broken in death in order to be distributed among the spiritually hungry; the poured-out wine tells us that His blood, which is His life, must be shed in death in order that its cleansing and quickening power may be supplied to needy souls."

From the very beginning of the Church, the gathered saints have joined regularly in their participation of communion, or the Lord's Table. It is one of the paramount reasons for you and me to be a part of an active church today, for there we fulfill Christ's command to continue the practice of communion.

The participation offers so many benefits. There we examine our inner souls and minds to see if unknown and unconfessed sins may be lurking there. Our spirit is nourished as we partake of the spiritual food as well as the emblems of communion. The observance enables us to draw closer to Christ and to each other, a most helpful benefit. Indeed, many have testified to being healed, physically, mentally, and spiritually in such services.

And, of course, as Paul wrote to the Corinthians, we observe the Lord's death until He comes. There is a constant reminder that Jesus will soon return. The Lord's Table here is a look into the future when we shall gather around the Marriage Supper of the Lamb that all eternity provided to extol His love and favor. So the communion service is truly a time of celebration and victory.

THE LORD'S SUPPER

Being a part of a church body molds me into a team member, a soldier in the ranks of the Christian Army. And participation in the Lord's Supper disciplines me for that endeavor. I must constantly survey my attitudes and thoughts. It is a time of self-examination, looking inside my own life to see if there are wrong motives.

Through the Lord's Supper, I have renewed within me the fact that, while I am a sinner, Christ's life has made me an heir of God. While I myself am unworthy, Christ makes me worthy. Praise the Lord for this marvelous spiritual exercise. Involve yourself in it regularly — only one more reason why you need to be a part of the Church.

Waking Giant
By: Dan Betzer

Believers should keep the Lord's supper. (I Corinthians 11:2)

1. It was instituted by Christ. (I Corinthians 11:23)
2. It is symbolic and representative. (Luke 22:19-20)
3. It is to be observed until Jesus returns. (I Corinthians 11:26)
4. The Church needs all of its members. (I Corinthians 12:22)
5. All believers need the Church. (Ephesians 4:12-13)

The Lord's Supper is a picture of the crucified life. Jesus gave us this picture of Himself as He wanted to be remembered. The fruit of the vine depicted His shed blood. The bread portrayed His surrendered body. Taken separately, they picture His death on the cross for human sin. Eaten, they symbolize the fact that the power of the cross has entered into every area of human living to redeem it and to become a vital energy in its daily living. (I Corinthians 11:25)

By: Elliott Horton

VIII-D: BAPTISM

THE ORDINANCES OF THE CHURCH

BAPTISM

Waking Giant
By: Dan Betzer

Water baptism is not a "take-it-or-leave-it" situation. Christ did not make it optional! He made it very clear that He did not want water baptism omitted from either the teachings or the practice of the Church. When He gave the Great Commission to His disciples, He commanded them to "Go ye therefore, and teach all nations, baptizing them in the name of the Father, and of the Son, and of the Holy Ghost." (Matthew 28:19)

There are different ways a person can be baptized. I believe the Bible teaches that immersion is the proper method of baptism. When Jesus was baptized by John in the Jordan River, the Bible says He came "up out of the water." When Philip baptized a believer, according to Acts, Chapter 8, they "went down both into the water" and "came up out of the water." The Greek word for baptism has the meaning of immersing, plunging, drenching, sinking and overwhelming.

When a believer is immersed in water, he is momentarily buried under the tide. Part of the object lesson, which baptism is, is that we show the world we have been buried with Christ and then raised to new life.

Let me ask you a question. Have you ever been baptized in water? It is not enough to be Christened as a baby, or dedicated by your parents. If you have become a Christian, then you need to be baptized. You should ask your pastor to baptize you before the congregation. This is a part of your public confession of faith to the world that as for you, you will serve the Lord.

THE MEANING AND IMPORTANCE OF BAPTISM
By: Dr. Samael J. Stoez

The primary meaning of baptism in the scriptures is a witness to the spiritual significance of the atonement in the death, burial and resurrection of Christ. When Jesus said to Peter and John, "I have a baptism to be baptized with and how am I straitened till it be accomplished!" (Luke 12:50), He was saying that He would be covered with afflictions and become "exceeding sorrowful, even unto death." (Matthew 26:3) The figurative expression of being plunged into deep water is used in Scripture to illustrate the sorrow and reproach of death itself (e.g., Isaiah 43:2; Psalm 69:14-15; Lamentations 4:54). Christ's baptism included death and burial, and it is this atoning baptism of Christ which becomes the objective in symbol for all other baptisms of the Bible. Redemptive atonement is the central theme of all Scripture. (Note Romans 6:4)

Since water baptism has a clear and definite purpose revealed in Scripture, two areas of Christian responsibility are evident.

First, baptism is necessary in order for the local church to exhibit a vital testimony. Baptism and the Lord's Supper are ordinances, and their observance witness to the spiritual and corporate nature of the church's fellowship. That baptism carries this significance is clear from Paul's evaluation of the Corinthian church: "I thank God that I baptized none of you, but Crispas and Gaius; lest any should say that I had baptized in mine own name" (I Corinthians 1:14-15). Because baptism testifies to the oneness of the Body of Christ and the Corinthian church was divided over loyalty to human ministers, Paul was thankful he had baptized only a few believers,

Paul was not making baptism an optional practice (cp. I Corinthians 14-15); indeed, he recognized the significance where the testimony of an established church was true and vital. The church which lightly esteems baptism will, in all probability, lightly regard carnal division, or vice versa. Identity with Christ in baptism should also demonstrate unity in the one Body of Christ. Until corrective measures are taken and the significance of the new birth is restored, the form of observance ought not to serve as a substitute for what it is supposed to represent.

The corporate nature of a church's responsibility is to be recognized in the ordinance of baptism and should constitute a testimony to its own faith, serving to strengthen the faith of a convert as he seeks identity in the local body. The process of discipleship as given in the Great Commission is teaching, baptizing and observing continually all that Jesus had commanded (Matthew 28:19-20). The church that fails to follow through in one aspect of this process will in that measure fail in its discipling process as directed by our Lord.

Second, baptism is necessary to a confession of obedience for the convert. The common expression that baptism is "an outward sign of an inward work" is incomplete. It is rather an outward confession of an inward commitment to discipleship and becomes both a safeguard for the church and a confirming experience for the believer, When Christ was baptized in the Jordan River the Father's voice affirmed Christ's identity and the Holy Spirit descended upon Him in the form of a dove (Matthew 3:16-17), witnessing to the significance of Christ's identity in the coming atonement. When a believer is baptized in the name of the Father, Son and Holy Spirit, he confesses his identity with Christ and the Triune God is present to affirm his confession.

God has provided an ordinance wherein witness to obedience of faith can be given to God, to the church and to one's own self. Baptism should bear witness to a full awareness of an actual death to one's old unregenerate life and to the resurrection of a new life in Christ. The convert thereby declares that he is to be counted in all that is necessary to discipleship. He is no longer "of the world" since he has committed himself to Christ and His service, cutting every tie that would bind him.

In such an act, both the church and the convert are strengthened and the commandment of the Lord is obeyed.

THE ORDINANCE OF WATER BAPTISM

The ordinance of water baptism was established by Christ himself for the benefit of the church. Water baptism is sometimes called the ordinance of initiation. This initial act of obedience to Christ will strengthen the new believer. Proper prearation for the act of baptism should occur soon after conversion. That water baptism follows conversion was a norm in New Testament times and should be in today's church. Baptism is not an option. It is a regular procedure of Christian discipleship.

The apostle depicts baptism as a symbol of the believer's union with Christ. Baptism also symbolizes the believer's identification with Christ in His death and resurrection. As an ordinance, it speaks of the radical inner change wrought by the regeneration. The believer rises from the baptismal water charged to walk in newness of life. That newness of life is the effect of being born again through the Holy Spirit.

The ordinance in this instance portrays the putting off of the old life and the putting on of a new life. In the practice of baptism one must change his garments. In a spiritual sense, the baptismal candidate is celebrating the change that has taken place in his own life as a result of accepting Jesus Christ as personal savior.

Water baptism is not an innovation of the church but an ordinance established by Christ. Christian baptism is unique among the religions of the world. It is not a magical rite which makes one a Christian. Baptism is an act which bears testimony to the world of God's grace and witnesses to the believer himself of the inner working of God in his heart.

CHAPTER XVIII

TITHING

I have a friend who has had many money problems in the past. She would overspend. She would borrow money from anyone she could. She could not keep her checkbook straight and she had many checks bounce. And, she would not tithe.

God dealt with her in many areas of her life, but it wasn't until she yielded this area of her life to the Lord that she began to experience real joy and victory.

Perhaps as a new Christian you don't know what tithing is. "Tithing is the giving of one tenth of your income to God. This is God's program to keep propagating the Gospel. Everything you possess comes from the hand of God. Do not be selfish with what God has given to you in the first place. You will want to honor God with your substance, but you have not even begun to give until you have paid your tithe or ten percent that belongs to God. "Will a man rob God? Yet ye have robbed me. But ye say, wherein have we robbed thee? In tithes and offerings. Bring ye all the tithes into the storehouse, that there may be meat in mine house, and prove me now herewith, saith the Lord of hosts, if I will not open you the windows of heaven and pour you out a blessing that there shall not be room enough to receive it" (Malachi 3:8, 10). If you are not a systematic tither, you may be robbing God. God will be no man's debtor, you cannot out-give God. God has promised to supply your needs, but try giving offerings and gifts after your tithe is paid and see how

God will open the windows of heaven to give back to you. Your church is your storehouse of spiritual food, blessing and service, so this is the proper place to give your tithe. The gathered funds carry on the work of God at home and on the mission field. If you cannot share your earthly possessions with God, God cannot possess much of you. How can your relationship and love to God be a complete oneness if you hold back of the material possessions that God has given to you in the first place? "Give, and it shall be given unto you: good measure, pressed down, and shaken together, and running over, shall men give into your bosom" (Luke 6;38).

Many people have problems letting go of their pocketbooks. As Christians, God has given us the privilege of sharing in the spread of the gospel. This should be a real joy for us.

I once sold some property I had. As a result I had $300 to use as tithe money. I asked the Lord where He would have me use it. I ended up letting a missionary friend in Indonesia use it for a need on the mission field. As it turned out, because of the people being willing to donate their labor, they were able to build an airstrip and a church. That was exciting!

People use many excuses for not tithing. My friend did. H.G. Lindsay, Jr. suggests six excuses:

1. Why give my money away? (Hag. 2:8, I Corinthians 6:19, Psalm 2:1, Psalm 50:10)
2. I am in debt.
3. I cannot afford to tithe.
4. Too hard on the poor. (Tithing has nothing to do with poverty or riches, but with the relation of man to God. It is not little money but little love that keeps us from tithing.)
5. Tithing is legalism,
6. Later I will tithe.

When we tithe, it is evidence that we are obeying God. It shows we have faith to believe that God will meet our needs when we obey Him. It also shows our love for the Lord and our surrender to Him.

(Homer G. Lindsay, Jr., *Spiritual Helps For The New Member,* Daniels Pub., Orlando, FL, 1969, p. 65-70)

HOW TO SUCCEED WITH YOUR MONEY

A. Three Ingredients for success
   1. Desire
   2. Time
   3. Plan

B. Criteria For True Success
   1. Worthy Goals
   2. Awareness of the Lord's Will
   3. Submission to the Lord's will.
   4. Initiative

C. The Trouble With Credit
   1. Artificial means to fulfill desire
   2. Makes it easy to overspend
   3. Causes additional debt
   4. Creates a false sense of security
   5. Unawareness of what has been spent

D. What Determines Value?
   1. Usefulness
   2. Durability
   3. Necessity
   4. Productivity

E. Importance Of Planning
   1. Thinking it over
      a. Do I need it?
      b. Can it fill my need?
      c. Can I afford it?
   2. Making a plan
   a. Consider it carefully
      b. Determine course of action
      c. Implement your plan immediately

F. Understanding What Causes Money Problems
   1. Seven Major Money Mistakes
      a. Debt
      b. Irresponsibility
      c. Wrong values
      d. Speculation
      e. Selfishness
      f. Cheating
      g. Wrong priorities

G. Four Cornerstones To Financial Freedom
   1. Recognize that God owns everything
      2. Giving as God has prospered you
      3. Establish a spiritual purpose
      4. Prioritize your goals

PERSONAL BUDGET WORKSHEET

Dr. Stoesz has said, "The issues of stewardship are at the heart of the Christian life ... Perhaps at no point is the issue as direct as in the matter of giving of tithes and offerings. This represents my life occupation, my investment in eternal things, my worship of God, and my covenant with him." In order to implement this truth practically into your life, list the following principles and consider each briefly:

a. Reckon on stewardship as a way of life.
b. Determine to give God the "firstfruits" of your life.
c. Live within the means God provides,
d. Determine to live debt-free.
e. Ascertain "real needs" versus "wants."
f. Purpose to use money wisely in order to have more for God.
g. Establish priorities,
h. Charge no more than you can pay at the end of the month.
i. Follow a personal budget scrupulously,
j. Pray for wisdom and discipline in the use of your money.

Consider the process of establishing a budget (or have someone qualified in this area do it) based on actual income and real needs. I want to point out that the tithe should always come off the top of the gross income. If we prayerfully and wisely budget the rest of our money, God often "stretches" the remainder so that it is more than adequate and even results in our having more to give to God's work.

PERSONAL BUDGET WORKSHEET

Read Needs Amount Budgeted	Actual Income
1. Tithe (10% Gross) $	$ Salary (net)
2. Housing – Rent $	$ Interest
3. Utilities $	$ Dividends
4. Food $	$ Miscellaneous
5. Clothing $	
6. Auto/Trans. $	
7. Insurance/Medical $	
8. Taxes $	
9. Savings/Recreation $	
10. Emergencies $	
TOTAL $	$

HOW AM I HANDLING MY MATERIAL POSSESSIONS?
"Do not conform yourselves to the standards of this world"
(Romans 12:2)
Author Unknown

	Yes	Somewhat	Actions for Improvements
1. The Bible and Material Possessions: Do I know Biblical teachings on material possessions?			
2. God's Purpose in Material Possessions: Do I realize God has created all material possessions and allows me to be a steward of them to bring glory to Him?			
3. Influences on Spending: Do I allow God – not goods – to motivate my spending?			
4. Have Nots: Do I give systematically to some individual(s) less fortunate than I?			
5. Success and Material Possessions: Do I honestly believe success is made up of elements other than accumulated material possessions?			
6. How Much Is Enough? Am I consistently cutting back my purchases in order to help my family and me discover how much is enough for us?			

7. Planning for the Future: Am I balancing my faith in God with caring for such matters as making a will and investing basics for the future?			
8. Sharing My Home: Do I freely open my home for Christian meetings and causes?			
9. Tithing: Am I regularly tithing my income?			
10. Gifts: Because God has blessed me through my church and denomination am I giving my monetary gifts to causes supported by them?			
11. Sacrificial Giving: Because Jesus has first claim on my life, am I prayerfully considering giving up something dear in order to give sacrificially to his cause – especially missions?			
12. Lifestyle/Commitment: Am I changing my priorities so that my commitment to Christ is reflected in everything I do – especially in the way I handle my material possessions?			

Signed:_____

Date: _____

GIVING TO GOD
Learning to Live
By: Dr. K. Bailey

God's Word says, "It is more blessed to give than to receive" (Acts 20:35). Sin makes one selfish. God gives the Christian a new mind so that he wants to give. A believer willingly gives his life, strength, time, money, and whatever he owns to the Lord,

God owns everything and you are just using what really belongs to Him. God is happy to give you whatever you need. Because of all that Christ has done for you it should be easy for you to give back to Him whatever He may ask.

The Bible teaches the believer to tithe. This means he should give to God at least ten percent of everything he earns (Malachi 3:10).

If every Christian would obey God by tithing, there would always be enough money for God's work. Start now to tithe. Obedience to God will bring rich blessings from the Lord.

The believer's love for God motivates him to give to God. That which is given above the tithe is a love offering to God,

A Christian must manage his money well in order to give as he should. Some Christians rob themselves of the joy of giving because they have made poor commitments of their money, so they have nothing to give to God.

Money is a necessary means of exchange in our modern world and Scripture recognized this reality. The Bible also recognizes the menace that money can be in the life of a believer. The sin of covetousness is deadly, twisting the personality so that the person in its grips lives to accumulate money.

The Word of God teaches the believer how to use his money for the glory of God. Money management for the Christian is not just for the purpose of giving, but because it represents a lifestyle compatible with divine standards.

Memorize II Corinthians 9:7 - "Every man according as he purposeth in his heart, so let him give; not grudgingly, or of necessity; for God loveth a cheerful giver."

Answer these questions from the Bible:

1. Should you give because you have to, or because you love the Lord and are happy to give to Him? II Corinthians 9:7.
2. Will God bless you and give you more as you tithe? Malachi 3:10.
3. God's Word says giving is like planting seeds because later you get back more than you planted. What will happen if you are selfish and forget to give? II Corinthians 9:6.
4. What day of the week should Christians bring their gifts for God to church? I Corinthians 10:2
5. Should Christians be selfish and try to save a lot of things just for themselves? Matthew 6:19-21.
6. Read the story in Mark 12:41-44. Why do you think Jesus was so pleased with what this woman did?
7. Read II Corinthians 8:9. What kind of example did Jesus give us by what He did for us?
8. Does God want you to help people who are poor and needy as well as give money in church? Psalm 41:1-3. Does He promise any reward for doing this?
9. Should Christians help send missionaries to other places and other countries to preach about Christ?

Do you need to make a commitment in this area? Maybe you need to say, "I trust God. I believe His word. Because of Christ's love for me, I will make full surrender of my life to Him. I will be faithful in my Christian stewardship."

The things which seem to be real problems disappear quickly when one is willing to seek God's will and do it. When a duty becomes clear, that is the time to begin performing that duty. The only way to go through with a Christian duty is first to begin and second, to continue.

Remember: YOU CAN NEVER OUT-GIVE GOD!

CHAPTER XIX

KNOWING GOD'S WILL AND MAKING WISE DECISIONS

We all have probably asked the question, "Can I know the will of God for my life and if so, how?" The answer is yes! One of our greatest privileges as God's children is knowing the blessedness and joy of this direct comminication of God's will. God cares so much for us that He wants to regulate the details of our lives. This is one of the greatest proofs of His love for us. Isn't it amazing that He would let us know how to live and walk so as to please Him? It seems almost too good to be true.

There are four ways in which God reveals His will to us.

1. Through the Scriptures.
2. Through providential circumstances,
3. Through the convictions of our higher judgment.
4. Through the inward impressions of the Holy Spirit on our minds.

When these four agree it is safe to say that God has spoken and is directing us.

Darwin E. Merril, in his book, *This New Life Of Yours,* suggests there are three areas of consideration for finding God's will for your life. It's easy to remember them by recalling three "Ps," - Preparation, Practice and Proof.

1. **Preparation**

The preparation needed for finding God's will is there must be a definite desire to know God's will and the place of service He has for you. John 7:17 assures us that if any man will do God's will (or is willing to do it), he shall know of the doctrine, whether it be of God. We must have a definite desire and concern to know the will of God, and we can be sure He will reveal it to us.

The person's heart, however, must be in tune with God before he can know the will of God. The Lord never reveals His will to someone who is not consecrated. In Romans 12:1,2, we find that we must present our bodies a living sacrifice to God, and be conformed to God, instead of to the world, before He will show us His good and acceptable and perfect will for our lives.

2. **Practice**

The practice used for finding God's will and your place of service. Read Proverbs 3:5,6. The secret for the way to find God's will is found in this passage.
- A. You must not have any preconceived convictions on what is God's will for your life — lean not toward your own understanding.
- B. You must consider all the facts involved, praying about them - trust in the Lord.
- C. You must not dictate the terms of the manner of God's revelation of His will - acknowledge Him in all ways.
- D. Reading God's Word will hasten the revelation of His will - He shall direct your paths.

3. **Proof**

The proof of having God's will. The impression, or what you felt was God's will becomes a conviction. There is a peace and rest in your heart and soul. You feel you can accept the decision of God with a heart of thanks. You can honestly look at God's revealed will and say that neither self, personal desire, human reasoning, nor human advice gave you God's will, but it came from the Spirit of God Himself. You are happy in your decision.

All of this may at first sound complicated. But if you will pray about these suggestions and consider them carefully, you will find that they will help a great deal in finding out what your place of service is for the Lord.

This New Life of Yours
By: Darwin E. Merrill

How Can I Know The Will Of God?
Make a list of those areas in which you would like to know God's will. Include both large and small areas. After you have made your list, spend 15 minutes in personal study applying the principles.

I. PREPARATION

II. PRACTICE

III. PROOF

PASTOR, HOW DO I KNOW I AM MAKING THE RIGHT DECISION?
By: Rev. D.J. Horton
Pastor of Anderson Mill Baptist Church
Spartanburg, SC
From their church paper.

Some questions seem to get asked more than others, and the one written above is one of the questions I hear most often. I would like to make a humble attempt at answering this question. Granted, all situations are different. This question is asked about important issues such as marriage, child-rearing reconciling a relationship, changing jobs, and even where and when to serve in the church. However, I would submit that no matter what the specifics around a decision are, there are some basic truths that will help us navigate our way to the right decision. I would offer the following:

1. **Live obediently.** When we are living according to God's word and will, we instantly put ourselves in a great position to discern more clearly what we are to do in any situation. There is nothing that obedience in our life does not help. In other words, you can't go wrong when you are living right. Mistakes will come but major sin caused by poor decisions will not be a part of our lives if we seek obedience on a daily basis,

2. **Determine what kind of decision you are making.** For example, the decision to intentionally hurt someone, or be dishonest about your taxes is a "no brainer." In fact, you don't even have to pray about it. God's word is clear that those things are wrong and should not be a part of our lives. These are moral decisions and many of them are cut and dry. However, life is not always that simple. Many decisions are not cut and dry. When there is no obvious right or wrong answer, then one must trust God to show him or her the right direction,

3. **Seek Counsel from three important places.** First, seek counsel from God through His word. Find Scripture that addresses your situation. If this is difficult, ask for some assistance from a pastor, Sunday School teacher, etc. Second, seek counsel from those closest to you. Your spouse and/or close relatives and friends only want what is best for you. They can be a powerful source of wisdom. Many people fail to do this because they believe they must appear to have all the answers and that asking for help shows vulnerability. This is not true. Asking for counsel shows wisdom and a strong desire to do what is pleasing to the Lord. Third, seek counsel from godly men and women in your life that you consider spiritual leaders. Use your pastor, Sunday school teacher, or mentor. Many

times these people have the gift of discernment and can serve as righteous prayer warriors on your behalf.

4. **Pray.** But do not just pray about the decision. Pray about your motivations, desires, and any prejudices that might exist within your heart. Ask the Lord to cleanse you of anything that might hinder clarity within your thinking. Pray for all others involved in the decision and ask for the ability to encourage them. Pray for the patience to wait on the Lord's timing in the decision. Pray for godly counsel to come your way and for the ability to recognize it when it does. Finally, ask the Lord simply and humbly what He would have you do and for the strength to do it.

5. Once you diligently complete steps one through four and you have determined that what you are deciding is not against God's will or His word, then **MAKE the decision.** God filled His Bible full of people who were not afraid to step out on faith. Be humble, be obedient, be prayerful, be wise, and **THEN BE DECISIVE.**

6. Once your decision is made look, listen, and feel for peace. God's peace is not always relief from burdens, nor is it instant gratification for a job well done. Rather, His peace is an inner calm and sense of assurance that you have done what is right and made a well informed decision to the best of your ability. If you do not sense His peace, do not be afraid to acknowledge that God could be calling you to reexamine your decision. No matter what you or I do, we will not always make perfect decisions. But we can live a life filled with the blessings of choosing God's best when life brings us to a fork in the road.

WILL OF GOD
The Glorious Journey
By: Dr. Charles Stanley

Ephesians 1:3-5

Blessed be the God and Father of our Lord Jesus Christ, who has blessed us with every spiritual blessing in the heavenly places in Christ, just as He chose us in Him before the foundation of the world, that we should be holy and without blame before Him in love, having predestined us to adoption as sons by Jesus Christ to Himself, according to the good pleasure of His will.

I think it is safe to say that the questions I am most frequently asked as a pastor revolve around the issue of the will of God. "How do I know the will of God for my life? How do I know, in a situation when I have two options, which way God wants me to go? How do I know which person I am supposed to marry? How do I know when to change jobs? How do I know if I should stay in the job I am in? What school should I put my kids in?"

As Christians, we believe that God is interested in these decisions and that, in fact, He has a plan for our life. We believe that God has a preference as to which direction we should take. But discovering His will can be a frustrating process.

God definitely has a will for you. If you were to take a concordance and look up the phrases "the will of God" and "God's will," you would find that, in the New Testament, the phrases fall into two categories. One category is "God's moral will." The other category is "God's personal will."

God's moral will in Scripture is the "dos" and "don'ts." "Thou shalt do this," "Thou shalt not do this."

For instance. Peter says that it is God's will that we obey human government. In I Thessalonians 4:3-4, Paul writes that it is the will of God that we be sanctified, that we abstain from moral impurity. There are almost a dozen other instances in the New Testament where God says, "This is My will."

The other category that we are usually interested in is God's personal will, which is His personal agenda for your life — the things that He has specifically designed for you.

Paul says in I Corinthians 1:1 that he has been "called to be an apostle of Jesus Christ through the will of God." God didn't call everybody to be an apostle. That was God's specific will for Paul.

Let's look at how to discover God's will. First, why do we even have to discover God's will? If I am His child and He is my heavenly Father, why doesn't He just make it plain? Why all the seeming mystery? Why all the tension? Why all the pressure? Why all the tears and the fasting and the praying?

The answer to that question lies behind this whole issue of knowing God's will. As you read the New Testament and the Old Testament, you find that God is always more interested in revealing Himself than simply revealing details about His will for us. God does not want to function simply as an information center in our lives; He wants to be involved in our lives in the most intimate of ways through a relationship that revolves around faith and trust. In times of pressure and questioning when we seek His will, God has the intention of drawing us into a more intimate relationship with Him.

Think about a time when you had to make a big decision; you prayed diligently and finally came to a conclusion about God's plan. Not only did you arrive at an action plan, but you also emerged from the situation amazed at the goodness and grace of God, You had not only more information about what He wanted you to do, but also an awareness of who He is and how much He loves you.

God is involved in this process. And while we might want simply information, He wants us to trust Him. The principle of discovering God's will is couched in the context of a relationship. He is working to reveal Himself to you because He wants you to walk away from the process with your faith greater and your relationship more intimate.

There is an island in the Bahamas called Inagua. And from that island they export salt. There is a harbor that has been dredged out and is large enough for big ships to dock and get the salt. The water is not very deep, so the ship captains have to be careful once they come inside the reef to stay inside the channels,

I was photographing in the area and noticed a very interesting phenomenon. On the mainland behind the harbor on this particular island was a large pole. About forty yards behind that one, farther inland, was another one. Another was positioned in alignment in the distance, I figured this had something to do with the ships' navigation but wasn't sure how it worked. I asked a man standing nearby to explain their function. He said, "Well, those are channel markers."

I responded, "Channel markers are usually in the channel. These are on the island. So how does this work?"

He responded, "What happens is, as a ship approaches the island, the captain of the ship can see these three poles. He has to keep maneuvering his ship so that all three poles line up. And once they are aligned he knows he is in the channel and can approach the island safely."

What God has done for us through His Word is give us channel markers that assure us that when these things line up, we can know we are following His will. I want you to be impressed with the incredible, practical approach God gives us to discern His will. It is not some kind of mysterious journey. He has given us objective channel markers to help us know whether or not our decisions agree with God's will for our life.

The first channel marker is God's moral will. God will never lead you to do anything that is in conflict with His moral will. Any decision you make or any option you are looking at that is in conflict with God's moral will is not of God.

He will never lead a husband to leave his wife for a more spiritual woman. It won't happen. That is not God. God will never lead a teenager to rebel against his or her parents. That is not God's way. God will never lead you to cheat on your income tax in order to give more money to the church.

God's moral will plays another important role. Obeying His moral will, the things that are clear, is the foundation for decision making in the more challenging arena of discerning His personal will. In John 14:21, Jesus puts it this way: "He who has My commandments and keeps them, it is he who loves Me. And he who loves Me will be loved by My Father, and I will love him and manifest Myself to him."

The man or woman who develops a lifestyle in harmony with God's moral commands will experience God's guidance in a special way. When you and I live lives of obedience, we are consistently in step with God's thoughts and God's ways. It makes sense that we are able to discern His voice more easily.

You are going to have a difficult time discerning God's personal will if you ignore His moral will. Why? Because as I said earlier,

God is not interested in simply being an information center. He is interested in an intimate relationship with you.

There is a second marker — the principles of God's Word. The difference between God's moral will and His principles is this: God's moral will is clear commands. "This is what you do. This is what you don't do." Principles, however, are more like equations — an equation where God says, "If a man does this, he can expect this to happen. If a woman does this, she can expect this to happen."

A principle is the law of sowing and reaping. We always reap what we sow. Another principle is this: things that you hold tightly to diminish; things that you scatter and give are multiplied and returned. "There is one who scatters, yet increases more; and there is one who withholds more than is right, but it leads to poverty" (Proverbs 11:24).

The Bible is full of principles. And here is the key: at some point in your decision making, your options will intersect with the principles of God's Word. The Bible is so incredibly packed with principles, there is no way for you to face any decision and not intersect with the principles of God's Word, God has given us His principles as a check and balance in the decision-making process.

Discovering the will of God is not the result of spending hours in a spiritual darkroom. That is not the picture. God has made it far simpler than that. He has given us principles that intersect with all the choices we must make. God wants to renew your mind with His principles. It is not a mystical thing. It is very practical.

Principles take precedence over a sense of inner peace. God does not want us to be slaves to vacillating feelings. He is far more practical than that. If you will keep God's moral will and constantly renew your mind to what is true, then, as the decisions come along, you will be able to sort out the options and discern what the will of God is for you. How practical. How wonderful.

Do you spend time in God's Word every day? If you don't and if you are not in some sort of systematic discipline to fill your mind with God's principles, you are going to have a difficult time making right decisions, because the key to decision making is the principles of His Word Promises have a role, but they are girded by the principles.

There is a third marker — wisdom, Ephesians 5:15 says, "See then that you walk circumspectly, not as fools but as wise." God has called us to ask of every invitation, every opportunity, every business transaction, every family decision, this important question: Is this the wise thing to do? In light of my present state of mind, in light of the present state of my relationship with my wife or my husband, in light of what's going on at work, in light of what's going on in my life right now, is this the wise thing for me to do? In light of where I want to be in the future, in light of the kind of marriage and the kind of family I want to have, in light of where I want to be financially, in light of where I want to be in terms of my career, in light of where I want to be in terms of my ability to serve God, is this the wise thing to do?

This question will quickly reveal your motive. It will reveal the selfishness in your relationships. It will reveal the greed in your financial decisions.

So in decision making, the place to start is measuring the decision against God's moral will. You have to measure it against the principles of His Word, and you have to measure it against this penetrating question: Is this the wise thing to do? If you do these things and still don't know God's mind, an example from Paul's missionary journeys is helpful.

Do you know how Paul decided which cities to visit? Paul apparently went where he wanted. He wasn't trapped by thinking, Oh, what if I do the wrong thing? What if I step out of God's will? He understood the incredible principle that God's will is not a tight-wire that we fall off of. Acts 16;7 gives insight: "After they had come to Mysia, they tried to go into Bithynia, but the Spirit did not permit them."

A key word is **tried.** They tried to go to Bithynia. It is where they wanted to go. We don't know how, but somehow Jesus said, "Paul, this isn't the right route."

Paul, in his own way, said, "Okay, no problem." He did not get depressed or discouraged; he just started out in a new direction.

God, through His Word, has demonstrated that if children of God are willing to be honest and, to the best of their ability, do what God wants them to do, He will intervene if they make faulty decisions,

Do you realize that God has made a commitment to tell us what we need to know when we are trying to make wise decisions? God doesn't want you making foolish decisions. Read the book of Proverbs. It is full of wisdom because He wants us to make wise decisions,

It is evident that God is interested in directing and guiding our lives, providing helpful wisdom for effective decision making. Let's ignore the ridiculous. Don't worry about what color socks you are going to wear. That is not the issue. We are talking about decisions in your life that matter — who you are going to marry, where you are going in your vocation, how you are going to spend or invest your time, what you are going to do with your money or your relationships with your family.

Remember, we belong to God. We do not have the right to make up our mind about what we are going to do and how we are going to do it independently of the will, the purpose, the plan, and the desire of God. You forsook that right when you said, "I receive the Lord Jesus Christ as my Savior." In that moment, He became the Lord of your life, whether you acknowledge it or not, whether you understood it or not.

We are to meditate on the Word of God. Scripture gives an understanding of the ways, the will, and the purpose of God. "Your word is a lamp to my feet and a light to my paths (Psalm 119:105). As we search and think deeply on the Word of God, asking God to speak to our hearts, He will work in such a way to help us understand His will.

The only way to know the mind of God is to know the Scriptures. The Scriptures sift, purify, and clear up our thinking process so we are able to think after God.

Sometimes God will give us wise counsel through others. However, you want to be sure that you are getting wise, godly counsel. Before you seek somebody's counsel, first examine his life. Is that person living in obedience to God? Is his lifestyle one of submission to the will of God?

A godly counselor is going to tell you the truth, whether you like it or not. If somebody is committed to God's principles, he is going to be honest with you. So counselors are often God's way of giving us direction.

The Holy Spirit has an essential role in helping us know God's will. "Now we have received, not the spirit of the world, but the Spirit who is from God, that we might know the things that have been freely given to us by God" (I Corinthians 2:12).

One of the purposes of the Holy Spirit is to show you the truth. Remember what Jesus said in the Upper Room? He said, "When He, the Spirit of truth, has come. He will guide you into all truth" (John 16:13).

There will be times when we are suddenly faced with a decision. In that moment, we may not be certain what to do, which way to turn. As one of His prescribed, designated, divine responsibilities, the Holy Spirit unfolds and unveils God's will for you by interceding in your behalf with God the Father to reveal the mind of Christ in that given issue.

You cannot trust your feelings when it comes to discovering God's will. "Oh, I just feel wonderful about this. I think this is what we are going to do."

"Well, is that what God wants?"

"Well, it looks like everything is working out."

"Well, have you asked God about it?"

"No."

If you have sin in your life — willful, deliberate sin — trying to discover God's will is frustrating. You are saying, "God, I really want to know Your will in my life in this area. Whatever You say to do, I am willing to do. But God, don't worry about this area of sin right now. I'll take care of that later. I have got to know Your will now. I'll deal with that later." God is not going to let you ignore sin. I am not saying you will never know the will of God if there is sin in your life. Sometimes God may show you exactly what to do, but then He will say it will never work until you deal with the sin problem. There is danger in praying and asking for God to show you His plan in a major decision when there is willful sin in your life.

Something is already wrong in your thinking process if you are tolerating sin. You have rationalized a given area that God says has to be dealt with. Here is the problem: our evaluation of sin is not the same as God's! He hates it. He wants it out of our lives, and He sees it as a stumbling block to His best for us.

Sometimes God delays revealing His will because He is getting us ready. He knows we are not prepared to fulfill His plan. You may lose your job and say, "Lord, what am I going to do?" God knows that in three months He has the most fantastic job ready for you, but He is working on some character traits such as perseverance and faith in your life in the interim.

CHAPTER XX

HOW TO HAVE CONSTANT VICTORY IN CHRIST
(Praise and How to Handle Pressure Biblically)

PRAISE

You see that this chapter on praise is entitled "How To Have Constant Victory in Christ" and "How to Handle Pressure Biblically." You may ask, "How is that possible?" I believe there are principles in God's Word that teach us that this is possible. If we believe that Romans 8:28 is really true, that "**all** things work together for good to them that love God, to them that are called according to His purpose," then when trials come we can still praise God because we know He is in control. If we are to have victory over adversity, then we are to consciously choose to praise God in everything, even when we don't understand. It isn't required that we understand, it's required that we trust God anyway.

When everything seems dark outside and our joy is gone, praise is the switch that turns the light of joy back on for us. When that light of joy is turned on, then others can see the glory of God in our lives. When we fail to praise, we fall short of giving God the glory that belongs to Him alone.

I was watching Christian TV one day, and Dr. Jack Hayford was speaking on Praise. He used an acrostic for praise and the following message:

P: Present your bodies. Romans 12:1-2

Kneeling, singing, standing in his presence, upraised hands, voice, be silent before Him, physical expressions. I present myself to you as a person of praise. James 4:10 — Humble yourself to the Lord and He will lift you up.

R: Raise holy hands in praise. Declaration of His worthiness. Is it pride that keeps us from it? It is not cultural. Thank you for the blood of Jesus that cleanses me from all sin. Psalm 63:3-4. A man said to Pastor Hayford, "What you said might injure someone's pride." Pastor Hayford said in response, "I don't want to injure it, I was hoping to kill it."

A: At all times. Psalm 34:1; Psalm 35:18.

I. Invite fresh Holy Spirit fullness. Operating where I am when I praise Him. Ephesians 5:18-20. Keep on being filled. Do it by speaking to yourself in Psalms, hymns, and spiritual songs.

S: Sing a new song in hope. Psalm 96:1; 98:1.

"In everything give thanks..." Not fatalism. Many things that happen to us are not of God. They are from Satan. The will of God is giving thanks. Praise me in the midst of problems (circumstances). How do you sing a new song? Just decide to sing your heart to the Lord. Sing His word back to Him.

When we sing, something happens in that situation even in the most trying circumstances. Songs in the night — Songs of deliverance.

I woke up the other night with a new song going through my mind. I couldn't remember it all, but it was about "Jesus is a true liberating friend."

E. Enter into each new day with faith. As your days, so shall your strength be. Start days with praise.

As we study praise in the Scriptures we find various methods of praise.

1. Using the mouth in praise. Revelation 7:10; Psalm 126:2; Ephesians 5:19; Revelation 19:1; Psalm 5:11; Psalm 98:4; Psalm 71:8.
2. Using the hands in praise,

      a. Lifting the hands - Psalm 63:4; Psalm 119:48; Psalm 134:2; Psalm 141:2.
      b. Clapping the hands – Psalm 47:1; Psalm 98:8; Isaiah 55:12.
3. Playing musical instruments – Psalm 33:2; Psalm 57:8; Psalm 144:9; Psalm 147:7; Psalm 150:3-5.
4. Using the posture or motion of the body in praise.
      a. Dancing - Ps, 30:11; Psalm 149:3; Psalm 150:4; II Sam. 6:14.
      b. Walking and leaping - Acts 3:8; II Sam. 6:16.
      c. Standing - Psalm 135:2; Psalm 134:1.
      d. Bowing and kneeling - Psalm 95:6; Ephesians 3:14.

All of these methods are used and encouraged in God's Word. But the method is not as important as the attitude of the heart.

If we desire to come to God, we must come through praise. You see, our praise delights Him. He enjoys it. It brings Him pleasure because it speaks of a warm relationship that we have with Him.

When we express our love and adoration to Him, it completes His enjoyment of being our Father. When our children crawl up on our lap and give us hugs and kisses, it brings us much delight. We don't have to have this, but it brings enjoyment to us. It's the same with God. He desires an intimate relationship with us where love and praise is expressed freely and willingly.

There was a time when I felt that God was talking to me about praising Him more. I was praising Him at times, but I felt I was just saying the same old thing over and over. I couldn't really express how I felt in my heart. I did a study on praise and I put one hundred verses on praise on three by five cards. I started memorizing some of them, and praying them back to the Lord. Others I would read back to Him. My expressions of praise began to change and it became easier to praise Him.

If we desire spiritual power in our lives, it comes through prayer and praise. Psalms 22:3 says that "God inhabits the praises of His people." Hebrews 13:15 — "By Him therefore let us offer the sacrifices of praise to God continually, that is the fruit of our lips giving thanks to His name." Psalm 34:1 - "I will bless the Lord at all times; his praise shall continually be in my mouth."

How can we **continually** praise God? Notice the word **sacrifice**. It may indeed be a sacrifice. We may not "feel" like praising, but we must not go by our feelings but make that conscious choice to praise God because it's the way to victory and it delights our Lord.

God wants us to praise Him in **all** things **all** the time. We can praise Him while we are driving the car, when we are putting gas in the car these days. We can praise Him when we are filling out the forms for our taxes. When we take out the garbage, we can praise Him. When we are taking a bath we can praise the Lord for warm water and a bathtub or shower.

Praise
The Mind Of Christ
T.W. Hunt
P. 169

Several years ago, during a particularly hard struggle, I stopped praising the Lord. For five days I brooded, then on the fifth day it occurred to me that when you praise the Lord on the mountaintop but refuse to praise Him in the valley, you are not praising the Lord, you are praising your feelings.

I did not feel like it, but in the strength of Christ I took possession of my thoughts and began praising the Lord in spite of my depression. His worth does not depend on our moods. It is a constant. I discovered that day a new definition for praise: Praise is insisting on the truth. Truth as a person is invariable.

I vowed that day that I would never again let my feelings dictate my awareness of my position in Christ. Our position is not a product of our feelings. Christ's victory is eternal, a constant, independent of our emotions.

When circumstances are dismal and gloomy, sacrifice praise! When sickness strikes our bodies and our will power is reduced to nil, sacrifice praise. Good days and bad days; in fair or foul weather;

whether we are up or down, in sickness and in health; sacrifice praise.

Praise is not optional for the Christian. God expects us to offer praise. I was not doing God a big favor by praising Him; I was simply obeying Him.

Psalm 50:23 — Our praises always glorify God. God wants us to use our voices to praise Him. Vocal praise is that which God requires. Psalm 66:8 - O bless our God, ye people, and make the voice of his praise to be heard.

When all else fails, praise prevails. Praise never fails to bring God's response to us, with our needs and circumstances.

Pastor Allen – "If you can't pray your way through, praise your way through."

Why does praise prevail? Because God inhabits our praises. Remember: praise is the language of faith, and faith is the victory.

Praising the Lord is right, scriptural, God-pleasing, an evidence of the true Spirit-filled life.

One of the biggest problems many of us face is praising the Lord openly. In order to do that, we need to overcome our natural inhibitions. We almost feel embarrassed to praise God, simply because no one else is doing it. The Holy Spirit needs to strip away our inhibitions which keep us from praising Jesus without embarrassment. Can we say we are proud of Jesus? Do we love to brag on Him, and tell others about His glories?

Many of us have lived most of our lives on "Grumble Street." But once we are saved and filled with the Holy Spirit, we should move to "Thanksgiving Street." If we don't have a thankful heart, we are hardly worthy of the name Christian. True thanksgiving is not complete until it is expressed. It must become vocal. Some say, "But I am grateful in my heart." That's good, but it is not acceptable to Jesus. Remember the 10 lepers of Luke 17?

People who have vitality and zest for living have learned the secret of praising God,

Practice praise power! Praising God has power to lift your spirit, loose you from your bondages and give you victory in every circumstance. Philippians 4:4 - Rejoice in the Lord always and again I say rejoice.

Psalm 95:1-2; Psalm 32:11; Psalm 150:6; Psalm 92:1; I Peter 2:9; Psalm 107:31.

God does not bless or fill grouchers.

A continual flow of praise characterizes the one who is truly Spirit-filled, (Ephesians 5:18-20)

Praise will bring the presence of God into our hearts in a blessed manner. When clouds of depression hang low, praise will drive them away. A lukewarm Christian won't praise the Lord, for they do not have an up-to-date fellowship with the Lord. Trying to exist on yesterday's blessings will not work.

True praise keeps us humble before the Lord, for humility is complete dependence upon the Lord.

Praising people have always been God's greatest saints.

One universal word is Hallelujah. It means Praise The Lord!

ACCEPT THE SITUATION AND PRAISE GOD
By: Mrs. H. Faust
Marrietta, PA

"... Those hard situations are put into your lives to change you. Stop praying for them to change, but pray that they may change you." - H. Markham

What a blessing the above has been to me since the Lord has been cleansing me of deep unwillingness to accept all He allows and to thank Him for it, seeing He is allowing it all to consume my dross and to refine my gold.

If I find I cannot accept any situation and thank Him for it, then I come to Him confessing, "Lord, I am not willing to accept this hard situation and I am not willing to thank you for it."

Then I begin to say as these difficult situations arise, or depression or heaviness come upon me, or I lose my peace over my own wrong doing or the wrong doing of others, or frustration, accidents or ill health, etc., "My Father, this is another one of these things you are allowing to consume my dross and to refine my gold and I thank you for it."

As I continue to confess the unwillingness and thank Him for all, just as often as it raises its ugly head, I soon see I am being changed, I am being delivered from the self-life. And now I would not have had the situation changed as I see what He has been doing in me through it as I learn to accept all with thanksgiving. Praise the Lord! Praise for the blood to cleanse and for Jesus who "took the cup of our iniquity and gave thanks," so now as we repent deeply He is also our enabling to take our cup and give thanks. Praise and Praise again!

There's Dynamite In Praise
By: Don Gossett

Here is a simple ten-point outline with supporting Scriptures, which will be a practical help to you in learning to praise God at all times. I suggest you commit this material to memory, and quote it aloud when you are feeling depressed, discouraged or indifferent. Then act on the instructions of the Scriptures, and victory will be yours!

1. God's command for New Testament Christians: "By him therefore let us offer the sacrifice of praise to God continually, that is, the fruit of our lips giving thanks to his name" (Hebrews 13:15)
2. The vow of David, the man after God's own hearts "I will bless the Lord at all times: his praise shall continually be in my mouth" (Psalm 34:1).
3. The practice of the first Christians: "And (they) were continually in the temple, praising and blessing God" (Luke 24:53).
4. The will of God for every Christian: "In everything give thanks: for this is the will of God in Christ Jesus concerning you" (I Thessalonians 5:18).
5. A vital proof of the true Spirit-filled life: "... be filled with the Spirit ... Giving thanks always for all things unto God and the Father in the name of our Lord Jesus Christ" (Ephesians 5:18, 20).

6. The chief function of the Royal Priesthood: "But ye are a chosen generation, a royal priesthood, an holy nation, a peculiar people: that ye should shew forth the praises of him who hath called you out of darkness into his marvelous light" (I Peter 2:9).
7. The way Bible believers begin every gathering: "Enter into his gates with thanksgiving, and into his courts with praise: be thankful unto him, and bless his name" (Psalm 100:4).
8. A message to be heeded from the throne: "And a voice came out of the throne, saying, Praise our God, all ye his servants, and ye that fear him, both small and great" (Revelation 19:5).
9. The Christian's obligation as long as he has breath: "Let every thing that hath breath praise the Lord. Praise ye the Lord" (Psalm 150:6).
10. A habit to be practiced all day long: "From the rising of the sun unto the going down of the same, the Lord's name is to be praised" (Psalm 113:3).

PRAISE
By: Frances Metcalfe

Praise unlocks heaven's portals;
Praise causes doubts to cease;
Praise brings precious blessings;
Praise leaves the sweetest peace.

Praise breaks all bands asunder;
Praise sets the captives free;
Praise lightens every burden;
Praise is the master key.

Praise changes circumstances;
Praise establishes the heart;
When praise becomes perpetual,
Praise Is a Holy Art,

I challenge you: practice the praising principle. Praise is precious. Praise is powerful. Praise is personal. Praise pleases God!

CHAPTER XXI

THE SECOND COMING OF CHRIST

THE BLESSED HOPE

The Way To Live
By: Dr. K. Bailey

The night before Jesus went to the cross, He met in an upper room with His disciples. He told them a wonderful secret. Though God's plan of salvation required that Christ die on the cross, be buried, be raised from the dead and then return to the Father in heaven, there was still another step in this great plan. Jesus promised His disciples He would personally come back again (John 14:3). Christ's second coming will occur in two phases. The first phase of this great event will be to gather all true believers to Himself.

Paul tells exactly how this will take place: "But I would not have you to be ignorant, brethren, concerning them which are asleep, that ye sorrow not, even as others which have no hope. For if we believe that Jesus died and rose again, even so them also which sleep in Jesus will God bring with him. For this we say unto you by the word of the Lord, that we which are alive and remain unto the coming of the Lord shall not prevent them which are asleep. For the Lord himself shall descend from heaven with a shout, with the voice of the archangel, and with the trump of God: and the dead in Christ shall rise first: Then we which are alive and remain shall be caught up together with them in the clouds, to meet the Lord in the air: and so shall we ever be with the Lord. Wherefore comfort one another with these words: (I Thessalonians 4:13-18)

For the Christian who is alive when Jesus comes, an instantaneous change will occur in his body. The perishable mortal body will be changed to a body like Christ's beyond the reach of death. At the time of Christ's return, the body of the dead believer will be resurrected and shall be caught up to meet Christ in the air. Paul spoke of Christ's coming for His own as the "blessed hope." The coming of Christ for His church is imminent. Jesus taught His disciples to live in constant readiness for the Lord's return.

The second coming of Christ is not only the believer's personal hope and answer to the future, it is also his key to understanding the world in which he lives. Christ gave insight into the signs at the end of the age and of His second coming. Jesus taught that wickedness would continue to worsen in the world system and that demonic activity would be intensified. The Apostle Paul described the last days as dangerous because of social unrest, violence and evil. Political systems will be devastated. Finally, in the dark hours of the tribulation (a period of judgment Christ has designed to deal with the nations of the world), Satan will bring forth his masterpiece: a world ruler called the Antichrist. This diabolic leader will bring the wickedness of the nations to its highest level.

Then the Lord Jesus will return to the earth with His saints to establish His kingdom. The power of Satan will be bound and the righteous government of Christ will prevail among all the nations of the world. The true believers will reign with Christ during the thousand years His kingdom will be on earth. At the end of the one thousand-year reign, the earth will be judged with fire. Christ will then judge the wicked from His great white throne. After these events, the new heavens and the new earth will begin. The saints will dwell in the city of God and enjoy the blessings of Christ's everlasting kingdom.

"And if I go and prepare a place for you, I will come again, and receive you unto myself; that where I am, there ye may be also." (John 14:3)

THE RAPTURE
By: Bruce Scott

At least seven years before He sets His feet on Planet Earth once again, Jesus Christ will descend from heaven. The bodies of Christians who have died during the Church Age will then be resurrected to join their spirits, already with the Lord. Church Age believers who are still alive will follow with new, glorified bodies. Both will be caught up to meet the Lord in the air. All of this will happen in a moment, as quickly as the twinkling of an eye.

This event is known as the Rapture. The primary texts describing it are John 14:1-35, I Corinthians 15:50-52; and I Thessalonians 4:13-18. (For non-church raptures, see Genesis 5:24; II Kings 2:11; Hebrews 11:5; Revelation 11:12.)

The word *rapture* is not in the English Bible. It is derived from the Latin translation of "caught up," found in I Thessalonians 4:17. Both the Latin and the original Greek word mean "to snatch or take something away by seizing it suddenly." Being snatched in this passage are both resurrected and living believers in Jesus Christ.

Even though the Church Age, or Age of Grace, does not technically end until the Second Coming of Jesus, the true church — the Body of Christ — will be raptured before then. The results are these:

(1) Through the Rapture, Jesus will receive His bride (the church), which will forever remain with Him.
(2) The church's salvation will become experientially complete by the glorification of each person's body.
(3) The "fullness of the Gentiles" will have come in, opening the way for God to continue His program with the nation of Israel (Acts 15:14; Romans 11:25).
(4) The Holy Spirit's ministry of baptizing individual Jews and Gentiles into the Body of Christ will cease.

(5) The church's stewardship for this age — walking under the control of the Holy Spirit, making disciples, and preserving the faith — will end. People will still become saved during the subsequent Tribulation, but they will not be part of the unique, spiritual union known as the Body of Christ.
(6) With the true church gone, only a false, apostate church will remain on this earth.

There is strong evidence the Rapture will take place before the Tribulation. For example, Scripture says the church is to be delivered from the "wrath to come" because God has not destined the church for wrath (I Thessalonians 1:10; 5:9). Since God pours out His wrath during the entire seven-year Tribulation, the church will be raptured before it. (See also Revelation 3:10; also note the church's conspicuous absence from the earth in Revelation 4-18.)

Also, the writers of the New Testament believed the Lord could return at any moment, without precursory signs (Philippians 4:5; Titus 2:13; James 5:8-9).

The Tribulation completes the remaining seven years of Daniel's 70 weeks prophecy for Israel (Daniel 9:24-27). Since God's programs for Israel and the church are distinct, it is fitting that the church be removed before God's program for Israel begins anew.

THE SECOND COMING OF JESUS CHRIST
By: Bruce Scott

The Second Coming of Jesus Christ is one of the cardinal doctrines of the Christian faith. It is sometimes confused with the Rapture of the church. However, there are distinctions between the two.

The Rapture occurs before the Tribulation. The Second Coming takes place after the Tribulation and before the Millennium. The Rapture will be instantaneous and invisible to the naked eye. The Second Coming will be gradual and visible to all. At the Rapture, believers will meet the Lord in the air. At the Second Coming, believers come with the Lord to the earth. At the Rapture, Jesus

Christ descends only as far as Earth's atmosphere. At the Second Coming, Christ sets His feet on planet Earth.

Certain events will take place after the Tribulation but before the Messiah returns (Matthew 24:29-30), There will be great cosmic disturbances. The sign of Jesus Christ will appear in heaven. Individuals from every people group around the globe will mourn, including those from Israel, from the realization that Jesus truly is the Messiah (Zechariah 12:10). Some will mourn with the sorrow that leads to repentance, while others will mourn out of regret (II Corinthians 7:10).

Finally, all people still alive after the Tribulation will clearly see the Messiah descend from heaven on the clouds. He will be riding a white horse, followed by the armies of heaven (Revelation 19:11, 14). Jesus' return will be literal, physical, and visible; thus He will return in the same manner and to the exact place from which He was taken into heaven (Zechariah 14:4; Acts 1:11).

The Second Coming of Christ will accomplish numerous purposes of God. It will officially close the Church Age, or Age of Grace. It will fulfill prophecies concerning the great and terrible Day of the Lord (Joel 2:11; Malachi 4:5). It will be the occasion on which the Messiah rescues and fights for Israel (Zechariah 14:2-3). It will be the occasion on which the Messiah, with His heavenly Kingdom, will smash the final manifestation of Gentile world power (Daniel 2:34, 44). It will also be the occasion on which Satan's rule over the earth, both personally and by proxy through the Antichrist and False Prophet, will end (Revelation 19:20; 20:2).

Christ's Second Coming will also prepare Israel to enter His Kingdom. The Jewish people will be gathered (fulfilling the prophetic aspect of the Feast of Trumpets), judged, cleansed (fulfilling the prophetic aspect of the Day of Atonement), regenerated, and established in their own land (Isaiah 27:12-13; Ezekiel 20:33-38; 36:25-28). The surviving Gentiles will also be prepared to enter the Kingdom. They, too, will be gathered and judged (Matthew 25:31-46). Whether they be Jewish or Gentile, only those born again will enter the Messiah's Kingdom (John 3:3,5).

THE MILLENNIUM

By: Bruce Scott

The Millennium is the term used to refer to the final dispensation in human history, when mankind's stewardship will be to live in harmony with the risen, glorified Savior. Despite Jesus' physical presence on Earth, however, sinful people will still rebel against Him (Revelation 20:7-8). Fire from heaven will consume the rebels; and Satan will be cast into the Lake of Fire, concluding this final epoch in human history (v. 9-10). When the Millennium ends and eternity begins, mortality will cease. Thus there will be no further need for God-given managerial structures (i.e., dispensations) for mortal human stewards.

As with all dispensations, the purpose of the Millennium will be to glorify God. His heavenly Kingdom will finally be established on the earth, once and for all (Zechariah 14:9). His rule will be literal, material, and spiritual (spiritual does not equate with immaterial), administered by Jesus Christ who will reign from the throne of David in Jerusalem (Isaiah 9:7; Ezekiel 43:7).

Jesus does not presently sit on the throne of David in heaven, as some claim. Scripture says He sits at the right hand of the Father on His Father's throne until His Father makes Jesus' enemies a footstool for His feet (Psalm 110:1; Revelation 3:21). As pictured by the stone cut without hands in the book of Daniel, Jesus' Millennial Kingdom will not be manmade; it will come from God and will fill the entire earth (Daniel 2:35, 44). It will serve as the radiant portion of the Day of the Lord and will be characterized by peace, prosperity, and righteous judgment (Isaiah 2:1-4; 11:1-10; Joel 3:18, 20; Amos 9:13).

Following the Millennium, there is a transition prior to the new heaven and new earth, during which the wicked are judged at the Great White Throne (Revelation 20:7-21:1).

God will also be glorified in the Millennium because all of the unilateral, eternal covenants He made with Israel will be brought to fruition (Abrahamic - Genesis 12:1-3; Land - Psalm 105:8-11; Davidic - Psalm 89:3-4; New - Jeremiah 31-34). When Israel is restored to its place of blessing during this time, even the Gentiles will benefit (Zechariah 8:23; Romans 11:12).

Finally, God will be glorified in the Millennium because it will be shown that despite an ideal environment, mankind will still rebel against God's rule, thus demonstrating God's righteousness in all His judgments (Isaiah 11:4; Revelation 20:8-9).

From: Israel My Glory

I personally have seen people come to a saving knowledge of Jesus Christ through biblical prophecy. For example, the Holy Spirit worked through the teaching of biblical prophecy to bring eight office workers and a school superintendent to saving faith in Christ at a conference I conducted in a church. Any Christian who avoids the study and teaching of biblical prophecy fails to use an effective evangelistic tool that God has given to us.

It is impossible to understand God's plan for Israel apart from prophecy.

1. **In the Past.** God established a unique relationship with Israel as a nation:

For you are a holy people to the LORD your God; the LORD your God has chosen you to be a people for Himself, a special treasure above all the peoples on the face of the earth (Dt. 7:6; cf. 14:2).

Furthermore, Scripture teaches that God established this relationship with Israel forever. King David said to God, "For You have made Your people Israel Your very own people forever" (II Samuel 7:24). In fact, the apostle Paul indicated that, despite Israel's unbelief, God's election, or calling, of the nation Israel for this unique relationship will never change (Romans 11:26-29).

God did not establish this relationship because Israel was greater than other nations. Moses told the Israelites, "The LORD did not set His love on you nor choose you because you were more in number than any other people, for you were the least of all peoples"

(Deuteronomy 7:7). Instead, God established the relationship because He loves the nation and has a unique, sovereign purpose for it (v. 8).

God sovereignly purposed that the nation Israel would play a strategic role in fulfilling His purpose for history. One aspect of that key role is to bring great blessing to the entire world through Abraham's physical offspring.

God promised Abraham, "In your seed all the nations of the earth shall be blessed" (Genesis 22:18). The fact that God repeated this promise to Abraham's son Isaac and grandson Jacob, whose 12 sons became the heads of the 12 tribes of Israel, indicates that God purposed to bring this promised blessing to the world through the nation Israel (26:4; 28:14).

God has already brought great blessings to the world through Israel. The Bible came through that nation. The apostle Paul wrote that to the Jews "were committed the oracles of God" (Romans 3:1-2). The Messiah-Savior came to the world by birth through Israel. Paul called the Jews the people "from whom, according to the flesh, Christ came" (9:5). Since the Messiah who provided salvation for all people was Jewish in His humanity, then salvation came through Israel. Jesus Himself said, "Salvation is of the Jews" (John 4:22).

2. In the Future. Biblical prophecy indicates that another aspect of Israel's key role is yet future. God will not totally crush Satan and his forces and establish His future theocratic Kingdom-rule in the world until the nation of Israel returns to God with all its heart and accepts its Messiah-Savior. Zechariah 12-14 reveals that, when the rulers and armies of all the Gentile nations will come against Israel in the future, the Jewish people will see the Messiah come out of heaven to rescue them (12:1-9). Gazing on the evidences of His past crucifixion, they will change their minds toward Him and mourn for Him "as one grieves for a firstborn" (v. 10). Then God will cleanse them from their sin (13:1).

Messiah will destroy the rulers and armies of the world and imprison Satan in the bottomless pit for 1,000 years (14:1-3,12-15; Revelation 19:11-21; 20:1-3). Then He will establish God's theocratic Kingdom and will rule as "king over all the earth," and Israel will become the spiritual leader of the world (Zechariah 14:9, 16-21; Revelation 20:4-6).

The people of Israel will "be named the priests of the LORD," and the Gentiles will call them "the servants [ministers] of our God" (Isaiah 61:6). "In those days ten men from every language of the nations shall grasp the sleeve of a Jewish man, saying, 'Let us go with you, for we have heard that God is with you'" (Zechariah 8:23).

Sadly, Christians who subscribe to Replacement Theology rather than Dispensational Theology insist that God did not establish His unique relationship with Israel forever. They believe that, because Israel rejected Jesus in His First Coming, God permanently severed His special relationship with the nation and replaced Israel with the New Testament church. They claim that God will save individual Jews but that He no longer has a national program for Israel.

This erroneous belief affects their thinking concerning Israel's right to exist as a national entity in the Middle East today. Such Christians neglect biblical prophecy or interpret it allegorically, which also causes them to reject the idea that God has irrevocably appointed Israel to play a future, key role in the fulfillment of His purpose for history.

God intends the study of biblical prophecy to purify our lives and change our priorities.

Two aspects of prophetic revelation serve such a purpose.

1. The Imminency of Christ's Return. The English word *imminent* means "hanging over one's head, ready to befall or overtake one; close at hand in its incidence." Thus an imminent event is one that is always hanging overhead, constantly ready to befall or overtake a person. It is always close at hand in the sense that it could happen at any moment. Other things may happen beforehand, but nothing else must happen. If something else must take place before an event can happen, the event is not imminent. Nor can you count on a fixed amount of time transpiring before the event occurs.

Thus the imminent coming of Christ means His next coming is always hanging overhead, constantly ready to befall or overtake us, always close at hand in the sense that it could happen at any moment. Other things may happen before His coming, but nothing else must happen.

Since we do not know exactly when He will come, we cannot count on a fixed amount of time transpiring before His arrival. Therefore, we should always be ready for Him at any moment.

Many Bible scholars from various church and theological backgrounds have concluded that the New Testament teaches or implies the imminent coming of Christ in the following passages: I Corinthians 1:7; 4:5; 15:51-52; 16:22; Philippians 3:20; 4:5; I Thessalonians 1:10; II Thessalonians 3:10-12; Titus 2:13; James 5:8-9; I John 2:28; Revelation 3:11; 22:7, 12,17, 20.

In James 5:8-9, the apostle James clearly indicated that, since Christ could return at any moment and confront His church saints as judge, Christians should be careful how they treat their fellow believers:

You also be patient. Establish your hearts, for the coming of the Lord is at hand. Do not grumble against one another, brethren, lest you be condemned. Behold, the Judge is standing at the door!

Christ's imminent return should make a difference in the way we live. We should live holy, godly lives every moment of every day because in the very next moment, Christ could step through the door of heaven and confront us face to face.

The apostle John emphasized the same truth when he wrote the following to Christians: "And now, little children, abide in Him, that when He appears, we may have confidence and not be ashamed before Him at His coming" (I John 2:28).

2. The Future Destruction of the Present Earth and Universe. The apostle Peter wrote, "The heavens will pass away with a great noise, and the elements will melt with fervent heat; both the earth and the works that are in it will be burned up" (II Peter 3:10). Peter foretold the future destruction of the present Earth and universe, including everything that mankind has designed and made during the history of this planet. All of our present material possessions will be destroyed.

In light of this certainty, Peter told believers, "Since all these things will be dissolved, what manner of persons ought you to be in holy conduct and godliness?" (v. 11).

His point was this: The fact that the present earth, universe, and all our material possessions will someday be destroyed should shape our values, priorities, and lifestyles. We should be holy in our daily conduct. Our desire to please and glorify God should motivate us and give us ultimate meaning and purpose in life — not money, material things, or the present world system. Because all earthly things are temporary and doomed for destruction, we should conform our values and priorities to things of the future eternal state (vv. 13-14).

Bible prophecy is an integral part of Scripture. Those who consider it irrelevant or fail to study it will wrongly divide the Word of Truth and fall into theological error.

"Even so come quickly Lord Jesus." Amen!

CHAPTER XXII

RECOMMENDED BOOKS FOR SPIRITUAL GROWTH

Other Book and Material I have Read and Studied

1. *Day By Day With God,* C.O, Rosenius.
2. *Assurance,* Bill Bright, Campus Crusade For Christ, Inc. 1976, U.S.A.
3. *The Way Of Life,* Norman R. Harrison, Christian Service Fellowship Pub., The Bible Meditations League, Columbus, OH 43216, k964.
4. *How To Begin Your Christian Life,* New Convert Study.
5. *How To Succeed In The Christian Life,* R.A. Torrey, Whitaker House, 1984.
6. *The Authority Of The Believer*, Dr. J. MacMillian, Christian Pub., Inc. Harrisburg, PA
7. *True Believing,* Ethel Meadows, Pilgrim Tract Soc., Tract.
8. *Prayer, Seven Minutes With God,* Navigators Inc., Colorado Springs, CO 80901.
9. *How To Be Sure You Are A Christian,* Bill Bright, Campus Crusade For Christ, Inc., U.S.A., 1972.
10. *How Christians Grow,* Russell T. Hitt, Oxford University Press, NY, 1979.
11. *A Know-So Salvation,* John R. Rice, Sword of the Lord Pub., TN, 1953-1973.

12. *That I May Know Him,* Evangelical Mennonite Conf., Man., Canada, 1976.
13. *Now That I Believe,* Robert Cook, Moody Press, U.S., 1949.
14. *How To Grow In The Christian Life,* B. Charles Hostetter, Moody Press, Chicago, 1960,
15. *Now That You've Been Born Again,* The Just Shall Live By Faith Mission, Inc. Inc., I. & J. Cook, Grand Rapids, MI 49509.
16. *Learning To Grow, First Things First,* Keith Parks.
17. *How To Have Constant Victory In Christ,* A.W. Tozer.
18. *Now That I'm A Christian,* Rich Yohn, Harvest House Pub., U.S.A. 1976.
19. *Five Steps Of Christian Growth,* Campus Crusade For Christ, Inc., U.S.A., 1976.
20. *Steps To Christian Commitment,* Charles Templeton, The Division of Evangelism, NY.
21. *Now What?,* Ralph W. Harris, Gospel Pub. House, Springfield, MS 65802, 1964.
22. *Steps To Christian Commitment,* Charles Templeton, The Division of Evangelism, NY.
23. *Assurance,* Bill Bright, Campus Crusade.

Recommended Books for Spiritual Growth

The Calvary Road, Roy Hession
The Corn of Wheat, Gladys Nash
The End of the Struggle, Daniel E. Friesen
How to Be Crucified with Christ, Bill McLeod
The Norman Christian Life, Watchman Nee
Absolute Surrender, A. Murray
Changed Into His Likeness, Watchman Nee
The Master's Indwelling, A. Murray
The Christ Life for Your Life, F.B. Meyer
The Christian Secret of a Happy Life, H.W. Smith
Keys to the Deeper Life, A.W. Tozer
When He is Come, A.W. Tozer

The Pursuit of God, A.W. Tozer
That Incredible Christian, A.W. Tozer
A Knowledge of the Holy, A.W. Tozer
War on the Saints, Jessie Penn-Lewis
How to Live the Victorious Life, Unknown Author
Filled with the Spirit – Then What?, Mable Francis
Freedom of Forgiveness, B. Augsburger
Crowded to Christ, L.E. Maxwell
We Would See Jesus, Roy Hession
How to Say No to a Stubborn Habit, Erwin Lutzer
The Prayer Life, A. Murray
Power Through Prayer, Bounds
How to Get Results Through Prayer, Bridges
How to Spend a Day in Prayer, Sanny
Beyond Ourselves, C. Marshall
Spirit-Controlled Temperaments, Tim LaHaye
Keys to Triumphant Living, Jack Taylor
Much More, Jack Taylor
Not I But Christ, Roy Hession
Victory Over Circumstances, Ruth Paxson
Five Vows for Spiritual Power, A.W. Tozer
The Larger Christian Life, A.B. Simpson

CHAPTER XIII

RECOMMENDED BOOKS FOR SOUL WINNING

How to Work for Christ, R.A. Torrey
How to Win Your Family to Christ, Nathanael Olson
More Power in Soul Winning, David M. Dawson
The Art of Personal Witnessing, Lorne C. Sanny
Evangelism, G. Campbell Morgan
Let's Go Soul Winning, Jack Hyles
The Spiritual Preparation of a Soul Winner, Charles G. Finney
Born to Reproduce, M.R. DeHaan, M.D.
Fishers, D.L. Moody
How to Give Away Your Faith, Paul E. Little
The Soul-Winners Fire, John R. Rice
Born to Reproduce, Dawson Trotman
How to Witness in the Spirit, Bill Bright
How to Help Fulfill the Great Commission, Bill Bright
How to Introduce Others to Christ, Bill Bright

BIBLIOGRAPHY

Aldrich, Willard M.: *Can You Be A Christian Without Becoming One?*
Alliance Witness. Aug. 1982-Nov. 1982. "Evidence of the Spirit-Filled Life."
"Confess Your Sins To One Another," Aug. 28, 1982.
Alpert, Ben; McQuaid, Elwood; Rosenthal, Stan; Varner, Will; Hartman, Fred; Weinbaum, Ron: "The Armor Of God." *Israel My Glory.* 1988.
Armin, George Wells: *Can Christ Be Savior Yet Not Lord?* Bible Research Fellowship, Inc. Chicago, IL 60666.
Back To The Bible Cor. School: *A Life That's Real,* G. Christian Weiss, U.S., 1973.
Bailey, Keith M.: *Learning To Live The Spirit-Filled Life.* Christian Pub. Inc., Harrisburg, PA 17101.
Bennett, Martin: *Are You Afraid?*
Betzer, Dan: *Waking Giant.*
Blackaby, Tom: "Four Ways To Be Neighborly." *Homelife.* 2007.
Bright, Dr. Bill: *How To Be Sure You Are A Christian.* Campus Crusade For Christ, Inc. 1972, U.S.A.
The Four Spiritual Laws: "The Two Divisions Of Mankind."
Brooke, Harold J.: *God's Recipe For Fellowship.*
Burkett, Larry: *Tithing.*
Caldwell, E.S.: "The Whole Armor Of God." *Advance.* Sermon Series, Sept. 1975.

Chapman, J. Wilbur: ***When Home Is Heaven.*** Fleming H. Revell Co.

Chilvers, Gordon: "Ask Questions Before You Pray," *Alliance Witness*, Feb. 18, 1981. (Article)

Christian Pub. Inc., Harrisburg, p. 45-46.: ***Learning To Live.***

Churches Of Christ In U.S.A., 475 Riverside Dr., NY, NY. *Decision: Helps For New Christians.*

Coleman, Robert E.: ***Established By The Word Of God.***

Daves, Michael: ***A Bible Reading Disciple.***

Davie, James E.: *The Second Coming Of Christ.* Sermon, 1954.

Dawson, Joy: ***Some Principles For Effective Intercession.***

Direction Correspondence School, Christian Direction Inc. Montreal, CAN. 1974. *I'll Take The High Road.*

Donoghue, Rev. Steve: *Fellowship.* Pastor Of Rives Junction Baptist Church, Rives Junction, MI.

Edman, Dr. V. Raymond: ***Ten Marks Of The Spirit-Filled Christian.*** Christian Life Pub., Inc., 33 South Wacker Dr., Chicago 8, IL.

Epp, Weiss, and Morrow: ***Praying With Authority.***

Flynn, Lester B.: ***The Gifts Of The Holy Spirit.*** Good News Broadcaster, Jan. 1979.

Good News Publishers: ***Joy And Peace In Believing.***

Gossett, Don: ***There's Dynamite In Praise.***

Harris, Ralph W.: ***Now What?*** Gospel Pub. House, Springfield, MS, 1964.

Henricksen, Walter A.: ***Disciples Are Made - Not Born.*** Victor Books, S.P. Pub. Inc., Wheaton, IL, 1977.

High School Evangelism Fellowship, Inc., NY, NY, 1951. *Commando Course.*

Homelife. "Simple Ways To Invest In The Lives Of People." 2007.

Horban, Michael P.: ***Now That You're A Christian.*** Full Gospel Pub. House.

Horton, Elliott: ***You And Communion.***

Horton, Rev. D.J.: *Pastor, How Do I Know I Am Making The Right Decision?* Anderson Mill Baptist Church, Spartanburg, SC. From their church paper.

Hour Of Prayer: *Prayer Outline.*

Humrichous, Joe C.: ***Why Should I Be Filled With The Holy Spirit?*** (A sheet he gives out)
Hunt, T.W.: ***The Mind Of Christ.***
Jackson, Bobby; ***Six Steps To Successful Christian Living.*** Nashville, TN, 1962.
Kazee, B.H.: ***Have You Been Saved or Deceived?*** Bible Baptist Church Pub., Clarksville, TN. A Tract.
Kenyon, Rev. Paul: "Superficial Believism." A tract in *The Alliance Witness Magazine.*
LaHaye, Dr. Tim: ***Spirit Controlled Temperaments.*** Tyndale House Pub., Wheaton, IL. 1966.
Laverne Tripp Ministries: *12 Steps To An Overcoming Life.* Song Revival Fellowship & Ministries, Inc., P.O. Box 527, Hendersonville, TN 37077-0527.
Lawrence, Arlyn: ***Spiritual Gifts.*** Sept. - Oct. 2005.
Life Action Ministries, P.O. Box 31, Buchanan, MI 49107, 2005: *31 Days of...Praying for Your Pastor.*
Traits Of Self.
Lindsay, Homer G., Jr.: ***Spiritual Helps For The New Member.*** Daniels Pub., Orlando, FL U.S.A. 1969.
Lutzer, Dr. Irwin: ***How To Say No To A Stubborn Habit.*** Victor Books, Wheaton, IL. 1979.
Maust, Mrs. H.: *Praise. Accept The Situation And Praise God.* Marrietta, PA.
McLeod, Rev. Bill: ***Starting The Day With God.*** Canadian Revival Fellowship, Box 584, Regina, Saskatchewan, Can. S4P 3A3.
Merrill, Darwin E.: ***This New Life of Yours.*** Baptist Pub., Inc. U.S.A.
Meyer, F.B.: ***The Christ-Life For The Self-Life.*** Moody Press, Chicago, IL.
Miller, Rev. Douglas: "The Self-life and How To deal With It," *The Alliance Witness,* Aug. 1982-Nov. 1982
"Death To Self." *Alliance Life.* Aug. 1982- Nov. 1982.
Morning Glory: "The Highway And Hedge Evangel."
Moody Bible Institute Correspondence School: *Youth Triumphant.* S. Maxwell Coder, Chicago 10, IL, 1946.

Now That I'm A Christian, 1968.
Moyer, Larry; **How To Present The Gospel.**
Myra, Harold: ***The New You.*** Zondervan Pub. House, 1976.
National Council of Churches, U.S.A.: ***Decision - Helps For New Christians.***
Pederson, Cliff: ***Christians Alive.*** Augsburg Pub. House, Minneapolis, MN, 1973.
Handbook For Spiritual Growth.
Peterson, Cliff: *How Can I Know The Will Of God?*
Pogue, Steven: ***The First Year Of Your Christian Life.***
Rice, John R.: ***When A Christian Sins.*** Moody Press, Chicago, U.S., 1954.
Rinker, Rosalind: ***Prayer: Conversing With God.*** Zondervan Pub. Co,, Grand Rapids, MI, 1959.
Scott, Bruce: "The Lord's Return." *Israel My Glory.* Spring 2008.
Shaver, Charles: ***Conserve The Converts.*** Beacon Hill Press Of Kansas City, Kansas City, MO.
Simpson, A.B.: ***The Christ Life.*** Christian Pub., Harrisburg, PA, 17101.
The Power Of Christ's Resurrection, The Self-Life And The Christ-Life.
Sipley, Richard M.: ***Understanding Divine Healing.*** Victor Books, Wheaton, IL 60187.
Smith, Hanna W.: ***God Is Enough.*** Francis Asbury Press of Zondervan Pub, house, Grand Rapids, MI, 1986.
Stanley, Dr. Charles: "Will Of God." ***The Glorious Journey.***
Stoez, Dr. Samuel J.: ***The Meaning And Importance Of Baptism.*** Christian Publications, Harrisburg, PA.
Stott, John R.W.: ***Being A Christian - Our Duty To God.*** InterVarsity Fellowship Press, Downers Grove, IL, 1976.
Sutera, Rev. Ralph: *Specific Questions To "Ask" About Questionables.* Canadian Revival Fellowship, Regina, Sask., CAN.
Reconciliation And Restitution Guidelines.
Sweeting, George: ***How To Begin The Christian Life.*** Moody Press, Chicago, IL. 1976.
Teichrob, Henry & Freda: ***Christian Reality.*** Canadian Revival Fellowship, Inc., CAN. 1975.

The Unknown Christian: ***The Kneeling Christian.*** Zondervan Pub. House, Grand Rapids, MI, 1971.

The Joyful Woman, Jan. and Feb.: "How To Pray For Missionaries."

Thomas, Dr. TV: ***Hindrances To Prayer.*** Canadian Revival Fellowship, Regina, SK, Canada, Message given at School of Revival and Prayer, July 18-20, 2007.

Tozer, A.W.: ***The Divine Conquest.*** Christian Publications, Inc. Harrisburg, PA.

Vander Klok, Duane: *Saying "No" To Addictions.* Walking By Faith TV program.

Wander Lugt, Herb: ***Filled With The Holy Spirit.*** Radio Bible Class Pub., Grand Rapids, MI, 1986.

The Spirit Filled Life.

Weiss, G. Christian: ***On Being A Real Christian.*** Moody Press, Chicago, IL. 1951.

Wilde, Paul And Carolyn: ***God, Why Am I Sick?*** Heartfelt Ministries, Box 350, Foley, AL 36535. 1986.

Woodcock, Eldon: "Prayer Motivation," *Alliance Witness.* Feb. 4, 1981. (Article)

Woychuk, N.A.: ***Keep In Memory.*** The Span Pub., 1978.

LaVergne, TN USA
24 August 2009

155704LV00004B/2/P